Cult Television

Cult Television

Sara Gwenllian-Jones and
Roberta E. Pearson, Editors

University of Minnesota Press
Minneapolis • London

Published by the University of Minnesota Press
111 Third Avenue South, Suite 290
Minneapolis, MN 55401-2520
http://www.upress.umn.edu

Library of Congress Cataloging-in-Publication Data

    Cult television / Sara Gwenllian-Jones and Roberta E. Pearson, editors.
      p.   cm.
    Includes bibliographical references.
    ISBN 0-8166-3830-6 (alk. paper) — ISBN 0-8166-3831-4 (PB : alk. paper)
    1. Television programs.   I. Gwenllian-Jones, Sara.   II. Pearson, Roberta E.
    PN1992.5.C85 2004
    791.45'6—dc22
                                 2003018986

12 11 10 09 08 07 06 05 04   10 9 8 7 6 5 4 3 2 1

Dedicated to my parents Jean and T. F. G. Jones,
and to my brothers Charles and Alun Gwyn Jones

S. G.-J.

Dedicated to Humphrey and Jennings

R. E. P.

Contents

Introduction

Sara Gwenllian-Jones and Roberta E. Pearson

■ Series as diverse as *Star Trek* (1966–1969), *Moonlighting* (1985–1989), and *Gilligan's Island* (1965–1967) might all be described as "cult television." One of the reviewers of the original proposal for this volume suggested rather forcibly that we include an essay on World Federation Wrestling, while colleagues questioned our exclusion of *The Simpsons* (1989–present) and other of their favorite shows. In the media, in common usage, and sometimes even in academia, "cult" is often loosely applied to any television program that is considered offbeat or edgy, that draws a niche audience, that has a nostalgic appeal, that is considered emblematic of a particular subculture, or that is considered hip. Such a variety of uses renders the term almost meaningless, since it allows much of television's output of fiction, and some nonfiction, to be described as "cult." So to what precisely does this collection's title, *Cult Television*, refer?

> The [cult object] must be loved, obviously, but this is not enough. It must provide a completely furnished world so that fans can quote characters and episodes as if they were aspects of the fan's private sectarian world, a world about which one can make up quizzes and play trivia games so that the adepts of the sect recognize through each other a shared expertise. Naturally all these elements (characters and episodes) must have some archetypal appeal. . . . I think that in order to transform a work into a cult object one must be able to break, dislocate, unhinge it so that one can remember only parts of it, irrespective of their original relationship with the whole.[1]

A reference to Umberto Eco's essay on cult movies and intertextual collage now routinely features in any definition of cult film or television; scholars of these still slightly disreputable texts invoke the celebrated Euro-theorist to locate their intellectual antecedents. Eco's essay focuses almost entirely on textual analysis of a single film, *Casablanca,* established in the United States as a cult object by the university film societies, urban repertory houses, and local television stations of the 1960s and 1970s. Eco predicates his own definition of a cult object on textual characteristics (archetypal appeal, completely furnished world) and reception (fans quoting and quizzing), but ignores the mechanisms (nontheatrical distribution, independent film and television exhibitors) that rendered *Casablanca* cult.

An understanding and definition of cult television must be predicated on the full circuit of communication, that is, texts, production/distribution, and audiences, rather than on an overvaluation of any one or two of these three factors. This entails asking the following questions: What distinguishes "cult" programs such as *Star Trek* and *The X-Files* (1993–present) from other series such as *Friends* (1994–present), which may attract larger audiences but do not inspire significant interpretive fan cultures? What characteristics do cult television programs share with other television dramas and what, if any, are the generic, textual, and metatextual characteristics specific to cult television? How do these characteristics function to engage avid audiences and inspire the production of tertiary texts? To what extent, how, and why does the television industry deliberately seek to develop, produce, and market programs as "cult"? Does the transmedial nature of cult television mean that the term must carry a wider set of meanings than its medium specificity suggests? What are the relations between the massive expansion of the cult television phenomenon in the 1990s and technological developments such as VCRs and the Internet? Are there grounds for distinguishing cult television fandom from other television and nontelevision fandoms? Why do text-producing fan cultures accrue to some series but not to others? We must also consider the ideological functions and impact of the most successful of the cult television texts: what can *Star Trek,* in its numerous manifestations, *The X-Files,* and *Buffy the Vampire Slayer* tell us about the societies that produce and consume them? Neither this volume's introduction nor its essays provide full answers to all these questions, but they do map the contours of the terrain to encourage further detailed exploration of the texts, production/distribution, and audiences of cult television.

Distinguishing cult television from cult film on one side and from non-cult television drama on the other may help to identify textual characteristics specific to the form. Cult films belonging to a "paracinematic culture" that "seeks to promote an alternative vision of cinematic 'art,' aggressively attacking the established canon of 'quality' cinema and questioning the legitimacy of reigning aesthetic discourses on movie art[2]" usually tell self-contained stories. They usually aspire to, if often fail to achieve, the narrative structure of the classical Hollywood cinema, a linear narrative predicated on forward temporal progression and the resolution of narrative enigmas. The individual films within cult series such as *Halloween* or *Friday the Thirteenth* conform to this model: the ending resolves the primary narrative hermeneutic of who lives, who dies, and who has been doing the killing. Of course, given that the term "cult" is used as indiscriminately with regard to film as with regard to television, some films to which the rubric is applied do not tell self-contained narratives. The individual entries in the *Star Wars, Aliens,* or *Crow* series do not entirely resolve narrative enigmas; rather each contributes to a longer narrative arc in which events in one film have consequences in the sequel (or prequel as the case might be).

Seriality distinguishes cult television from cult film, yet is a characteristic shared with the many other American television dramas that follow the serial format with which programs of the early 1980s such as *Hill Street Blues* and *St. Elsewhere* first experimented. The 90 to 120 minutes of a single film, or even the several hours of a series such as *Star Wars,* cannot possibly provide the scope for narrative developments offered by the hundreds of hours of a long-running television program. To quote Sconce again, this time from an article contrasting film and television adaptations of the works of Charles Dickens:

> Dickens' (and the nineteenth-century novel's) emphasis on serial narrative and episodic emplotment . . . has proven a . . . lasting influence on . . . television. . . . Hollywood sacrificed the narrative pleasures of serialised delay, diegetic expansion, and heteroglossic play. Long-running television series . . . face the problem of *filling* time (or even killing time)—often hours, days, and even months of diegetic time and space. . . . A popular series in any medium . . . must balance repetition of successful (i.e., commercial) story elements with a search for forms of difference that will provide novel variation and interest. . . . Television's episodic seriality and textual density allow for a narrative elasticity unavailable to Hollywood cinema.[3]

Seriality and narrative elasticity permitted *ER*'s fourth season premiere to take the form of a "mocumentary," and *The West Wing*'s third season premiere to temporarily abandon the narrative arc concerning Jed Bartlett's illness in favor of responding to the events of September 11. But narrative elasticity would not have permitted *The West Wing*'s writers to continually ignore the president's multiple sclerosis. The linear structure of "realist" television dramas, both within individual episodes and within overarching narrative arcs, proceeds in a relatively straight line, following a chronological temporal progression (although allowing for flashbacks and, in some rare instances, even flashforwards) that deals in turn with narrative hermeneutics and arrives at eventual resolution. As the essays in this collection reflect, cult series usually—though not exclusively—belong to one or another of the fantastic genres of science fiction, fantasy, horror, or speculative fiction. These genres permit non-linear narratives that can go backward and sideways as well as forward, encompassing multiple time frames and settings to create a potentially infinitely large metatext and sometimes the seemingly infinite delay of the resolution of narrative hermeneutics. A seriality not constrained by a linear narrative structure allows series such as *Star Trek, Babylon 5* (1993–1998), and *Xena: Warrior Princess* (1995–2001) over a period of time to establish multiple back stories, parallel histories that may be periodically revisited, characters and peoples who appear for the duration of an episode or two and disappear again into other "lives" and possible futures. Interconnected story lines, both realized and implied, extend far beyond any single episode to become a metatext that structures production, diegesis, and reception. Cult television's imaginary universes support an inexhaustible range of narrative possibilities, inviting, supporting, and rewarding close textual analysis, interpretation, and inventive reformulations.

The deliberate production of cult television programs that occurred in the 1990s relates to a reconfiguration of the American television industry that began in the 1970s. In their essay "Rewriting Popularity: The Cult *Files,*" Jimmie Reeves, Mark Rodgers, and Michael Epstein discuss a shift from the centralized "network-era television" of "TVI" to the diffused, multichannel, post-Fordist, and postmodern "TVII."[4] Syndication, globalization, the rise of multichannel cable, satellite and digital television, and domestic technologies such as remote control handsets, videocassette recorders, and networked personal computers have, Reeves, Rodgers, and Epstein argue, created an increasingly fractured television audience. This caused programmers to seek small but demographically desirable "niche audiences" or to commission shows that "put together a series of interlocking appeals to a number of discrete but potentially interconnected audiences."[5] Channels such as the Sci-Fi Channel constitute and target "cult" audiences by defining their program content in terms of genre. Such strategies allow them to establish their own brand identity and attract audiences that constitute a relatively identifiable, specific, and consistent demographic that can be further targeted by advertisers. In a multichannel environment, success is achieved through specialist and not generalist program content.

1990s cult television evidences this same commercial logic, addressing not the "homogeneous mass" audience but rather a variety of interconnected subcultural and special interest groups.

In countries with populations as large as that of the United States, or even that of the United Kingdom, however, amalgamating the fragmented audience around cult television programs results in viewing figures in the millions. Hence, unlike many low-budget cult films aimed at niche audiences of aficionados, cult television is fairly mainstream fare. Produced by Hollywood studios or major corporations such as the BBC that can afford high production values and broadcast on major channels, often in prime-time viewing slots, series such as *The X-Files* or *Buffy the Vampire Slayer* (1997–2003) address a sizable television audience with the aim of both attracting and maintaining regular viewers and fostering among them a high proportion of avid fans. Yet these programs' economic viability does not stem mainly from their first-run audiences; the multichannel universe offers outlets for endless circulation, each repeat showing garnering further profits for the producers. Cult programs recycle endlessly as local stations and satellite channels screen the syndicated episodes. At the present moment in the United Kingdom, the Murdoch-owned Sky One cable and satellite channel slots episodes of *Star Trek: The Next Generation, Star Trek: Deep Space Nine,* and *Star Trek: Voyager* throughout its schedule. The BBC rotates *The Next Generation, Deep Space Nine,* and *Voyager* in its "tea-time" early evening slots. In New York City, Channel Eleven, WPIX, has been rerunning *The Next Generation* for years, a practice common among local stations around the country. The new domestic technologies provide further opportunities for commercial exploitation via video and DVD sales aimed at the avid fans. The most successful of cult television programs—e.g., *Star Trek, The X-Files,* and *Buffy the Vampire Slayer*—also circulate in other forms intended for fans (specialized magazines, novels, licensed merchandise) as media conglomerates such as Paramount/Viacom and Fox use their flagship franchise to maximize profits across all divisions. *Star Trek,* of course, also exists as a profitable film series, a status to which *The X-Files* producers may have aspired with the release of *The X-Files* film. The first-run broadcast of a single episode of a successful cult television program forms but one small component of a vast franchise empire.

Star Trek was not the first television series to achieve cult status, being preceded, among others, by *Quatermass* in the 1950s and *The Avengers* (1961–1969), but it did establish the pattern for the cult television program. *Star Trek* began its long life just at the wrong time, before the industrial reconfiguration of the 1970s, when American network executives still sought the largest audience rather than the most desirable demographics. Despite inspiring intense loyalty among some viewers, whose dedication was enough to save the program for a third season through a massive letter-writing campaign, it was canceled in 1969. But the fan network responsible for extending the original run kept the series in the public eye. *Star Trek* continued to make money for its producers long after the original series had gone out of production as local stations showed the seventy-nine episodes again and again, satisfying current fans, attracting new ones, and ensuring the program's place in the pop culture Hall of Fame. Paramount, which had acquired the rights to the program after buying out the Desilu Studios, considered reviving the series with the original cast, but after the first *Star Wars* proved the viability of the science fiction blockbuster, decided instead to make *Star Trek: The Motion Picture* (1979), the first in a series that eventually included ten feature films. In 1987, Paramount exploited the possibilities of the new TVII mediascape with *Star Trek: The Next Generation.* Bypassing the three powerful American television networks (ABC, CBS, and NBC), the studio sold the series directly to local stations, gambling on making the bulk of its profits not through first-run showings but through eventual syndication. The gamble paid off well enough to inspire the production of three more *Star Trek* series: *Deep Space Nine, Voyager,* and *Enterprise.* The Star Trek franchise by now includes the ten feature films and the five television series, as well as a vast collection of official novels, episode guides, and other series-related books, comics, magazines, and a full range of commercial merchandise such as dolls, models, collectors' cards, posters, photographs, calendars, jewelry, costumes, and so on. Perhaps more important, *Star Trek* occupies such a central place in popular culture that three feature films, *Galaxy Quest, Free Enterprise,* and *Trekkies* pay homage to its status as the ur–cult television show, while Star Trek phrases have entered common parlance: "beam me up," "phasers," "warp speed," and the like.

    Star Trek's commercial success and longevity have inspired a plethora of series seeking to capture something of its magic and to emulate its success. What the producers of the original *Star Trek* series did unknowingly, other producers have attempted to replicate. Three years after *The Next Generation,* ABC made a deliberate bid for cultdom with *Twin Peaks,* the brainchild of cult movie director David Lynch. Promoted as "the series that will change TV,"[6] *Twin Peaks'* subject matter and narrative form are wholly different from those of *Star Trek,* but the series used a variety of textual and marketing strategies with an excess that, with hindsight, may be considered typical of cult television as a metagenre. Intertextuality, metatextuality, ironic and/or surreal humor, eclecticism, pastiche, and self-referentiality combine to draw viewers into intense imaginative and interpretative engagement with the series. But *Twin Peaks,* for all its calculated aspiration toward cult status, failed to win the large, avid audience that it desired. The hype around the show ensured that the first few episodes won it a large share of the American television audience, but thereafter its ratings plummeted, and the series was canceled after just two seasons and thirty episodes.[7]

Twin Peaks' failure was soon superseded by the extraordinary success of a second deliberate cult series, *The X-Files.* In the shared ambitions and divergent destinies of these two series, it is possible to identify some of the strategies that make a television series "cult." *Twin Peaks* was essentially a murder mystery that hinged its imaginative appeal around the single central enigma of "who killed Laura Palmer?" While such a premise can easily sustain a miniseries, it was not, it seems, enough to maintain the interest of large numbers of viewers over a long period of time. *The X-Files* adopted a very different narrative strategy, combining self-contained episodes with an ongoing story arc or "mythology" concerning UFOs and a vast government conspiracy. It could offer the pleasures of both story line resolutions within single episodes *and* an endlessly deferred resolution to the overarching puzzle constructed through the series as a whole. Unlike *Twin Peaks, The X-Files* plugged into a variety of subcultures and subcultural discourses, including science fiction, the paranormal, conspiracism, and ufology. The fortuitous timing of the series' dark subject matter resonated with the wider zeitgeist of paranoia that followed the end of the Cold War and the countdown to the new millennium. At the same time, *The X-Files'* release in 1993 coincided with the rapid expansion of the Internet in the mid-1990s, allowing it to take advantage of the possibilities the Internet presented for word-of-mouth promotion, connectivity between subcultures, and, above all, the rapid expansion of active fandom affected by the accessibility and attractiveness of on-line fan cultures. Perhaps more than any other single phenomenon, it is the success of *The X-Files* that ensured that from the early 1990s onward cult television has become an industry in and of itself. Series such as *Dark Skies, Millennium, Hercules: The Legendary Journeys, Babylon 5, Xena: Warrior Princess, Roar, Ultraviolet, Buffy the Vampire Slayer, Angel, Dark Angel,* and *Farscape* have all attempted, with varying degrees of success, to win not just large audiences but large *avid* audiences—audiences that will not only treat the series as "appointment viewing" but also become consumers of a full range of officially produced merchandise.

"Cult television" has become a metagenre that caters to intense, interpretative audience practices. Reeves, Rodgers, and Epstein argue, "What distinguishes cult shows from typical fare is that a relatively large percentage of the viewers are avid fans and that these fans have relatively high visibility compared to the avid fans of other shows."[8] This "visibility" arises from the distinctive practices of cult television fans, which include the formation of loose interpretative communities and the production of tertiary texts such as fan fiction, scratch videos, cultural criticism essays, filk music, Web sites, and fan art. These intensive and interpretative audience practices, we would argue, stem from an imaginative involvement with the cult television narratives that afford fans enormous scope for further interpretation, speculation, and invention. Cult television programs' dense intertextuality ranges from 1930s Hollywood serials to 1950s television shows, to classical mythology and Shakespeare. The programs formulate complex internal logics, combine realistic and archetypal characters, and construct fantastical worlds where philosophical and ethical issues can be explored and grand gestures enacted free from the obscuring trivia and mundane concerns of everyday reality.

To date, academic research on cult television has focused mainly on the avid fans, since cult television emerged as a metagenre coincident with cultural studies' reevaluation of audience reception paradigms. Reacting against Marxist and social science traditions that portrayed audiences as passive dupes, such scholars as John Fiske celebrated the "active" audience who rejected a text's dominant meanings in favor of manufacturing their own. Some scholars, such as Henry Jenkins and Constance Penley, have argued that cult television fans engage in semiotic resistance by appropriating the diegetic universes and characters owned by giant corporations such as Paramount/Viacom and Fox to construct their own oppositional texts in which characters engage in activities, such as homosexuality, prohibited by the authorized texts.[9] We would not deny that the pleasure of resistance figures in the activities of some avid fans; for example, writers of romantic stories about *The Next Generation*'s Captain Picard and Dr. Beverly Crusher or about *The X-Files'* Fox Mulder and Dana Scully often claim to rectify the wrongs inflicted on the characters by the corporate owners who refuse to permit them to have a sexual relationship. But we would hazard that the vast amount of fan fiction writing, together with the production of

Web sites, fan art, and the like, stems not from resistance to capitalism but rather from an imaginative engagement with cult television programs encouraged by the textual characteristics we discussed earlier. The collective episodes of the original text have themselves established a metaverse rich with spatial/temporal narrative settings and character possibilities; fans can, if they wish, indulge in an imaginative extension of the metaverse that conforms in spirit, if not to the letter, to the "canon." As Sara Gwenllian-Jones argues elsewhere,

> Cult television's serial and segmented forms, its familiar formulae, its accumulated multiple storylines, its metatextuality, its ubiquitous intertextuality and intra-textuality, its extension across a variety of other media, its modes of self-reflexivity and constant play of interruption and excess, work together to overwhelm the processual order of cause and effect, enigma and resolution, extending story events and other narrative and textual elements across boundless networks of interconnected possibilities.[10]

Seriality, textual density, and, perhaps most especially, the nonlinearity of multiple time frames and settings that create the potentially infinitely large metatext of a cult television text create the space for fans to revel in the development of characters and long, complex narrative arcs both within the commercial texts and their own, noncommercial spin-offs.

We have grouped the twelve chapters in this volume into three separate parts: "Cult," "Fictions," and "Fans." The first part deals with the specificity of cult texts, production, and audiences. Philippe Le Guern, working in the French sociological tradition of Pierre Bourdieu, argues that the concept of cult is neither a linguistic game nor a reality but rather a socially constructed representation. Mark Jancovich and Nathan Hunt, as well as Petra Kuppers, are also explicitly or implicitly indebted to Bourdieu, asserting that fans position themselves against the mainstream not through "textual poaching," in Jenkins's phrase, but by valorizing the "quality" of texts that seem opposed to the debased commercialism of the television industry. Jancovich and Hunt say that fans' "persistent interest in scripts and the ways in which they develop characters and story lines shows the insistence on literary values, as does the concern with the devices and techniques of storytelling." Petra Kuppers makes similar if more specific claims about the fans of *Babylon 5:* "The [fan and fan-oriented] writings around *B5* continually stress the program's quality status, celebrating the complexity of its literary and self-aware approach and rejecting as undemanding the formulaic nature of much television science fiction." Roberta E. Pearson's contribution uses Patrick Stewart of *Star Trek: The Next Generation* as a case study to consider the relationship between a cult television star and his character, arguing that cult television conflates character and actor to an even greater extent than other television drama, but that specific aspects of Stewart's star image have enabled him to some extent to break free of Captain Jean-Luc Picard.

The chapters in "Fictions" focus on the imaginative worlds of cult television programs. Sara Gwenllian-Jones argues that the dense texts of such programs as *Xena: Warrior Princess,* together with their commercial and noncommercial spin-offs, constitute deterritorialized fictional worlds that approximate virtual realities, supporting immersive and interactive viewer engagements. David Black shows that fans of the original *Avengers* television series were so fully invested in the program's imaginative universe that they deeply resented the changes wrought by the Warner Bros. feature film. Karen Backstein and Mary Hammond show how cult television programs provide the perfect vehicle for the metaphorical exploration of social concerns. Backstein looks at issues of race and ethnicity in *The X-Files,* and Hammond considers the ways in which *Buffy the Vampire Slayer* condenses the anxieties of both its adolescent audience and its adolescent country.

The four chapters in "Fans" all focus on the fandoms of particular cult programs. Alan McKee's analysis of Doctor Who fandom suggests that the distinction between the cultural production of fans and that of television producers is not nearly as clear as those who celebrate the active audience have asserted. Paradoxically, scholars such as Henry Jenkins, by granting power to the institutions that originate the television programs, have returned "precisely to the binaries of 'production' and 'consumption' from which they explicitly want to escape." Toby Miller mounts a rather more acerbic attack on the active audience paradigm, asserting that *Avengers* fans are not semiotic guerrillas but pathetic trainspotters. Jeffrey Sconce's chapter in some ways serves as a riposte to Miller. Sconce investigates the connection between the Heaven's Gate suicide cultists and Star Trek fandom, concluding, "If only they had spent less time reading the Bible and more time watching *Star Trek,* they might still be alive today." Sconce's facetious conclusion masks a serious point: far from the deluded fantasists of the popular imagination, cult television fans inhabit imaginative worlds and actual communities that vastly enrich their lives. Eva Vieth's chapter concerns *Starship Orion,* a program from the 1960s little known outside its native Germany that stands as a strange doppelgänger for *Star Trek*. How do fans maintain their enthusiasm and their community for more than thirty years sustained only by eight original episodes and a few novelizations, rather than the ever-expanding universe of the Star Trek franchise?

The cult television phenomenon is a fluid and evolutionary process. The essays collected here do not attempt to provide definitive answers to the questions the phenomenon poses, but rather to map its major contours and dynamics at a particular historical moment. As television industries, particularly in the United States, responded to the challenges of an ever-fragmenting audience and ever-evolving technologies, cult television became increasingly central to their strategic positioning in a marketplace that includes not only the television texts themselves but all the ancillary products and spin-offs associated with them. Cult television, like blockbuster films such as *Star Wars,* is symptomatic of a shift away from medium specificity and toward the production and marketing of transmedial fictions through the diversification of corporate interests. The study of cult television provides an important means of exploring wider issues concerning the culture industries and the circulation and consumption of cultural texts. Much remains to be said on the topic, and we hope that this book will serve as a foundation for further investigation.

Notes

1. *"Casablanca:* Cult Movies and Intertextual Collage," in Umberto Eco, *Travels in Hyperreality,* trans. William Weaver (London: Picador, 1987), 198.

2. Jeffrey Sconce, "'Trashing' the Academy: Taste, Excess, and an Emerging Politics of Cinematic Style," *Screen* 36, no. 4 (winter 1995): 374.

3. Jeffrey Sconce, "Oh My God, They've Killed Dickens . . . You Bastards!" in *Dickens on Screen,* ed. John Glavin (Cambridge: Cambridge University Press, 2003).

4. Jimmie L. Reeves, Mark C. Rodgers, and Michael Epstein, "Rewriting Popularity: The Cult *Files,*" in *Deny All Knowledge: Reading the X-Files,* ed. David Lavery, Angela Hague, and Marla Cartwright (London: Faber, 1996), 22–35.

5. Jim Collins, "Television and Postmodernism," in *Channels of Discourse, Reassembled,* ed. Robert C. Allen (London and New York: Routledge, 1994), 342.

6. Ibid., 343.

7. See David Lavery, ed., *Full of Secrets: Critical Approaches to Twin Peaks* (Detroit: Wayne State University Press, 1995).

8. Reeves, Rodgers, and Epstein, "Rewriting Popularity," 27.

9. Henry Jenkins, *Textual Poachers: Television Fans and Participatory Culture* (New York: Routledge, 1992).

10. Sara Gwenllian-Jones, "The Sex Lives of Cult Television Characters," *Screen* 43, no. 1 (2002): 84.

Part I
Cult

Toward a Constructivist Approach to Media Cults

Philippe Le Guern

Translated by Richard Crangle

■ Today, the term "cult" is widely applied in relation to television series *(The Prisoner, The X-Files, Friends)*, films *(The Rocky Horror Picture Show, Pink Flamingo, Titanic, Casablanca)*, novels (John Kennedy Toole's *A Confederacy of Dunces*, David Lodge's *Small World*),[1] and the world of music (Elvis Presley, the Beatles, the Velvet Underground,[2] Joy Division).

The term is just as readily applied to "classic" texts as it is to creations in the lower reaches of the cultural hierarchy (1970s children's television programs such as *Goldorak* or Christophe Izard's *L'île aux enfants*, gore or psychotronic films, second features or B movies). It can indicate a heterogeneous range of audiences: a fan culture of segmented or specialized audiences, generational affinities or youth culture (for example, the cult status of Luc Besson's *Le grand bleu*), or the interest of a mass audience that acquires the aspect of a social phenomenon, as with the film *Titanic*. In common usage, the term "cult" has even wider application and refers to a common cultural background; the Volkswagen Beetle, Solex moped, and Citroen 2CV[3] are described as "cult objects" because they evoke nostalgia for a common cultural background. For example, on 17 July 2000 the French newspaper *Libération* compared Queniborough, an English village affected by outbreaks of "mad cow disease," to *"The Village of the Damned,* the cult science fiction film of the 50s";[4] the following day, an article about the TV game show *Tournez manège* referred to "games that become cults."[5] In each of the cases described, cultural relationships with texts seem to be sites of genuine social and cultural interplay. Even where the texts concerned seem to be devoid of artistic legitimacy, they are invested with aspirations or claims to identity: they unite members of the same generation around a common lifestyle; they forcefully translate strategies of position and opposition; they express cultural preferences by emphasizing potentially distinctive values.

However, the semantic elasticity of the term "cult" in contemporary usage, its intimate connections with vocabularies of religiosity,[6] and its ambiguity from a functional point of view—where the "cult" gathers together a community but also distinguishes between values, cultural preferences, and social positions—make any attempt at definition and delimitation of the concept and its uses particularly difficult.

Defining the Cult: Textual Features, Religious Metaphor, or Distinctive Culture?

At first sight, it might seem that there exists an objective agreement surrounding cult texts: for example, in books that list the corpus of cult films or TV series;[7] the French TV program *Culte fiction,* which pronounced Jimi Hendrix "cultissime";[8] and so on. However, such descriptions are clearly just as heterogeneous as are the definitions of "cult" that their authors offer for the typologies they adopt (classifications by genre, period, and so on). They indicate texts that may be rare (unscreened episodes or "secret" films) or may be widely distributed; they refer sometimes to membership of a fan culture that is a restricted community and other times to a much wider spectatorial experience.

Should the concept of cult therefore be reduced from a nominalist perspective to the product of a linguistic game, to one of those classification schemes created by the observer but devoid of reality? Or perhaps the cult is no more than a representation arising from a project of constructing social reality, and the interplays of definition and classification with which the idea of the cult is loaded should not be brought to light. Is it, in the end, the usage of the concept of the cult, its mobilization, and its varying interpretations by audiences that should be examined, independently of the question of whether the cult corresponds to an objective reality and a proven body of work? When an individual refers to his or her own cult films or records, what do we learn about the individual's tastes and values, identification with one or more social generational communities, and cultural practices?

It is not a question of making the relativity of the concept of the cult vanish, nor of erasing the historical paths that compose it. However, it is useful here to bypass two sociologically unsatisfactory alternatives: rejection of the point of view of the participants, or consideration *only* of the point of view of the participants (which runs the risk of overlooking the fact that the cult is also a social construct).[9] From this perspective, constructivist perspectives offer ways of evading "the almost insurmountable difficulties which beset the work of definition and establishment of 'objective' criteria"[10] by repositioning the question of the cult as a dynamic culminating in a socially constructed representation, without eclipsing its symbolic effectiveness:

> One may say without contradiction that social realities are simultaneously social fictions with no other basis than social construction, and that they exist in reality, in as much as they are collectively recognised.[11]

The scarcity of texts dealing with the concept of the cult in relation to media and contemporary cultural forms testifies to the difficulty of objectivizing this volatile concept, which simultaneously implies a value judgment (to describe a work as "cult" is to admit it to a pantheon) and certain forms of connection to cultural objects (its functions in a community of appreciation). In addition, the concept of cult depends partly on a social world—that of fans—that is difficult to study because an approximative sociology can attribute to it a subordinate position in the social environment and an inability to reflect the meanings of its own practices.

A second difficulty concerns the analogy of media cults and religious cults. Walter Benjamin, analyzing the subjects of authenticity and reproduction, presents the idea that an art such as cinema can only exist at the level of reproduction (as opposed to unique production) in which reproducibility invalidates the "cult value" of art.[12] Benjamin defines the religious aura as the unique presence of the original, whose authenticity is dissolved by reproduction. Of course, my intention here is not to discuss the coherence of Benjamin's ideas[13] but to investigate whether his definition of cult value clarifies the premises of contemporary cults. At first sight, it certainly appears that cinema or television produces effects that contradict the essential characteristics attributed to classical art. The association of uniqueness with cult value is abolished; cinema and television are mass media. It is, however, possible that the *organization* of artistic rarity through single screenings, "underground" projections, and cinephilic rituals for audiences of initiates organized in particular cinematographic contexts may lead to artistic cult value, for which Benjamin emphasizes the need for difficulty of access.

On the other hand, the study of fans, their tastes, and their practices frequently leads to the use of schemas that borrow from religious *doxa*. This involves metaphorically registering the formation of communities of spectators,[14] the deployment of media rituals, and the supervaluation of objects (such as TV stars) around which the audience dedicates a cult. But the utilization of these religious categories and the numerous epistemological distortions that it generates, even in the scientific field, are rarely viewed objectively.[15] Jean-Claude Schmitt emphasizes the limits of the analogical model and hagiographic comparisons, starting with the attitudes of devotion that surround the memory of the French singer Claude François:

> one might think of the attitude of the faithful towards the saints, in a quite different context. But . . . the stars of today are not the inheritors of the saints. There is no doubt that they have borrowed some of their features, but they participate in a social system, indeed a religion, which is profoundly different. . . . As for the ephemeral stars whom the media lay on the altars of "show business" today, are they not just the plaything, along with their followers, of those impresarios and financiers who hold the reins of their success and destiny?[16]

More generally, although the term "cult" is widely used by journalistic commentators, who use it to describe—partly contributing, according to a truly tautological logic, a social consistency to a representation that they simultaneously observe and generate—the audience success achieved by numerous television series (such as *The X-Files*) from the mid-1990s onward and the related phenomena generated by this success (growing numbers of fan cultures; interest in the series amplified by the development of Internet discussion groups that promote new forms of appropriation, socialization, and usage by "youth" audiences; increase in merchandising via spin-off products), it remains largely foreign to academic critics.[17] With the exception of a few short notes or passing mentions, the concept of cult is almost completely absent from French media research. Dominique Pasquier is one of the few authors to mention the concept of the cult, identifying "popular movements of the fan club type, elitist movements which form around cult series."[18] By limiting cult culture to an audience of the "happy few," however, this definition poses another question: can we describe a successful blockbuster film like *Titanic,* for example, as a cult text? Daniel Dayan and Elihu Katz define cult programs by distinguishing them from ceremonial programs:

> certain films which, like *Woodstock* or *The Rocky Horror Picture Show,* become the object of a true cult, with the accompanying obligation to witness and record in a communal register the habitual behaviour of members of the cinema audience.[19]

But by restricting the concept of cult texts to ritualized and communal practices, does this definition not pass silently over the cultural claims with which the forms of cult membership are loaded? François Jost, considering the connection between "filmicity" and genre, suggests a radical heterogeneity between the status of the book and that of the film, from the point of view of both the location of its construction and its modes of appropriation: "a novel one considers to be a great work is a 'bedside book,' while a film one worships is a 'cult film,' whose value is proportional to the difficulty of seeing it."[20] This analysis corresponds to those that make reading the book the product of a belief system in which the book is perceived as a condition of cultural status:

> For the old respect for the book, whose rarity governed its price, is substituted the attraction and respect for "rare" texts. . . . The quest for cultural status can in this way appear in the sacredness with which the book object is surrounded, in the ways of its reading and in those texts which are chosen.[21]

The sociology of the social uses of culture, taking into account the modifications induced by the extension of audiovisual practices, encourages a grasp (with many shades of meaning) of the opposition of book versus film or TV that underlies that other opposition of culture versus entertainment.

For reasons that probably relate to an older interest, which is less marked by prejudices concerning popular cultures and practices,[22] and are probably also influenced by cultural studies and related approaches that take into consideration interactions between cultural forms and community groupings (the concepts of camp and kitsch and so on have in this way been related to cultist culture), studies dedicated to the world of fans and to cult phenomena have enjoyed a much less limited development in North American research contexts.[23] In particular it is worth mentioning the work of Jonathan Hoberman and Jonathan Rosenbaum on midnight movie screenings and the collection of essays on cult films edited by Jean-Pierre Telotte.[24]

Umberto Eco's essay on the film *Casablanca* seems to have played a particularly formative role in research into cult films, sometimes as a dominant model, sometimes as a reflective foil.[25] In summary, it asks whether cult texts are reducible to the presence of specific textual features.[26] Eco proposes cult films as texts saturated with references and cinephilic and narrative clichés that turn it "into a museum, so to speak, for moviegoers."[27] In other words, it is the narrative structure itself—separable into segments of quotation that are likely to intersect with the cultural background of each spectator—that is the condition of a text's status as "cult." This thesis leads Eco to deduce that *Hamlet* and *The Rocky Horror Picture Show* are cult texts while the *Decameron* is not. The blind spot of such a proposition is clearly the spectator her- or himself and the latitude in the definition that guides the choice of cult texts. It is notable that the cultist relationship with texts frequently presents itself as a cultivated response to a noncultivated culture (that is, a culture with little legitimacy).

Cult texts are often, though not exclusively, little-recognized or underground films (gore films, B movies, second features, and genre films, whose narrative structures include highly predictable elements), or films or television series that display more of the logic of industrial production than the politics of individual authors (at least in the most dignified sense of the term, which disqualifies Ed Wood and John Carpenter). To a certain extent, the cultist relationship with texts can be defined as a form of inversion of traditional value and a valorization of less "respectable" elements. This may involve, for example, the presence of "low" aesthetic elements (notably kitsch) or again the repetition of recurrent motifs that indicate genre films that capture the attention of cultist audiences. Productions that come to be regarded as cults are frequently those that have "escaped" the critics, which have not benefited from distribution resources, or whose production has been controlled by economic limitations that are particularly visible on the screen. The example of the B movie is sufficient to illustrate the nature of the constraints that apply to this type of production: "Often the characters were not even centred in the frame; but it would have cost too much to shoot another take, so that would do."[28] At the same time, the absence of resources or the slim credibility of the special effects can define style for cultist audiences.

The essays collected in J. P. Telotte's *The Cult Film Experience* address this ambiguity very well. Most of these authors agree on a typology that places cult films regarded as classics (*Casablanca* being a prime example) as "midnight movies," that is to say, films that become the object of a ceremony of appropriation, such as *The Rocky Horror Picture Show*. Several authors identify internal characteristics of cult films while trying hard to divine a social origin for cultist phenomena:

> The property of being a cult film, whatever that turns out to be, is not necessarily inherent in *Casablanca,* which is basically a romantic political melodrama that happens to have been elevated to cult status. But

it *is* an inherent property of a film like *Evil Dead II,* which has been designed to please a cult audience.[29]

Or:

On this point I differ from Eco, who argues that these films "are born in order to become cult objects." No film, I would say, is naturally a cult film; all cult films are adopted children.[30]

The authors attempt to respond to the question of whether the cult film is a genre, that is, a supertext, or whether particular genres are predisposed to become cults, while also examining the interactions between cult films and their audiences. A cult film can indicate a private experience or, on the contrary, a collective experience: "these are films with which we, as solitary or united members of the audience, feel we have a relationship."[31] It sometimes encounters relatively marginal and cinephilic audiences, sometimes vast general audiences. It may or may not generate ritualized practices. In the end, the diversity of approaches and the apparent heterogeneity of (and sometimes contradictory) results obtained is less an indicator of a defective methodology or the inability of authors to propose a once-and-for-all definition of "cult" than an indicator of the mutability of a concept that varies according to the nature of the texts, contexts, accompanying discourses, periods, and audiences concerned.

The epistemological relativism that the examination of such a concept invites does not, however, prevent the location of recurrent traits and the construction of a sort of idealized cult. Generally speaking, it is possible to say that

1. the cult expresses the attribution of a value;
2. it functions as a unifier that produces groups and communities of spectators;
3. these groups are most often limited to audiences of a "happy few" but can also unite members of the same generation (the cult then takes on a countercultural value);
4. the group maintains enthusiasm for the cult text;
5. the concrete manifestation of this relationship is expressed in the practice of rituals.

Cult texts will therefore be those that display a form of rarity, with low accessibility—works rejected at the time by cultured spectators as outside the world of legitimate culture and by the "mass audience" for their disappointing lack of special effects, the weakness of their scripts, or the absence of the major stars expected in spectacular cinema—but which in some way oppose the uses of the most distinctive works of art operated by dominant groups, the methods of their appropriation and expression of taste, and the supreme affirmation of the excellence of "high culture."[32] This involves making "low culture" sufficiently distinctive to put in place the elements of a structural opposition between certain categories of audience.

But unlike those "enlightened" individuals whose degree of familiarity with mainstream culture authorizes the wisest knowledge and recognition of legitimate texts, devotees of cult texts practice a form of false cultural allodoxy. This consists not of mistaking "operetta for great music," to borrow a phrase from Pierre Bourdieu,[33] but of finding interest and value in the material that critics and "good" taste have left by the wayside: defects become qualities, kitsch becomes a stylistic effect, and stereotypes become a maker's mark. From this point of view, cultism could be described as a practice, more or less conscious and often ironic, of putting into perspective judgments of value and taste and submission to the hierarchy of works produced by mechanisms of consecration. The irreverent response to cult films that finds expression in ritual (creating noise, throwing objects) evidences a new way of responding to texts in opposition to dark and silent auditoria or that other location of cult, the museum. Whereas the museum presents objects removed from private appropriation and intended for appreciation at a distance, cultism entails intervention by the audience, where the show takes place as much in the auditorium as it does on the screen.

Equally striking is the extent to which cultist culture is also a type of cultivated culture: it mobilizes an encyclopedic knowledge based on exhaustiveness and scholarship—particularly valorized in the identification of intertexts to which spectators frequently apply themselves—which requires a heavy investment of time and money. John Tulloch remarks, "the standard knowledge of minute details of the series' history is prodigious, and is a major marker of being accepted as a 'real' fan."[34] My own observations of members of French fan clubs of TV series[35] confirm the extent to which the symbolic "profit" that a hyperspecialized knowledge of such products offers has a practical cost that is often very high.

> The dominant groups do not have a monopoly on the uses of the work
> of art objectively—and sometimes subjectively—driven by the search
> for exclusive appropriation, vouching for the unique "personality" of

the owner. But the conditions of material appropriation are lacking; nothing remains of the search for exclusivity other than the singularity of the mode of appropriation. To like the same things in different ways, or to like other things in the same way which are less strongly designated for admiration, by strategies of intensification, excess and displacement which, by a principle of the permanent transformation of tastes, allow dominated groups, less economically well off and therefore devoted almost exclusively to symbolic appropriation, to ensure an exclusive possession at any moment. Intellectuals and artists have a particular liking for the most risky (but most profitable) strategies of distinction, those which consist of confirming the power which is theirs alone to constitute insignificant objects as works of art or, worse, those already treated as works of art but in another mode, by other classes or sections of classes (as in kitsch). In this case, it is the method of consumption which creates, in that the object of consumption and secondary delight transforms everyday goods supplied for common consumption (westerns, comic strips, family photos, graffiti) into works of distinguished and distinctive culture.[36]

Such an analysis seems hardly removed at all from a definition of the cultist relationship with culture and the modes of appropriation (in a secondary manner) of texts, even if to make the cultist relationship with texts the consequence only of a socially dominated position is somewhat debatable. More broadly, it is the way in which cultural industries are likely to offer symbolic benefits and the development of distinctive strategies that needs to be questioned here.

A Participatory Culture: Communities, Fans, and Rituals

Traditionally perceived as an irrational and excessive form, the cult relationship with the text is frequently described in terms of an enthusiastic, indeed even pathological, attachment:

> The fan is consistently characterized (referencing the term's origins) as a potential fanatic. This means that fandom is seen as excessive, bordering on deranged, behavior.[37]

The concept of the cult is in this way spontaneously associated with that of the fan, sustaining the most common preconceptions of the fetishistic behavior attributed to fans, a form of hysterical identification with the idol. But on the contrary, scrupulous observation of the world of fans (which only an approximate sociology would dare to describe as homogeneous, in either the social properties of the participants or the practices that define them and the interests that motivate them) suggests an approach to the comprehension of cult phenomena with many shades of meaning and without giving in to the commonsense pseudo-evidence that makes the cult relationship with texts the automatic expression of dominated tastes, that is to say, the counterpoint of legitimate texts and the legitimate way of dealing with texts. From this point of view, it helps to think of cult practice as a specific type of constitution of a cultural heritage (to which the arrival of the video recorder contributed a great deal), as the distinctive assertion of tastes that are too often summarily labeled as kitsch or immature, and as the valorization of new forms of cultural expression and mediation (in particular television) that call into question the oppositions between popular and high culture and between minor and major arts and genres, as well as the passivity attributed to popular audiences.

In one respect, the conditions of access to texts constitute a central element of cultism as a form of participatory culture: the late-night screenings described by Hoberman and Rosenbaum, in particular, appear from the start to attract a secret audience of the "happy few." In accordance with the rules of the symbolic economy, the use-value of films distributed via such showings is strictly dependent on their rarity. The choice of films (unreleased and underground films, sometimes without a distributor, difficult to see outside late-night screenings) and the specificity of the conditions of access, due partly to the late hour of such screenings or the specialized nature of the venue, are just as much elements that constitute the rarity and therefore the attraction of these showings.

In another respect, cultism manifests itself through ritualized practices: the cult is a unifying phenomenon and implies a cooperative effort that defines a communal membership. Discourses and behavior patterns are enacted according to often specially codified modalities that allow a definition of the boundary between those who are "one of us," the initiated, and those who are "not one of us." The terminology attached to the cult of *The Rocky Horror Picture Show* refers in this way to "virgins," spectators attending for the first time, as opposed to "regulars." Pasquier also observes that TV series such as *Hélène et les garçons* are just as capable of assembling audience groups as "in general, cult programs reaching more targeted audiences."[38] Quantitative and qualitative data are unfortunately either nonexistent or too approximate to provide sufficiently precise information on the composition of audiences during cult film showings.[39] The secretive nature of cult showings is a recurrent doxic element, but one that does not necessarily go without saying. According to Laurent Aknin, "in Los Angeles, the *Rocky Horror Show* sold out almost every evening, but for the most part it was the same spectators who came back every time."[40] Robert Schlokoff describes how the Paris Festival du Film Fantastique, first organized in 1974, had a full house from the outset; a quarter of the audience, from Paris and the suburbs, was composed of fans.[41] Descriptions of the rituals that accompany each showing are more numerous and often very detailed, particularly in the case of *The Rocky Horror Picture Show,* which perhaps owes its emblematic status[42] to its ability to fulfill every last element on the cultist checklist: critical praise; audience devotion that emerges as a social phenomenon; countercultural themes such as sex, drugs, and rock music; and so on. The relations between rituals and interactive responses—throwing rice, using water pistols, recitation of dialogue—lead commentators to wonder about the social and anthropological meanings of such transgressions of the norms of viewing (violations of the rules of the darkened auditorium, participation of costumed spectators). The performance of the audience becomes a sort of supertext with its own rules and constraints, implying a complete apprenticeship through its assumption of a previous knowledge of the film and its dialogue.

The contextualization of cultist phenomena must also be considered: how are the codes that govern the rituals established and distributed in a scheme of repetition and variation?[43] From town to town or country to country, the structure and meaning of the rituals relating to the same film may vary considerably. For example, a large part of the ritual in Britain and the United States consists of entering into a dialogue with the film, even adding one's own responses. Aknin notes,

> such a performance is difficult to achieve for a non-anglophone
> spectator, who makes up for it by playing with the subtitles. In Paris,
> the physical performance takes precedence over the verbal. This has
> sometimes led to certain deviations and to practices (flour in place of
> rice, for example) which are roundly condemned by the holders of the
> orthodoxy of the cult.[44]

On a more general level, it is the whole culture of late-night screenings and cult projections that needs to form the object of study, varying according to national contexts. Gregory A. Waller, for example, emphasizes the importance of "drive-in" culture to American teenagers' interest in cult films and the link between cinemas showing cult films and FM rock radio stations—neither of which have an equivalent in France:

in exchange for free advertising, the station was billed as co-promoter
of the midnight movies and split whatever profits remained after the
theatre recouped its operating expenses and rental costs.[45]

Finally, in the light of the development of domestic audiovisual practices,
it must be considered whether cult rituals have adapted to the world of
television. Observations suggest that activities associated with cinema
auditoria can be re-created around the video recorder in the context
of fan clubs or conventions dedicated to television series. In the same
way, cult series can give rise to forms of linguistic contamination, to
practices of exchanging objects, and to the mastery of codes by "initiates." Videocassette recorders allow cumulative modes of viewing
identical to those described in relation to cinematographic screenings,
but at the same time use of video recorders modifies the conditions of access to texts and results in a logic of inheritance with multiple effects.[46]
Like books, videotapes can be kept and archived, presenting conditions
for new relationships with television series that cease to be "instant
television" or "TV events." At the same time, video recording confers
legitimacy on television series. Whereas once the BBC destroyed whole
episodes of the series *Doctor Who*[47] for want of a conservation policy,
cult series are today sold on video and the market is organized to create
collections and collectors. In the same way, television programs become
"texts"; they gain in complexity because the technological ability to
record and freeze images[48] opens the way for interpretive activities that
are more in-depth than those permitted by the one-off broadcasts of the
1960s. They legitimize the figure of the "auteur"—Patrick McGoohan
for *The Prisoner,* David Lynch for *Twin Peaks*—which is traditionally
absent from productions subject to the imperatives of industrial production and standardization.

The Social Construction of Cults

Bourdieu quotes Weber's invitation to take account of the agents and
their interests in the study of symbolic systems:

> Weber notes that, in order to understand religion, it is not sufficient to
> study the symbolic forms of a religious type . . . nor even the immanent
> structure of the religious message, the mythological corpus or the "dis-
> courses," as the structuralists do; he addresses himself to the producers
> of the religious message, to the specific interests which motivate them.[49]

Weber's invitation can be applied to the concept of the cult as a social
construct. Rosenbaum, for example, emphasizes the attempts at (cul-

tural and economic) rationalization that the label "cult" has brought into play:

> Now that it is becoming more and more difficult to distinguish between criticism and advertising in American cinematographic culture—each practice doing its best to conceal or rationalise the progressive deterioration in a social contract which was firmly established between an audience and an industry from the 1950s . . . now this erasure has left a void, a blind gaping emptiness, which only hyperbole and "star fucking" can fill—the idea of a truly *spontaneous* cinematographic cult automatically becomes suspect.[50]

The diagnosis that brings Rosenbaum to the systematization of a politics of cultification involves, it seems to me, two major suppositions that it is important to examine. First, there is the question of relocating the concept of the cult and its different uses in a historical evolution that will run—loosely put—from an original and spontaneous form of appropriation to the planning of products that are cults a priori, that is to say, even before the audience has access to them. This suggests a movement from "authentic" cults to the production of "inauthentic" cults, and clearly such an approach could be something of an irritant for defenders of an idealistic conception of culture. Simon Frith, addressing how values initially conveyed through rock music are exploited by the contemporary advertising industry, emphasizes a shift "from the counterculture of youth to the counterculture of the shop":[51]

> The use of classic rock, soul, even blues, as sound tracks for advertisements . . . has become so common that the only thing still capable of shocking me is the industrial character that the process has now taken on. . . . If it is so easy to use snatches of rock and rock stars to indicate rock during the "commercial breaks" on television, what does rock itself mean today? The answer is "the same as it always meant," but in a context in which the old values of rock—unbridled individualism, immediate community, youth in rebellion, the joy of the senses—are in future heard in playback, as memories and desires that one may only now attain by spending money to purchase other goods.[52]

To mention cult albums or bands comes back toward a postmodern reading of a cult culture that takes a retrospective look at itself with the aim of satisfying two types of audience: on the one hand, nostalgic baby boomers;[53] on the other, young consumers in search of "authentic" lifestyles and therefore "authentic" products.

This analysis is probably transposable to the area of media and especially to the world of television production. Even if, unlike rock music, there is little question of redeploying the values of emancipation and counterculture for which television has never been a favored outlet, the contemporary re-presentation of old television series, in particular, offers occasion to promote the idea of a golden age of the small screen. But more recent series also benefit from this systematic cultualization. For example, transmission of the series *Lexx* on the French channel Canal Plus was preceded by the trailer, "Welcome to the galaxy of Kitsch. *Lexx,* your new cosmic cult rendezvous."[54] This is a case not of noting the previous existence of the cult but rather of calling it into existence and inciting it, of recruiting its audience and programming its meanings in advance. The concept of the cult and the categories that ac-company it—notably kitsch—operate according to a performative logic just as much as by advertising claims aimed at audiences who have in-teriorized cult's cultural and social meanings and integrated them into their values and practices. In this way, it is possible to use terms like the "TV generation" or the "Canal Jimmy way of life."[55] Cult television series have become synonymous with participative and distinctive cul-ture: a pronounced taste for original versions and unseen episodes, an initiatory culture based on hyperknowledge of textual or paratextual elements, challenges to the domination of the written text and the strict distinction between major and minor arts, a claim of cultural indepen-dence for youth accompanied by a valorization of audiovisual elements that become the dominant elements of a new form of culture to be consecrated.[56]

The appeal of (re)discovering "cult" television series is connected to the development of domestic audiovisual technologies, which has been through two distinct phases: first, the equipment of households with television sets at the start of the 1970s; then, in the mid-1980s, the multiplication of channels and the use of the video recorder and remote control.[57] By addressing an audience of "enfants de la Télé"—to bor-row the title of a successful TF1 show whose stock-in-trade is nostalgia for a small-screen golden age—consultants and marketing specialists are simply recognizing the progressive homogenization of audiovisual prac-tices, the removal of restrictions concerning television, and its increas-ingly central cultural position. At the same time, the television industry legitimizes itself by awarding honors to aspects of television culture and thereby consecrating its own productions. This self-legitimization—which most frequently takes the form of rapturous histories of the small screen and its golden age—is completed by the "heritigization" that drives the marketing of products on video. Just as there are video series of "masterpieces of the cinematographic art," so too are there commercial video collections of the "great works" of television: twenty "anthology series of the great moments of ORTF" are available today, from *Rocambole* to *Janique Aimée* via *Les chevaliers du ciel*. By assessing the position that economic logics hold in the construction of cult phenomena, we can gauge the importance of the financial stakes represented by the video market for organizations such as Gaumont, Columbia, Warner Home Video, and even TF1 Vidéo. The strategies that underlie the marketing of commercial video collections are a useful indication of how the television industry addresses different categories of purchaser: for example, two boxed sets (three cassettes each) of the series *Ally McBeal,* priced at 249 francs each, are currently available on the French market, in both original and French-language versions; there are also two boxed sets (six cassettes each) at 199 francs per box for the series *Urgences* (the French title for the American series *ER*), but only the French version of the latter is available, suggesting a more general audience of wider age range than that of *Ally McBeal.*

The distinction between authentic/original cults and inauthentic/ planned cults, based on a historical concept whose point of transition is the rationalization and exploitation of tastes, must however be relativized in order to be understood. In one respect, even if it appears difficult to question the movement toward rationalization of the cult, this must be located in the procession of successive generations, their cultural practices, and the conditions and contexts of these practices. The cultural landscape of the early 1970s was very different from that of the early 1990s; the conditions that made possible the development and success of midnight cinema screenings and their related cult rituals are not comparable with the distribution of domestic audiovisual technologies and a relationship with culture in which the mediation of the "prescriber" has a notably reduced importance. The now ubiquitous nature of television, the spread of technologies for home use, and the use of video recorders are all factors that favor the (relative) independence of cultural choices and a greater individualization of practices. If the counterculture of the 1960s finds in *its* cult films the expression of its own values, the culture of the 1990s certainly finds in television series other values and other methods of intervention. In this sense, the cult probably expresses no more than the view that the participants have of themselves, their tastes, and their cultural and social identities. This indicates the fragility of an overly radical historicization of the cult, even if it is assumed that denunciation of the cult is partly linked to competition between the baby-boomer generation—which participated in the counterculture and is returning to its "old" values—and contemporary youth whose world is organized around a rereading of cultist figures[58] so that (to quote Frith) the cult *"cannot* any longer say what it means"[59] for those for whom it has ceased to be an exclusive property. This dispossession is perhaps exacerbated by the difference in conditions of access to cult objects: objects that were previously rare and therefore valuable to the baby boomers ("collectible" films that could only be seen at midnight screenings) are today more easily accessed. Rarity no longer functions as an automatically distinctive sign, even if the production of rarity in contemporary cults may become the object of an economic rationalization through the distribution of limited editions and the marketing of collectors' versions.

Cult phenomena seem inseparable from the position occupied by some television channels, fanzines and magazines, publishing houses, repertory cinemas, and so on. The label "cult," for example, has become a trademark and a central identifying element for those conventional or thematic French television channels that target youth audiences: channel M6, whose content includes a high proportion of series, responds directly to the aspirations and interests of fan culture as evidenced by its production and marketing of the M6 Ciné Culte video collection and by the program *Fan de* . . . Cult can function as a constitutive element of the symbolic capital of a channel: for example, by claiming the "discovery" of series such as *Friends* (Canal Jimmy) or *The X-Files* (M6) and by broadcasting series in their original (non-French) versions, certain channels place themselves in opposition to mainstream culture by pioneering a youth identity.[60] Being known as a cult channel is an important means of valorization and distinction that allows niche audiences to be euphemized through claims of counterprogramming according to a classic process that consists of denying economics as a sign of quality and makes cult series (as opposed to sitcoms and mass-audience series) a criterion of selectivity.[61] At the same time, cult can function on Canal Plus (whose audience is mainly male and educated) as a criterion of originality (a distinct taste for secondary culture and for cultivated readings of media culture) in a particularly competitive market, or as a symbol of the countercultural spirit originally claimed by this channel. It could be argued, too, that the identity of a channel also functions as a constitutive element of cult phenomena and that a series may become "cult" because it is associated with the image of a particular channel. In any case, it is clear that cult phenomena and the judgments made about cult works depend also on the "prescribers" (commentators, critics, programmers, and so on) who participate in the construction of cults at the same time as they accompany them, comment on them, or situate themselves in relation to them.[62] A similar analysis could be carried out in relation to the internal and external organization of the market for publications, the press, and the specialized bookshops devoted to TV series that have played a decisive part, at least in France, in the valorization of televisual culture at the same time that they have constructed and/or responded to the expectations of new audience groups.

Conclusion

To examine the concept of cult media—its origins, the phenomena it claims to describe, and the position it occupies in the contemporary media world—appears at first to be a considerably more complex process than can be based on an analogy that associates the anthropology of religion or of contemporary ritual with the sociology of the media and its audiences. It is possible to question the heuristic value of such an analogy—structuralist in its inspiration, it proposes that rituals are never "new"—as soon as the specificity of groups of fans or the market situation of cultural goods are taken into account. On this point, it is worth noting,

> "ritual" and "rite of passage" are, paradoxically, among those terms that belong to specialized areas and disciplines, among those who have acquired the greatest popularity in the usage of the press and the educated public, but in a manner that is somewhat vague, allusive, metaphorical, negligent.[63]

As a consequence it is possible to question those movements in the field that "flush out the sacred in the smallest formalization of individual or collective behavior."[64]

On the other hand, the constructivist approach that I have endeavored to adopt allows, it seems to me, a break with classic oppositions of the objective/subjective or nominalism/substantialism kind. In this way it becomes clear that to a certain extent "cult" is a social construct that constructs socially. It is not necessary to deny the existence of the concept of cult that appears in discourses and practices and that expresses values, but it is advisable to appreciate the social work of definition and delimitation (with a large contribution from the politics of rationalization of media cults developed by those participants—video distribution companies, publishers, television channels—who have vested interests) that results in the naturalization of this concept. The question is therefore less one of knowing what "cult" is, if the essence of "cult" actually exists at all, than one of bringing to light the uses that are made of it. From this perspective, is it necessary to attempt to unify at any cost a concept that in practice displays multiple and even contradictory uses? Finally, in the cultist relationship with texts, the dichotomy popular culture/cultivated culture partly loses its power, just as it appears difficult to encapsulate fans in simplistic statements that make them into dominated social groups not in control of their own practices or population groups that are completely homogeneous in their social properties.

This essay closes, however, by noting a blind spot that future works on cult media would do well to examine in greater depth. Is it possible to establish links between social milieus and cultural worlds—between, on the one hand, generational similarities, levels of qualification, social position, and so on, and, on the other hand, the principles of cultural and social identification on which the variable forms of the cultist relationship with texts are based?

Notes

1. In his preface to the French translation of *A Small World* (David Lodge, *Un tout petit monde* [Rivages], 7), Umberto Eco describes it as a "cult" text: "Even though it was only published in 1984, this book is a *cult book*. The reasons why a book becomes a cult object are many and I have no wish to discuss them here."

2. According to Lou Reed, the Velvet Underground were "the only example of a cult group." Lou Reed, cited in Declan Lowney, *Curious,* TV documentary, 1993.

3. Jean-Michel Normand, "La Volkswagen New Beetle tente de séduire les nostalgiques," *Le Monde,* 9–10 August 1998, 13.

4. *Libération,* 17 July 2000, 7.

5. *Libération*, 18 July 2000, vi. *Tournez manège* was a successful 1980s game show in which single individuals were brought together to form a winning couple.

6. Edgar Morin's book *Les stars* (Paris: Seuil, 1957) has played a dominant role in spreading the use of religious vocabulary to describe the connection between fans and their idols: "The stars are beings comparable, in certain respects, to the heroes of mythology or the gods of Olympus, giving rise to a cult, even a sort of religion. . . . Among the cinema crowds can be detected the tribe of faithful relic carriers, dedicated to devotion, the fans." On the hagiographic portrayal of stars by their fans, see particularly the articles by Jacques Berlioz on Patti Smith and by Marie-Christine Pouchelle on Claude François, in *Les saints et les stars,* ed. Jean-Claude Schmitt (Paris: Beauchesne, 1983). See also John Frow, "Is Elvis a God? Cult, Culture, Questions of Method," in *International Journal of Cultural Studies* 1–2 (1998): 197–210; and Eric Maigret, "Religion diffuse ou dissolution du religieux: La question des 'fans' des

médias," in *Médias et religions en miroir,* ed. Pierre Bréchon and Jean-Paul Willaime (Paris: Presses Universitaires de France, 2000).

7. See, for example, John E. Lewis and Penny Stempel, *Cult TV* (London: Pavilion, 1993); or Alain Riou, *Les films cultes* (Paris: Éditions du Chêne, 1998).

8. *Culte Fiction,* France 2, 21 July 2000.

9. Pierre Bourdieu, *Ce que parler veut dire* (Paris: Fayard, 1982), 142: "In fact, there is nothing to choose between an objectivist judgement which measures representations (in every sense of the term) against 'reality' while forgetting that they can cause what they represent to come to pass in reality, by the very effectiveness of their evocation, and a subjectivist engagement which, in privileging representation, ratifies on scientific terms the falsehood in sociological writings by means of which the militants move from the representation of reality to the reality of representation."

10. Luc Boltanski, *Les cadres: La formation d'un groupe social* (Paris: Éditions de Minuit, 1982), 49.

11. Pierre Bourdieu, *Raisons pratiques: Sur la théorie de l'action* (Paris: Seuil, 1994), 137.

12. Walter Benjamin, "L'oeuvre d'art à l'ère de sa reproduction mécanisée," in *Écrits français* (Paris: Gallimard, 1991), 116–192. For a critical reading of this text, see Antoine Hennion and Bruno Latour, "L'art, l'aura, et la technique selon Benjamin ou comment devenir célèbre en faisant tant d'erreurs à la fois," in *La querelle du spectacle, Les cahiers de médiologie* 1(Paris: Gallimard, 1996), 235–41.

13. See Hennion and Latour, "L'art, l'aura, et la technique selon Benjamin."

14. The concept of the de-Christianization of contemporary societies has supported the idea of retribalization around new "pagan" cults such as fan clubs. See Michel Maffesoli, *Le temps des tribus: Le déclin de l'individualisme dans les sociétés de masse* (Paris: Méridiens Klincksieck, 1988).

15. For a critique of the analogy between religious and media cults, see Eric Maigret, "Du mythe au culte . . . ou de Charybde en Scylla? Le problème de l'importation des concepts religieux dans l'étude des publics des médias," in *Les cultes médiatiques: Culture fan et oeuvres cultes,* ed. Philippe Le Guern (Rennes: PUR, Coll. Le Sens Social, 2002).

16. Jean-Claude Schmitt, ed., *Les saints et les stars,* 17, 19.

17. The term "cult" is frequently used in the "Télévision" section of *Le Monde.* See, for example, the edition of 4–10 November 1996, devoted to cult TV series, or that of 12–18 June 2000 on the marketing of videocassettes of the series *Ally McBeal.* See also "Soupçons sur la série-culte," *Télérama,* 14–20 December 1996; and "Touche pas à mon culte," *Marianne,* 28 December 1998–3 January 1999.

18. Dominique Pasquier, *Les scénaristes et la télévision: Approche sociologique* (Paris: Nathan Université, 1995), 101.

19. Daniel Dayan and Elihu Katz, *La télévision cérémonielle* (Paris: Presses Universitaires de France, 1996), 15.

20. François Jost, *Un monde à notre image: Enonciation, cinéma, télévision* (Paris: Méridiens/Klincksieck, 1992), 124.

21. Gérard Mauger and Claude F. Poliak, "Les usages sociaux de la lecture," *Actes de la recherche en sciences sociales* 123 (June 1998), 22.

22. A simple comparison of the numbers of works relating to television programs and their audiences produced in France on the one hand, and the Anglo-Saxon countries on the other, is all that is needed to measure the gulf that exists between these two traditions of research.

23. Good starting points for the reader interested in becoming familiar with this area of study in France are the works of Dominique Pasquier and Sabine Chalvon-Demersay. For work on Anglo-Saxon contexts see the works of Henry Jenkins and Lisa Lewis, which include substantial bibliographies.

24. Jonathan Hoberman and Jonathan Rosenbaum, *Midnight Movies* (New York: Da Capo, 1983).

25. Umberto Eco, "*Casablanca:* Cult Movies and Intertextual Collage," *SubStance* 47 (1984): 3–12.

26. For an internalist and externalist reading of cult texts, see Philippe Le Guern, "The Ideological Project between Representation and Metaphor: The Television Example of a 'Cult Series,' *The Prisoner,*" in *Sociocriticism, Images,* ed. Monique Carcaud-Macaire, 12, no. 1–2 (1997): 159–75.

27. Umberto Eco, *Six Walks in the Fictional Woods* (Cambridge: Harvard University Press, 1995), 127.

28. Interview with Larry "Buster" Crabbe, quoted in Stéphane Bourgoin and Pascal Mérigeau, "La série B américaine," *La revue du cinéma* 380 (February 1983): 63.

29. Bruce Kawin, "After Midnight," in *The Cult Film Experience: Beyond All Reason,* ed. Jean-Pierre Telotte (Austin: University of Texas Press, 1991), 18.

30. Timothy Corrigan, "Film and the Culture of Cult," in *The Cult Film Experience,* ed. Telotte, 26.

31. Kawin, "After Midnight," 20.

32. On the relationship between lifestyles and methods of appropriation of works of art, see Pierre Bourdieu, *La distinction: Critique sociale du jugement* (Paris: Éditions de Minuit, 1979), especially 301–64.

33. On cultural allodoxia, see ibid., 370ff.

34. John Tulloch and Henry Jenkins, *Science Fiction Audiences: Watching "Doctor Who" and "Star Trek"* (London: Routledge, 1995), 134.

35. Philippe Le Guern, "Un certain sens de la distinction? Les fans de la série TV *The Prisoner,*" in *La culture du culte.*

36. Bourdieu, *La distinction,* 321.

37. Joli Jenson, "Fandom as Pathology: The Consequences of Characterization," in *The Adoring Audience: Fan Culture and the Popular Media,* ed. Lisa A. Lewis (London: Routledge, 1992), 9.

38. Dominique Pasquier, *La culture des sentiments: L'expérience télé-*

visuelle des adolescents (Paris: Éditions de la Maison des Sciences de l'Homme, 1999), 188.

39. Jean-Pierre Telotte, "Beyond All Reason," 10: "The former's audience is usually the middle-class teenager and young adult, the seventeen-to-twenty-four-year-old group."

40. Laurent Aknin, "'I was a Regular Frankie Fan': *Rocky Horror Picture Show,* mode d'emploi," *Vertigo* 10 (1993): 102–5. It is notable that the author's only bibliographic reference is Bill Henkin, *The Rocky Horror Picture Show Book* (New York: Hawthorn-Dutton, 1979).

41. Nicolas Saada, "'La porte!' Les heures du Grand Rex," *Vertigo* 10 (1993): 106–8.

42. It is necessary to take account of the structural effects that such a paradigmatic film produces on research into cults by imposing itself as the dominant model—and by imposing a certain number of characteristic traits—with regard to the observer. Gregory A. Waller rightly notes the extreme diversity of films that are projected at midnight movie screenings and likely to become cults, ranging from comedies to rock films ("Midnight Movies, 1980–1985: A Market Study," in *The Cult Film Experience,* ed. Telotte).

43. Jonathan Rosenbaum, in "The Rocky Horror Picture Show, 'cult-film,'" *Cahiers du Cinéma* 307 (January 1980): 33–38, notes that these rituals "represent a text in continuous change and evolution—an assemblage formed by layers which are deposited at each showing, consisting simultaneously of a traditional catechism and a series of fresh or relatively fresh contributions." The author indicates both the universality of the ritual, performed at the time in more than 180 venues across the United States, and the method by which meanings and rules of localized ways of performing the cult, that is to say, of interpreting the film, circulate.

44. Aknin, "'I was a Regular Frankie Fan,'" *Vertigo* 10 (1993): 104.

45. Gregory A. Waller, "Midnight Movies, 1980–1985," 170.

46. Olivier Donnat, *Les pratiques culturelles des français: Enquête 1997* (Paris: La Documentation Française, 1998), 315: "Might not the tendency to extend the range of collectible objects, observed in France since the start of the 1980s, in fact be seen as a replica of what takes place in the public space, that is a means of constituting one's own heritage in order to resist the compression of time and space, an attempt at a response to the sense of loss of reference points which results from that?"

47. Chris Gregory, *Decoding "The Prisoner"* (Luton, England: University of Luton Press, 1997), 187.

48. Freezing the image is a practice often mentioned by fans, who often demonstrate mastery of cinematographic language.

49. Bourdieu, *Raisons pratiques,* 129.

50. Rosenbaum, "The Rocky Horror Picture Show, 'cult-film.'"

51. Simon Frith, "Souvenirs, souvenirs . . ." in *Rock: De l'Histoire au Mythe,* ed. Patrick Mignon and Antoine Hennion (Paris: Anthropos, 1991), 250.

52. Ibid., 248–49.

53. "La Volkswagen New Beetle tente de séduire les nostalgiques," *Le Monde*: "Among those age groups with high purchasing power and increasing influence at the heart of society, the nostalgic discourse strikes a particularly sensitive chord. . . . Confectioners reinstall their bowls of strawberry Tagada, the 'Nutella generation' is appealed to, cult TV series soar up the ratings and the Solex [moped] is back in fashion." Olivier Donnat, in *Les français face à la culture: De l'exclusion à l'éclectisme* (Paris: La Découverte, 1994), 237, notes with regard to music that "the music boom . . . appears more fundamentally the result of a meeting, over the course of the last decade, between a certain sociological reality (the arrival at adult age of the generations of the music boom), a commercial strategy by the record companies (release on CD of the 'greats' of classical music, jazz, and rock), and a political willingness, perfectly symbolized by the *Fête de la Musique,* to decompartmentalize and extend the range of the forms recognized as legitimate." With the exception of that final point—the intervention of public politics—this analysis is largely transposable to the world of the small screen. It is also notable that in France, promoters of cult culture on the small screen have found it possible to associate with the valorization of rock culture, following the example of Jean-Pierre Dionnet, former presenter of *Enfants du rock* and currently presenter of *Cinéma de quartier* on the TV channel Canal Plus.

54. Trailer, Canal Plus, 4 July 2000.

55. The title of an article published in *Le point* 1320 (3 January 1998), xx–xxii, in reference to the French TV channel Canal Jimmy.

56. "'I don't understand those who find it ridiculous that you may be enthusiastic about a TV series, who criticize you and end up by regarding you from a great height, convinced that you will always remain a hopelessly stupid moron,' complains Frédéric, 23, treasurer of a fan club, otherwise a student of history at the Sorbonne, to whom this misfortune has occurred." Quoted in ibid., xxi.

57. See Donnat, *Les pratiques culturelles des français,* 346–50.

58. This rereading is fed by the release of numerous sets of old cult series such as *Mission Impossible: 20 Years,* following or preceding the broadcast of series that already existed several decades previously (such as *Les mystères de l'Ouest, Chapeau melon et bottes de cuir, Amicalement vôtre*).

59. Frith, "Souvenirs, souvenirs . . . ," 250.

60. "We do not have the budgets of TF1 and France 2, but we make up for it with a commando spirit" (Nathalie Drouaire, director of acquisitions at M6).

61. See, for example, the channel Série Club, discussed in the newspaper *L'Express,* 9 March 2000, 11: "Fiercely negotiated, these already cult series (like *Twin Peaks,* snaffled up by Canal Jimmy in 1997) are the pride of the channel and contribute to its fame."

62. On this interaction between cult phenomena and their commentators who are also in part their producers, see Philippe Teillet, "Les cultes musicaux: La contribution de l'appareil de commentaires à la construction de cultes, l'exemple de la presse rock," in *La culture du culte,* ed. Le Guern.

63. Pierre Centlivres, "Rites, seuils, passages," in Martin de la Soudière, ed., *Seuils, Passages, Communication* 70 (2000): 33.

64. Ibid., 33.

2

The Mainstream, Distinction, and Cult TV

Mark Jancovich and Nathan Hunt

■ The British magazine *Cult Times* describes itself as "The Best Guide to This Month's Cult TV" and presents its readers with a format composed of news, features, reviews, and a guide to "programmes on the UK's terrestrial, satellite and cable channels."[1] However, it does not simply provide a schedule of *all* programs on these channels; it lists shows that it defines as "cult TV." The precise criteria for this selection are not specified, but the magazine does refer to itself as a "telefantasy guide" for "science fiction, fantasy and horror." Unfortunately, such generic categories do not define "cult TV." Not all science fiction, fantasy, and horror is defined as cult TV, and not all cult TV is an example of these three overlapping genres. Not only have shows such as *I Love Lucy, Leave It to Beaver, The Andy Griffith Show, The Mary Tyler Moore Show,* and *The Professionals* all attracted cult followings, but even *Cult Times* includes discussions of shows that would not fit these categories.

Indeed, the problem is that cult TV is defined not by any feature shared by the shows themselves, but rather by the ways in which they are appropriated by specific groups. There is no single quality that characterizes a cult text; rather, cult texts are defined through a process in which shows are positioned in opposition to the mainstream, a classification that is no more coherent as an object than the cult and is also a product of the same process of distinction that creates the opposed couplet mainstream/cult.

In other words, conceptions of cult TV are the product of what Sara Thornton has termed "subcultural ideologies," and rather than simply accepting this distinction between the mainstream and the cult, the purpose of this essay is to examine the ways in which these categories are constructed within cult TV fandom and to demonstrate that the distinctions between them are the product of specific competences and

dispositions. Although cult subcultures present themselves as oppositional through their distinction from the mainstream, their specific reading
strategies not only are the product of a situation of relative privilege and
authority within the cultural field, but also frequently reproduce relations of power and authority within it.

For example, as we have argued elsewhere, cult fandom is usually
based on a rejection of the middlebrow rather than the legitimate, and
often employs reading strategies that are specifically based on the privileging of form over function that distinguishes bourgeois taste.[2] In other
words, cult fandom opposes itself to the easy and transparent readings
that distinguish popular taste and draws on the terms and strategies
of legitimate culture. In the process, fans not only ridicule the naïve
and easy pleasures of "ordinary" people in a way that reproduces the
authority of bourgeois taste over popular taste, but can also engage
in extremely viscous internal struggles. The cult fandom oppositional
community presented by some writers is actually ridden with factional
animosity; the need to maintain a clear sense of distinction between the
authentic insider and the inauthentic outsider breeds hostility and contempt not only for the more obvious outsiders but also for other fans.[3]

The value of community membership stems from a sense of exclusivity and rarity that can, of course, easily be lost. Many fans present
themselves as opposed to the media, but also present the media as constantly trying to incorporate and commercialize them. As Thornton
puts it, the very notion of "'selling out' means 'selling to outsiders.'"[4]
The widening popularity of what were originally deemed cult TV shows
threatens to blur the line between the authentic subcultural insider and
the inauthentic outsider. This produces a policing of the boundaries of
the subculture, with fans constantly looking out for the cultural inter-
loper. Though fans may depict their subcultures as tolerant and supportive communities, the constant attempt to protect internal purity by
identifying inauthentic outsiders who must be rejected and shunned be-
lies this. Related to policing is the search for a new authenticity. The exclusivity that gives value to a cult text may not be sustainable. As others
come to appreciate the text, fans must either find new forms of exclusive
appreciation or reject or relegate the text to the passé. *The X-Files* on
BBC2 in Britain (a channel catering to small selective audiences) maintained a devoted following, but as soon as its prominence persuaded
the British Broadcasting Corporation to move the show to BBC1, with
its larger mainstream audience, fans began to worry about the show's
fate and to shift their allegiance to other shows. Championing the show
no longer produced subcultural value and cache. Conversely, being a

fan of *The Six Million Dollar Man* in the 1970s, when it was still a hit show with a large audience, produced little value. Now, when it is screened only on minor network channels such as the Sci-Fi Channel and its production values have come to appear hopelessly outdated, the program not only has become a rare taste but also has developed a cult following.

Cult TV fandom also polices boundaries and defends exclusivity through opposition to both the media and the academy. This essay will examine the reasons for this hostility and demonstrate that these institutions have been "instrumental in the congregation of [fans] and the formation of subcultures,"[5] providing systems of communication that produce and maintain a sense of community. We will show that the similarities that many critics have noted between fan discourses and academic writing stem not only from these groups sharing similar competences and dispositions deriving from their middle-class and well-educated status, but also from their development being intimately interconnected in intellectual terms.[6]

Mediating Exclusivity: Communication, Cultural Competences, and the Construction of Fandom

In spite of fans' hostility, the media act to produce fandom. The media provide the systems of communication that bring fans together and create the impression of an imagined community. Many cult television publications offer guides to the exclusive and elusive world of fandom, offering the knowledge necessary to make distinctions, to appreciate the value of a cult text, and to delineate between insider or outsider status. Cult TV fan publications give background details on shows and characters to establish the context necessary to make sense of them in specific fannish ways, while at the same time answering questions and supplying news to keep fans up-to-date. Ironically, however, the media also threaten to dissolve these fan communities, since the very process of dissemination that enables the production of fandom undermines the sense of exclusivity on which it is based. Disseminating too widely the exclusive competences and dispositions on which fandom is based may destroy the sense of exclusivity that these competences and dispositions provide.

This inherent contradiction presents a problem for fan media. One way to solve it is by presenting themselves not as part of the media but as an organic element of fandom itself. In the first edition of *SFX*—one of Britain's biggest-selling science fiction fan magazines—the editors were careful to position themselves as fans with knowledge, not journalists doing a job, and to describe the magazine itself as a labor of love:

> The idea for *SFX* has been burning away on the back boiler for more years than I care to remember now. Both deputy editor Dave Golder and myself have done proposals for it (or something very much like it) in the past, had them rejected, waited a few more years, then suggested them again.

They list their professional credentials to assure the reader of the operation's professionalism and establish their fannish commitments and competences:

> Now the people. Well, there's me, the editor—Matt Bielby. Last year, I launched a little Internet magazine called *.net,* and before that I was behind the launches of computer game mags like *Amiga Power, Super Play* and *PC Gamer.* However science fiction is my first love. Deputy editor Dave Golder has a similar background and, if anything, is an even more ardent SF admirer.[7]

The editors present themselves as fans talking to fans and simultaneously police the authenticity of their readership. The attacks and jibes directed at readers' letters together with the more generalized attacks on hypothetical inauthentic fans, which pepper the pages of fan magazines, are intended at least as much to reassure fans of the exclusivity of the magazine as to actually scare off outsiders. These magazines address the "genuine" insider, distancing themselves from "the media's" incorporation of the scene or its dissemination of fan knowledge to the broader public.

Constructing Cultural Distinctions

Fans' frequent complaints about the industry most clearly illustrate the representation of the mainstream as the inauthentic other of the cult fan. While identifying with specific shows, cult TV fans often present the industry that produces these shows as representing everything they despise. The executive, a figure who is seen to value commercial success over the quality of the shows themselves, epitomizes everything wrong with the industry. As one writer puts it: "So who has the power of life and death over our favourite characters? . . . Ultimately it has to be the ratings obsessed executive."[8] Cult TV fandom claims that the industry's commercial considerations lead to a lack of originality in the development of shows and a tendency to ruin established shows in the pursuit of the mainstream audience:

> Cult TV is fortunate in its fans, who have broad tastes and a high toler-
> ance level and invariably give a show a chance. . . . Lack of creativity
> is pervasive, with everyone sticking to the "tried and tested" route to
> success. . . . So lack of belief in the genre [science fiction] threatens to
> overwhelm it, as everyone gropes for the next show that will cross the
> barrier and become a mainstream hit.[9]

The executives, associated with mainstream consumerism by virtue of
their supposed adherence to the profit motive and interest in numbers,
are placed in stark contrast with fandom's appreciation of quality shows.

The selection of quality shows helps to create the rarity and exclusivity so often central to cult status. Censorship can render a text valuable;
within fandom never-before-seen footage has particular cachet. The
BBC shows *Buffy the Vampire Slayer* twice, once in an early evening slot
edited for violence and again in a late night slot complete and unedited.
One episode of *Buffy* acquired greater value when refused transmission after the Columbine shootings in the United States. Its status as a
banned object suddenly made it essential viewing. Sometimes programs
are cut to fill time slots or because of cultural differences; even this kind
of editing gives the "original" acquired importance. As one fan notes:

> I recently visited Vancouver and through friends was lucky enough to
> have a guided tour of the *ReBoot* studios . . . seeing new work from
> their upcoming CGI show, *Transformers*. In the UK and Europe,
> however, we get the full uncensored version—and, since the show is
> transferred to tape in the PAL format, we also get the full 100 extra
> lines resolution. So there *are* benefits to living in the UK![10]

Sequences therefore get retroactively defined as important and valuable
through the knowledge that they are exclusive to the UK and Europe.
Even the PAL system's one hundred extra lines become a sign of exclusivity as part of a supposedly complete and unabridged original. Magazines
often act as gatekeepers to authenticate some versions of programs and
warn against others. For example, in the UK, Channel Four's screening
of the first series of *Angel,* heavily censored in a prewatershed[11] family
time slot, was greeted with hostility by fan publications who made it
their business to warn fans of the changes made to the authentic and
original episodes. The series was promptly rescreened unedited at a later
time, illustrating the strong connections between television programmers and fan communities.

Fans' opposition to the mainstream is not restricted to their attacks
on executives or the industry but also extends to other fans. The figure

from whom most fans want to distance themselves is "the anorak," often identified as the epitome of the cult fan by those who distinguish themselves *from* cult fandom. The anorak is seen as nerdish, asexual, and obsessive, an image from which many fans are concerned to distance themselves: "*SFX* is great! Congratulations on writing something that is informative, funny and doesn't treat SF fans as though we're total anoraks."[12] Many fans resist being seen as taking things too seriously by ridiculing the behavior of other fans. As one fan writes:

> At last, a magazine . . . that's glossy, hip and literate . . . offers a good broad range of articles, and doesn't take itself *too* seriously. . . . And that latter point, I think, is very important. Too often fans of the science fiction *oeuvre* come across as anoraks of the highest order. . . . And this, I feel, is what keeps the genre so ghettoised in the eyes of the masses—Trekkers and Whovians will always be treated as cretins because they take it all too seriously![13]

The generalized criticism becomes a direct personalized attack on Doctor Who and Star Trek fans, central to the external image of fandom.

In another issue of the same magazine, the following appears under the heading "Generic Letter," although we cannot tell whether the letter actually represents one reader complaining about others or is an invention of the editors.

> Dear *SFX,*
>
> Please help me! I'm a huge fan of [insert show here] and I'm totally in love with [insert actor/actress here] who plays [insert character here]. Please could you send me any picture of him/her? Or any info you can get your hands on? Or could you send me an address at which I can write to him/her?
>
> > [insert fanboy/fangirl's name here]
> > [insert fanboy/fangirl's address her][14]

The letter purportedly represents the emotionally or intellectually stunted "inauthentic" fans who don't really "get it," in contrast to the normal, healthy "real" fans. Fandom defines itself through opposition not just to the construction of the mainstream but also to the mainstream's construction of fandom. Sometimes these oppositions are deeply gendered so that the mainstream is often attacked for being a feminized form.[15] It is hardly surprising that women within fandom are often either attacked or dismissed. For example, when one female fan writes in to complain about the magazine's coverage of *The X-Files, SFX* insults her "and any other X-Files fans who share her views."[16] Here female fans are dismissed for having "girly" tastes, and it is suggested that female X-Files fans are indistinguishable from female Take That fans, who are obviously seen as inherently beneath contempt.[17]

These magazines direct their ridicule against the competences and dispositions of other fans, against the ways in which they read the shows. As we have seen, some fans are derided for "fancying" cast members, despite the fact that magazines like *SFX* clearly use the pinup potential of stars such as Sarah Michele Geller as a means of increasing sales. The derision of those who "fancy" cast members suggests that sexual attraction should not be the primary terms of evaluation. Preferences for shows, it suggests, should be based on other notions of value and the reading strategies appropriate to them.

Assigning Value

A common debate between fan cultures concerns the relative merits of film versus television. For example, certain sections of horror fandom see television horror as inherently inauthentic by virtue of its appearance on such a mainstream medium.[18] Films such as *Scream* and *I Know What You Did Last Summer* and shows such as *Buffy the Vampire Slayer* are attacked because of their stars' associations with television. For these horror fans, television, the home of safe, sanitized programming, is opposed to "real" horror—low budget, dangerous, and distinguished by its handling of taboo material. A language of subversion and political resistance that represents horror as dealing with dangerous materials that society wants to repress and contain confers value on the fan who transgresses the prohibitions against viewing this material.[19]

Science fiction fans, on the other hand, tend to prefer television to films. *SFX* celebrated its fiftieth issue with a list of "The Top 50 SF Shows of All Time" rather than the top fifty films.[20] Fans believe that the constraints of television place the emphasis on ideas rather than the special effects of science fiction movies. Star Trek fans have tended to be highly ambivalent about the film versions of the franchise. The BBC Cult TV Web site refers to the first Star Trek film as an "oddly soulless movie debut" that places the emphasis on "indulgent (but impressive) special effects." By contrast, the second film, *Star Trek II: The Wrath of Khan,* "restores the character-driven heart to Star Trek."[21] Special effects are not irrelevant, as seen in the title of one of the leading cult TV magazines, *SFX.* Fans talk at length in its pages about the special effects on display in films and television programs. They nonetheless privilege ideas, characters, and the arc story lines of television series over special effects, condemning texts that give special effects precedence over these other considerations. This is not simply because, as with *Star Trek,* the television series is seen as the original and the films as sellouts. In the case of the *Robocop* franchise, the film came first. But although many science fiction fans hold the original in high regard, one writer claims that the shift to television actually helped the franchise:

> The most obvious upshot of this is that the TV incarnation of "the Future of Law Enforcement" is a lot more *creative* about how he appre-hends his suspects—utilising techniques that are interesting to watch yet devoid of all that brain-splattering action.

This writer does not dislike the violent action of the first film, but approves of the fact that the need to tone down the violence for television forces the series to be more creative or idea-driven. By contrast, the writer views the toned-down violence of the third film as a negative development:

> The Robocop films suffered badly from the law of diminishing re-turns. . . . the only significant thing about Robocop 3 was that it came with a chillingly mainstream 15 rating.[22]

The writer sees television's prohibition on excessive violence as forcing the program makers to be more inventive, but believes that the absence of violence in the third film stems from the desire to make a bland and sanitized film suitable for a general audience.

The concentration on the creative aspects of TV can also be seen in publications such as *Cult Time, TV Zone,* and the BBC's own *Cult TV* Web pages, all of which focus on character and arc story lines. These publications provide summaries of the characters and the arcs and speculate on the ways in which they will develop over time. They also single out specific episodes that are seen as key or classic moments within the series: e.g., the *Star Trek: The Next Generation* two-parter "The Best of Both Worlds." This episode is seen as a central moment in the development of both the series arc and the development of one char-acter, Captain Jean-Luc Picard. Such focus on character and story arc as the creative core of a cult show opposes the concentration on canons and directors within horror film fandom. On many horror Web sites, a display of knowledge of a canon of horror greats is coupled with an auteurist appreciation of directors such as Wes Craven, John Carpenter, and Sam Raimi.[23] With TV series, writers and stories become the focus for validations of quality, since directors often change.

This focus on arc and character also places an emphasis on the literary values associated with legitimate culture. As argued elsewhere, cult movie fandom often tries to lend itself legitimacy through association with the formally challenging and antirealist aesthetics of the avant-garde.[24] Cult TV fandom, however, focuses on ideas and imagination, rather than on taboo material. This leads to a language based on originality and invention instead of independence, subversion, or resistance, and results in a tendency to draw on the legitimate rather than the avant-garde, particularly as regards literary values. The persistent interest in scripts and the ways in which they develop characters and story lines shows the insistence on literary values, as does the concern with the devices and techniques of storytelling. For example, an episode of *Buffy* is criticized because "the moments of pleasure don't excuse the unconvincing central conceit."[25] The tracing of literary references and origins is central to cult television fandom, not just with regard to *Star Trek: The Next Generation,* where Shakespearean and other references abound, but in the discussion of other shows and films. For example, one fan writes listing the numerous parallels that he has found between Frank Herbert's series of *Dune* novels and the *Star Wars* series.[26]

Star Wars has a stronger following among cult TV fans than other films precisely because it is a *series.* The emphasis on literary values places a special premium on the long-running story over the individual film, as seen most clearly in discussions of *Babylon 5.* As *SFX* puts it, "Babylon 5 remains one of the best-loved science fiction TV series of the last decade, combining Star Trek–style space operatics and character interaction with a complex, novel-like storyline."[27] It is also significant that *SFX* notes, "Babylon 5 had become only the fourth TV series to win a Hugo in the awards' 43 year history."[28] The Hugo awards, usually bestowed on science fiction literature, possess the legitimacy to confer respectability on a TV show. The focus on literary values carries over into the concern with characters and the actors who embody them, with continual references to the quality of performances almost entirely absent from cult movie fandom, where one might find occasional cracks about wooden acting, but rarely if ever encounter terms such as "fine performances"[29] or "beautifully played."[30] Cult TV fandom often evaluates shows simply on the basis of the quality of the performances. For example, "Warhead," an episode of *Star Trek: Voyager,* is praised because "it simply played to the strengths of its actors."[31]

This overall emphasis on quality entails a concern with production values. Cult TV fans are rarely averse to big budgets despite their association with the tendency to privilege special effects over story and character. While excusing the poor production values of shows such as *Doctor Who* or *Blake 7* in terms of the concentration on ideas, fans believe that cheesy special effects may contribute to cult television's low esteem and to the nerdish image of its fans. Referring to *Neverwhere,* for example, the *SFX* letter editor comments:

> It's a shame that the show was all shot in dodgy, overlit video tape. General audiences would have taken one look at it and gone, "*Dr Who?* Cheap tat.*" Please, BBC, the next time you do a fantasy or SF series, do it on film.[32]

The Media, the Academy, and the Development of Cult TV Fandom

Similarities in the tastes of supposedly mainstream or legitimate culture are hardly surprising. Despite the fact that cult TV fans frequently present themselves as "somehow outside the media," as "grass roots cultures [that] resist and struggle with a colonizing mass-mediated corporate world,"[33] cult fandom is not the product of an authentic self-generation or affinity that is then threatened with incorporation by "the media." On the contrary, both the media and the academy have been central to the formation and maintenance of cult TV audiences.

However, cult audiences first emerged in relation to film rather than television, and from the start their development was intimately connected with the economics of the cultural industries and intellectual developments rather than opposed to them. Cult movie fandom developed out of the art cinema and repertory theater movements of the postwar period. These cinemas developed as cinema audiences declined, and certain cinemas began to service a small, highly educated, economically exclusive audience that was not only middle-class but also restricted to specific metropolitan areas. These sites of exhibition not only provided the initial places for the congregation of new audiences, but also often acted as the gatekeepers of this new scene. It was their programming policies and advertising materials that acted to classify and reclassify films, processes that were central to the development of the cult movie as a form.[34]

Rather than being, as is commonly suggested, opposed to the commercialism of mainstream cinema, the art and repertory cinema developed out of economic motivations. The art cinema managed to legitimate cinema as an art form through its use of foreign films, but it was later joined in the 1960s by the repertory theaters, which developed out of the college film societies of the late 1950s and early 1960s. These theaters largely showed reruns of old movies, but in the process they recontextualized films that had largely been dismissed as the products of a formulaic mass or mainstream culture and claimed them to be previously undiscovered gems of film art.

These developments were therefore directly connected to intellectual developments in the period such as the work of Dwight Macdonald, who presented European cinema as independent in opposition to the supposedly standardized mass culture of Hollywood.[35] The repertory cinemas, on the other hand, followed a similar strategy to auteur theorists, such as Andrew Sarris, who sought to reevaluate the Hollywood cinema and demonstrate their powers of discrimination by making distinctions where others had seen only an undifferentiated mass.[36]

Like the emergence of the cult movie, cult TV was also largely a product of changing audience demographics, but for this reason it developed later than the cult movie and in different ways. In the 1980s, the proliferation of video, cable, and satellite threatened the audiences for network or terrestrial television programming, and this development created two different, but related, tendencies.

First, video distributors and cable and satellite channels were all desperate for material, and they turned to old television shows as one of the ways of cheaply satisfying this need. While there is little direct correlation with the emergence of the art cinema, this development shares many features of the college film societies and repertory cinemas. Old television shows were recontextualized, reappraised, and reread. While there had been groups of fans associated with specific series before this development, these new channels needed to change the meanings of these shows: to convert them from simply old shows and to make them the center of new fan cultures. As a result these industries developed a new relationship with cult audiences who were not seen as simply irrelevant or annoying, but actively courted and serviced. Furthermore, these channels could not survive on the basis of these existing cultures alone; they sought to develop and promote them to increase their size and to encourage the development of new fan cultures centered around shows that had not previously enjoyed the attention given to shows such as *Star Trek* or *Doctor Who*. In other words, like the repertory cinemas, they acted as gatekeepers, which classified and reclassified old shows through their schedules and their advertising.

Second, these developments affected the strategies of terrestrial television stations and network television. In the United States, for example, the networks adopted new strategies for securing their audiences. In the late 1940s, Hollywood found that it could not rely on a regular attendance to secure its market and turned to the blockbuster, the big budget event picture that would appeal to the relatively affluent middle-brow consumer who was not a regular moviegoer but had the disposable income to go for a big night out once in a while. In a similar way, as their own audiences dwindled, network television gradually focused on "must see TV": television programs that people did not watch simply because they were habituated to television viewing, but because these shows were events. The shows were designed so that viewers would go out of their way to watch them and to organize their schedules around them, shows such as *ER, Seinfeld,* and *The X-Files.* In this way, the networks used them as anchors: they drew people to the channel and kept them there. The intent was not to get the biggest audience, but to attract specific audiences. Often identified as "quality" television and seen as a "literate peak" when contrasted to early periods in American television,[37] these shows are aimed at relatively well-educated, middle-class audiences with a spending power that makes them valuable to advertisers. It is therefore hardly surprising that cult audiences developed around these shows.

Cult audiences became increasingly important to the industry in other ways as well. In Britain, the News Corporation–owned satellite company Sky built itself through the use of established U.S. cult shows such as *The Simpsons* and *Star Trek: The Next Generation* to which it had exclusive rights. News Corporation also used a similar technique to establish its American network, Fox, after which is named one of the most important figures in cult television, Special Agent Fox Mulder. In a period of high competition between channels, one of the central problems is that shows are canceled quickly and rarely have time to find an audience, leading to fans' complaints about networks. In this context, Fox used shows that were designed to appeal to cult audiences because, although they might not take off immediately, they might be able to generate a dedicated following that would enable them to hold their own in the schedules and so give these shows the time to develop a broader audience.

This is not to suggest that there were no cult TV audiences before these developments, or that cult TV audiences are simply the product of some industrial conspiracy, but to illustrate that, despite the rhetoric of these audiences declaring their opposition to the media and cultural industries, they are rather intimately and intricately related to them. Indeed, cult TV has virtually acquired the status of a market category, and this is demonstrated by the British Broadcasting Corporation, which not only directly addresses cult audiences through its advertising but also has dedicated a section of its Web site to "Cult TV."

These developments are related to changing academic attitudes to television within the period, but these attitudes developed differently from academic attitudes to film. Film studies largely developed as an aesthetic discipline concerned with the study of film texts, while television studies already had a long tradition in the social sciences before academics started to make claims for the aesthetic merit of particular texts.[38] It is precisely the process of aesthetic reevaluation through which previously despised texts are introduced into the canon and so transgress, disrupt, and eventually revise established strategies of reading and evaluation that is at issue here. It is through this process that new generations of scholars present themselves as oppositional while actually demonstrating their cultural authority by showing that they do not slavishly conform to existing aesthetic evaluations but have mastery of the pure gaze.[39] In other words, they convert their own cultural competences into cultural capital, and then use them to confer aesthetic value onto objects.

The conference of value also stems from the development of semiotic and structuralist analysis within television study, which opens the door to the analysis of a whole series of cult forms. Cult audiences developed in relation to literary and film genres such as science fiction and the crime thriller, and critics with an investment in these genres began to study them in relation to television. Early work on popular television at the Open University, for example, provided analyses of *Doctor Who,* a program that also became, in 1983, the topic of a book-length study by John Tulloch and Manuel Alvarado, *Doctor Who: The Unfolding Text.*[40] In a more recent volume, Tulloch is clearly identified as someone who was a fan of the series, whose authority on the matter came from the competences that he had acquired as a result of this relationship to the show: "John Tulloch, a keen follower of science fiction films, comics and novels in his childhood, watched *Doctor Who* from its very first episode in December 1963, and continued to follow each episode for the next twenty-five years."[41]

The idea that popular television fiction could be defined as "quality" was soon well established within television studies, if nowhere else. Like Tulloch, other critics returned to their old loves and reenshrined them as classics, and some became aware of the development of new "quality" shows made for American television, many of which were produced by MTM, such as *Lou Grant, Hill Street Blues,* and *Cheers,*[42] but which also included shows such as *Cagney and Lacey.*[43] These critics usually drew on their competences as fans self-consciously, but they were not uncritical of these shows. As with cult movies, the influence of structuralism allowed them to read these shows symptomatically as revealing the contradictions and tensions of the dominant *ideology,* as texts that differed from the mainstream and offered a resistance to it but in a way that was neither straightforward nor univocal. Nonetheless, they still maintained the idea of a dominant, undifferentiated mainstream culture against which subcultural forms could offer a resistance. They presented a clear instance of the "subcultural ideologies" that Sara Thornton has criticized within both fan cultures and academic criticism, ideologies that, as Thornton demonstrates, rely on a sense of opposition to, and difference from, the "mainstream," which usually proves entirely inconsistent and contradictory.

Indeed, the very inconsistent and contradictory way in which the mainstream is imagined results in an entirely inconsistent and contradictory sense of those texts that oppose it. While some texts are viewed quite simply as classics or as texts of quality, others are viewed as objects with an altogether more precarious status. Some texts, such as *Leave it to Beaver* and *The Brady Bunch,* for example, are seen as trash texts, which like films such as *The Phenix City Story* (1955) or *Reefer Madness* (1936) are praised not for their inherent quality but for what is seen as a remarkable lack of quality—their supposedly formal ineptness or their supposed bald, contradictory, and even hypocritical ideological positions—and they can be treated either with virtual contempt as trash to be ridiculed and denigrated, or as grotesque and pathetic objects that evoke a kind of patronizing affection for their various failings. This latter strategy also shades into the camp readings that developed during the 1980s, particularly in relation to shows such as *Dynasty,* which were seen either as so bad that they were funny or as offering a more challenging critique to the values of mainstream realist television.[44]

This sense of opposition between the industry and the subcultural fan was also evident in critics such as John Fiske, who drew on the work of de Certeau. In this work, the industry is seen as a force of domination and control and also as one against which consumers struggle (although presumably not all viewers). Consumers have no control over the industry but take the texts that it produces and subvert them for their own ends. They appropriate the fruits of the cultural industries but in ways that resist the controlling power of the media.[45] Although significantly different from Fiske in many ways, these ideas have been used by Henry Jenkins to talk about fandom. Fans are "textual poachers" who steal from the domains of the dominant culture and use its texts to produce a resistant, alternative, participatory culture.[46] Writing predominantly about Star Trek fans, of which he is one, Jenkins specifically justifies not only the academic study of *Star Trek* but also seeks to demonstrate that fans and academics share very similar strategies of reading. However, rather than simply trying to legitimate his own cultural competences as a fan within the academy, Jenkins uses the fan to criticize the academy and calls for a greater sense of academic engagement with the popular.

If in these cases fandom provided new ways of reading to the academy, it is also the case that the academy offered fandom ways of legitimating itself. This can perhaps most clearly be seen in the ways in which fans appropriated the language of postmodernism in their celebration of shows such as *Twin Peaks*.[47] Associated with the auteur director David Lynch, *Twin Peaks* had a diverse following from the start. Lynch's earlier film *Blue Velvet* was already the darling of academics and one of the touchstones in debates about postmodernism.[48] Lynch had a large cult following, who frequently used the language of postmodernism in their discussions of the director and his films. The launch of the television series cemented this relationship and allowed the emergence of a broader cult following centered on the show itself. People who had not previously been fans of Lynch's work became fans of the show and learned to legitimate their taste for it through the academic terminology of postmodernism.

In this way, the history of aesthetic television study can be seen as crucially bound up with fan cultures. Far from being defined in opposition to one another, fandom and the academy have always been deeply interconnected as fans try to legitimate themselves in terms of the academy and new generations of academics establish themselves through the act of aesthetic transgression.

Conclusion

Cult TV fandom is not the product of an opposition to either the cultural industries or the academy but the product of a series of economic and intellectual developments that have produced a series of niche television markets. Indeed, cult TV fandom's claim that it is outside of economics is one of the key features that it shares with bourgeois aesthetics more generally, and it is this claim that we need to criticize. Rather than being some natural predisposition, the tastes associated with cult TV fandom need to be seen as not only socially defined, but as "closely linked to the structural inequality of access to society's resources."[49] Far from being natural, these tastes are themselves the products of economic investments in books, magazines, videos, and so on, and on positions of social and economic privilege. Nonetheless, fans use these tastes to justify their sense of distinction from, and superiority to, those who are damned by their preference for the mainstream and the commercial: those who do not know better.

Notes

1. At http://www.bbc.co.uk/cult/, accessed 11 May 2000.

2. Mark Jancovich, "Cult Fictions: Cult Movies, Subcultural Capital, and the Production of Cultural Distinctions," *Cultural Studies* 16, no. 2 (March 2001): 306–22.

3. For a more idyllic view of fandom see Henry Jenkins, *Textual Poachers: Television Fans and Participatory Culture* (New York: Routledge, 1992); and Jeffrey Sconce "Trashing the Academy: Taste, Excess and an Emerging Politics of Cinematic Style," *Screen* (1995) 36: 4, 371–93.

4. Emphasis in original; Sara Thornton, *Club Cultures: Music, Media, and Subcultural Capital* (Oxford: Blackwell, 1995), 124.

5. Ibid., 121.

6. On this point, see Jenkins, *Textual Poachers;* and Sconce, "Trashing the Academy."

7. *SFX* 1 (June 1995): 29.

8. *Starburst* 263 (July 2000): 22.

9. Ibid., 22–26.

10. *SFX* 16 (September 1996): 18.

11. In Britain, "the watershed" refers to a time after which it is supposed that younger viewers have gone to bed and so it is permissible to show more adult material; "prewatershed," therefore, refers to the period before this time, when broadcasters are supposed to be more careful about sex, violence, swearing, and so on.

12. *SFX* 50 (April 1999): 43.

13. *SFX* 2 (July 1995): 36.

14. *SFX* 16 (September 1996): 19.

15. Mark Jancovich, "A Real Shocker: Authenticity, Genre, and the Struggle for Cultural Distinction," *Continuum: Journal of Media and Cultural Studies* 14, no. 1 (2000): 23–35; and Joanne Hollows, "The Masculinity of Cult," in *Defining Cult Movies: The Cultural Politics of Oppositional Taste* (Manchester: Manchester University Press, 2003).

16. *SFX* 13 (June 1996): 19.

17. Hollows, "The Masculinity of Cult."

18. See Jancovich, "A Real Shocker."

19. See ibid. and Jancovich, "Cult Fictions."

20. *SFX* 50 (April 1999).

21. At http://www.bbc.co.uk/cult/, accessed 11 May 2000.

22. *SFX* 1 (June 1995): 70.

23. See, for example, Absolute Horror, at http://www.smackem.com/horror/; Arachnia's Den of the Deceived, at http://www.arachnia.com/; Horror Haven, at http://www.horrorhaven.net; Horror Movies, at http://www.horrormovies.com/home.html; House of Fright, at http://www.geocities.com/Hollywood/Theater/5514/; the Horror Site, at http://www.free4all.co.uk/free0002654/horror_1x.htm; and Vault of Horror, at http://www.geocities.com/Hollywood/Hills/5409/, all accessed 11 May 2000.

24. Jancovich, "Cult Fictions."

25. *TV Zone* 129 (August 2000): 74.

26. *Starburst* 251 (July 1999): 17.

27. *SFX* 5 (October 1995): 22.

28. *SFX* 18 (November 1996): 8.

29. *Cult Times,* at http://www.visimag.com/culttimes.

30. *TV Zone* 129 (August 2000): 74.

31. *Starburst* 251 (July 1999): 68.

32. *SFX,* 19 December 1996, 18.

33. Thornton, *Club Cultures,* 116.

34. Jancovich, "Cult Fictions."

35. Dwight Macdonald, "Masscult and Midcult," in *Against the American Grain* (London: Gollancz, 1963), 3–75.

36. Andrew Sarris, *Confessions of a Cultist: On the Cinema, 1955–1969* (New York: Simon and Schuster, 1970); and "Towards a Theory of Film History," in *Movies and Methods,* ed. Bill Nichols (Berkeley: University of California Press, 1976).

37. David Marc, *Comic Visions: Television Comedy and American Culture* (London: Unwin Hyman, 1989).

38. David Morley, *Television, Audiences, and Cultural Studies* (London: Routledge, 1992).

39. Pierre Bourdieu, *Distinction: A Social Critique of the Judgement of Taste* (London: Routledge, 1984).

40. John Tulloch and Manuel Alvarado, *Doctor Who: The Unfolding Text* (London: Routledge, 1983).

41. John Tulloch and Henry Jenkins, *Science Fiction Audiences: Watching Doctor Who and Star Trek* (London: Routledge, 1995), 22.

42. Jane Feuer, Paul Kerr, and Tise Vahimagi, *MTM: "Quality Television"* (London: British Film Institute, 1984).

43. Julie D'Acci, "Defining Women: The Case of *Cagney and Lacey,*" in *Private Screenings,* ed. Lynn Spigel and Denise Mann (Minneapolis: University of Minnesota Press, 1992), 169–202.

44. Mark Finch, "Sex and Address in *Dynasty,*" *Screen* 27, no. 6 (1986): 24–42.

45. John Fiske, *Television Culture* (London: Routledge, 1987), and *Understanding Popular Culture* (London: Unwin Hyman, 1989).

46. Jenkins, *Textual Poachers*.

47. Jim Collins, "Postmodernism and Television," in *Channels of Discourse Reassembled*, ed. Robert Allen (London: Routledge, 1992).

48. Norman Denzin, *Images of Postmodern Society: Social Theory and Contemporary Cinema* (London: Sage, 1991).

49. Nicholas Garnham, "Towards a Political Economy of Culture," *New Universities Quarterly*, summer 1977, 347.

Quality Science Fiction:
Babylon 5's Metatextual
Universe

Petra Kuppers

■ The formats of contemporary fan culture series such as *Babylon 5 (B5),* which spin their yarns over years, do not bear out Marshall McLuhan's predictions of a short but intensive attention span for the television (and computer) generation. A predetermined story arc spanning five seasons forced viewers of *B5*'s weekly episodes to wait years in order to unravel plot elements hinted at in the early episodes.[1] So-called arc episodes, in which the overall narrative is developed, are interspersed with more traditional episodes that develop shorter narratives in a familiar soap opera format. As this chapter will show, within its diegetic universe *B5* very self-consciously comments on the program's long narrative arcs and their position within the commercial politics of media networks. How does the content of particular episodes comment on and frame the arc episodes and the narrative they constitute? In which ways, beyond the pleasure of suspense and resolution, does the arc structure reinforce viewing pleasures and fan identification? This paper addresses these questions by investigating intertextual (between the diegetic universe of *B5* and extratextual discourses ranging from publicity to fan comments) and intratextual (within the diegetic universe) references within the texts. The essay will also look at fan writing about a series with a narrative predetermined over a wide span of time and ambitious in its viewer address. Many fans define themselves through the arcane knowledge of the arc in all its complexities. In one form of fan discourse, they prove their metanarrational ability to puncture holes in *B5*'s narrative fabric, exposing the fraying edges of the tightly spun cloth. These fans negotiate a range of knowledges and inhabit a range of positions. What kind of animal is the contemporary sci-fi fan? Maybe we can answer the Vorlon Kosh's question, "Who are you?"

Who am I? Perhaps more pertinently for the purposes of this paper, what is my knowledge base and involvement with the metatext of *B5*? I came to *B5* as a serious and dedicated sci-fi fan and writer with a regular column in a professional popular genre magazine (*Moviestar,* a German science fiction and horror publication). Like many genre commentators, I also publish stories in small press magazines, have taught genre material in university classrooms, and am a long-standing reader of sci-fi material. I religiously watched the first two full screenings of *B5* on British television, read B5 stories in the movie magazines and the B5 spin-off books, and commented on B5 gossip in my column. For many years, I have dropped occasionally into some of the many B5 Internet sites and e-lists, but not as an academic researcher of the subject. This kind of anecdotal evidence of living the life of a moderate B5 fan informs my findings here, but my main intertextual material comes from a more focused, research-oriented attention to B5 publications and Web sites between July 1999 and July 2000. The wealth of material is overwhelming; this essay maintains a tight focus on the representation of the B5 narrative structure in publicity material (mainly UK-based), some fan discourse from Web discussions, and textual material.[2]

Authors and Origins

Babylon 5 is produced by J. M. Straczynski, series creator and co-executive producer (from here on referenced as JMS, the signature he adopts on the Web). A large part of the fan culture surrounding this cult TV phenomenon centers around JMS as authorial figure, with Warner Bros., the producing studio, seen as secondary to the series' origin: "*B5* is the brain-child of one dedicated man—ex-novelist and TV-writer J. Michael Straczynski, who takes on the role of executive producer, chief scriptwriter . . . and, it seems, pretty much everything else too."[3] As with the ur–cult series *Star Trek* and its auteur-creator Gene Roddenberry, fans identify *B5* not with a network or an industrial work process, but with the ingenuity, creativity, and stubbornness of one man: "understanding *Babylon 5* is more or less understanding Joe Straczynski."[4] The secondary literature surrounding *B5* makes much of the "warrior status" of JMS, the core creator; his main appeal to fans can be attributed to his liminal status in between "TV hierarchies" and the "true fan." Fan culture around cult TV has often defined itself in opposition to the TV/network apparatus, which is equated with rabid commercialism and a paternalistic approach to its audiences (see, for instance, the us versus them stories surrounding the Star Trek universe, and the publicized and romanticized struggles with Paramount over copyright and fan Web sites). JMS refers to this oppositional stance in his own narrative of his journey to *B5*:

> It is 1983, and I am interviewing the producers of the television series Victor for the Los Angeles Herald Examiner. Not the creators of the original miniseries, which dared to touch wonder, but those brought on to produce the series proper. Or improper, in this case. In the course of the interview, one of the producers said, "As long as we have aliens, ray guns, and space ships, we're guaranteed the Sci-Fi audience automatically. What we have to do is broaden out to mainstream viewers.
>
> Their disregard for the science fiction community was undisguised and unmitigated. Plug in the hardware and the snazzy effects, and we'll come uncritically a'running.[5]

This and other accounts of the birth of *B5* cast the small guy with the big vision against the giant corporations, their cynical vision of fandom, and the evils of modern television. Eventually, *B5* emerges from the struggle between JMS and the industry, seemingly subverting "normal" science fiction television with its original and demanding narrative structure, the five-year arc.

The mythology of the marketing and development of *B5* mirrors aspects of the B5 narrative arc, which describes the struggle of the crew of the B5 space station, a lonely outpost, to expose a galactic threat (the ancient race of the Shadows), which disrupts space and seeds discontent among "the younger races," including humanity. The arc includes a second plot concerning a struggle among humanity. On one side are the anti-alien conservatives, who take control of Earth, effectively mind-controlling the planet's population through control of the media. On the other are the tolerant personnel of B5, whose commander eventually becomes president of the mixed-race federation. Mind control, totalitarianism, bigotry, and media involvement are major themes in the B5 universe. The struggle of individuals, carriers of a long tradition of valiant fighters, against a monolithic media conglomerate alluded to in JMS's narrative resonates with these aspects of the B5 saga.

This resonance of inter- and intratextual concerns occurs in other areas of the B5 world and format. In his history of *B5*'s becoming, JMS describes the industry's lack of respect for sci-fi's history, highlights, and special requirements—"to them, sf writing meant that nothing had to make any sense. Sf meant writing for juveniles, computer nerds and other cases of arrested development."[6] JMS realized that reinvigoration of the sci-fi genre would result from different marketing that would make industry personnel see sci-fi and its audiences in a different (more profitable? more respectable?) light.

> [W]hy had no one ever done a full-blown saga—something on the order of the *Lensman* books, or *Lord of the Rings,* or the *Foundation* books—for television? The British had done it, with *The Prisoner,* with *Blake's 7* and *Tripods* and some elements of *Dr. Who.* Why not us?
> Answer: simply because no one had ever done it.
> Someone had to try it.
> Might as well be me as anyone else.[7]

This David versus Goliath scenario, casting JMS, who had been writing for television since 1984, as part of the dedicated, "quality" sci-fi community in opposition to the industry, has influenced a lot of fan writing about the series. JMS claims authenticity and hard-earned respect: "I am a pretty good judge of this [going overboard on humanist sentimentality] by virtue of the fact of being a Science Fiction fan for as long as I can remember and I have very little patience for things that are treacley. Hence my ban on things that are cute in this show."[8] This concept of internalized quality control has set the tone for celebrating *B5*'s achievements. The identification of *B5* with JMS evokes notions of purity stemming from authority—the auteur's stern control of all aspects of the series.[9] By linking the production of TV texts to the production of literary sci-fi material, *B5* interpellates its viewers as purveyors of quality, not nerds stuck in front of the television for five years.

Echoes of Quality

The writings around *B5* continually stress the program's quality status, celebrating the complexity of its literary and self-aware approach and rejecting as undemanding the formulaic nature of much television science fiction. This publicity strategy rehearses older arguments about mass-produced "rubbish"—from Adorno's critique of popular music and his celebration of difficult, complex texts that demand consumer's labor to the criticisms of women's supposed mindless consumption of undemanding, escapist soap operas. High versus low arguments have their own history within the sci-fi critical community in terms of the contrast between the classical form and the space opera. The way in which Gary Westfahl discusses the controversy casts an interesting light on the B5 debate. Westfahl outlines how Hugo Gernsback, a classic science fiction writer and commentator in the 1920s and 1930s, imbued the genre with two highly ambitious sets of aspirations: . . . writers were urged to be scrupulously accurate in their presentations of scientific fact and to be impeccably logical in extrapolating and developing their scientific speculations. . . . [W]riters were urged to improve their style of writing, to emulate and even surpass classic writers such as Edgar Allan Poe, Jules Verne and H. G. Wells.[10]

Gernsback's first exhortation still retains some power within the science fiction community, as the popularity of books on the science of *Star Trek* or on the mechanics of science fiction series "ship manuals" can attest. His second, Westfahl writes, has shaped the vision of science fiction critics such as "Damon Knight, James Blish, Judith Merril, Michael Moorcock, and Harlan Ellison,"[11] the last being a creative consultant on *B5*. According to Westfahl, space soap does not aspire to either scientific or literary excellence. In terms of the discourses surrounding *B5*, the producers JMS met in his crusade to rescue sci-fi can clearly be identified as "space soapers": "nothing has to make any sense," "aliens, ray guns, space ships."

B5's publicity discourse addresses the commandments of "good" sci-fi in a number of ways. In relation to scientific excellence, *B5*'s technical arsenal resembles that of other contemporary series (hyperspace, jump gates, mind melds, organic technology, alien thinking crafts), but the program does not foreground them as particularly interesting or innovative. The publicity stresses extratextual rather than textual technical achievements, such as computer graphics publicity stories that generate discussion in science fiction circles. The show prided itself on not using the miniature models relied on by many science fiction television programs at the time, instead employing computer graphics for its special effects, including complex space battle scenes:

> [T]he team were able to consider abandoning the use of special effects miniatures in favour of revolutionary CGI techniques. [Visual effects designer] Ron Thornton was the one who made the big discovery about what he could do. We discovered there was stuff that would allow us to do matte painting and composites in a computer. As more and more desktop stuff came along it became more apparent there were applications that we could use. We've done some things that I don't think anybody else has ever done.[12]

This description of the visual effect designer's learning curve echoes the language of technological discovery and technical breakthrough more familiar from the textual universes of science fiction. We see that the intertextual discourse of *B5* provides different forms of reaction to the classical laws of quality science fiction writing—the story of *B5* is the whole story, not merely the internal story of the fictional universe.

B5 publicity material repeatedly stresses the "literary excellence" Gernsback demanded of quality sci-fi. By employing veteran novelist Harlan Ellison as creative consultant, the series immediately gained status within the genre. JMS says about Ellison's contribution: "Harlan keeps us honest, and helps keep the standard of the show high."[13] In return, Ellison comments on JMS's decision to write a significant run of scripts not only himself, but *all by* himself:

> It's like Bill Shakespeare saying to the Globe Theatre, "Well, we've done some other people's stuff and there's been some pretty good stuff, but in fact here's what I want to do with the Globe Theatre.[14]

Quality literature references abound in publicity materials: "*B5* is a lot like a Russian novel, that has a lot of characters in it that come in and out. It's epic."[15] The novel serves as JMS's model of literary production: "we've diverged from our outline here and there, but there isn't a novelist who doesn't do that once he actually gets into writing his book."[16] The grand arc of JMS's career is seen as culminating in novel writing: "he intends to abandon TV for novels once *B5* is complete."[17]

This respect for cultural forms "superior" to television pervades the diegetic universe of *B5*—like other series before (in particular, *Star Trek: The Next Generation* and its Shakespeare complex), *B5* is intertextually dense. The original opening of *B5*'s pilot episode was intended to focus on the naming of a newly discovered star after J. F. Kennedy, including a cut to one of his rousing speeches.[18] Quality pop culture (the film *Casablanca*) enters in the form of "sooner or later, everybody comes to *Babylon 5*" (episode 1). Tennyson's *Ulysses,* references to Isaac Asimov, Santayana, some Shakespeare, the Holy Grail, the Bible, the Flying Dutchman, General Schwarzkopf, Patrick Henry, Charles Dickens—they all crop up, some in starship or character names, others in short verbal quotations. As both printed materials and Internet sites show, fans love to ferret out these references, this metatextual engagement with the text, seeing *B5* not as a stand-alone narrative but rather as connected to the myriad texts and genres it references. And with its own "Koshisms" (seemingly deep utterances from B5's resident mystic alien), the B5 universe creates its own quotation canon, which gradually unfolds and becomes meaningful as the story arc unfolds (examples include: "Who are you?"; "How will this end?"; "In Fire"; "You do *not* understand"; "And so it begins"; "The avalanche has already started. It is too late for the pebbles to vote."). Fan activities can take up these textual strategies in complex fashion, as this posting to a B5 news group by Jennifer Lynn Dailey-O'Cain describing her and her friends' appropriation of the Koshism "He's the One" shows:

> Two friends and myself went to a Halloween party as "the one" last weekend. It was basically a walking in-joke. We all wore all black with brightly-colored "ones" (the number one) stapled or pinned to our clothes, and "ranger pins" ("Sinclair" and "Delenn" had lentils glued to theirs—don't ask—and "Sheridan" had a big question mark on hers). We also all wore red buttons that said "not 1/3" (meaning that none of us were part of the 1/3 who would agree with the Shadows' motives).
>
> In addition, we had some other "accessories." "Sinclair" had a cloak, a scar, greying hair, and a sign that said "erat" ("was" in Latin). "Delenn" had a feminine vest, a triangle on her forehead made out of silver glitter, a Halloween "snow globe," and a sign that said "est" ("is" in Latin). "Sheridan" had a black star on one cheek and a white star on the other cheek, a parachute, and a sign that said "erit" ("will be" in Latin). Whenever someone didn't understand the costume, we called over another friend of ours who always does a really good "Zathras voice," and he would explain to others who we were.[19]

B5's relationship to "quality" is reinforced through discourses on production practices and textual references. All science fiction series have to define themselves with succinct sound bites in the publicity material. For *Star Trek* the original series and its spin-offs, Gene Roddenberry's humanitarian ideals and utopias formed a core text of the Star Trek discourse. For *B5*, "quality" in its various manifestations constituted a core text of the discourse. *Babylon 5* allows for inattentive viewing by retaining some formulaic structures and providing frequent reinforcements of narrative developments, while simultaneously its intra- and intertextual discourses emphasize the complex, involved, intertextual, multilayered nature of its story line and audience involvement. In Andy Lane's *The Babylon File*, Lane precedes his episode guide with an in-depth look at the B5 universe and story line through the lens of Jungian psychology. He justifies this approach by citing JMS's rather begrudging comment on the subject:

An analysis of some of the stuff in Jungian terms is not entirely un-
productive. It really is a hodge-podge of bits and pieces, a Frankenstein
monster assembled from elements of myth, and archetype, and history
that I've been kind of subconsciously assembling over a long, long time.[20]

JMS's statement also shows an awareness of semiotic and psychological analysis, while his description of his creative process stresses highly
personal involvement and the length of *B5*'s gestation time. Lane's
Jungian framing of JMS's grudging acknowledgment further reinforces
the connection of *B5* to discourses of artistic creativity rather than industrial production. Some fans believe that the audience engagement
demanded by *B5* resembles that elicited by "high art" rather than by
mass-produced texts:

Unlike anything else ever made for American television, *Babylon 5* is
a multi-layered experience that demands repeated viewing and deep
analysis if one of to get the most from it.[21]

Within the episodes themselves, reflective references to layeredness,
writing process, and symbolism multiply and signal "privileged moments" for the viewer to store away and reflect on later. Examples
include the Koshisms, flashbacks, and, rarer in television series, flashforwards, liberal use of dreams, a shower sequence where a dead character miraculously reappears for a night ("Day of the Dead," season 5),
as well as highly self-aware references to narrative structure: "Problems are solved in pieces"; "Just think of what a symbol this would
make"; "It is a parallel"; "This is where it begins to go badly for all of
us"; "Everybody tries to kill each other here" (all from one episode,
"Strange Relations," season 5). This may make for somewhat difficult
viewing, but the discourse of art and creativity justifies it. The emphasis
on "work" and reflection as appropriate forms of audience engagement
with the text recalls the Kantian categories of art and beauty, and differs from the kind of identificatory, phantastical pleasures explored by
other critical writers on sci-fi soap fandom. Lane doesn't deny that sci-
fi has a range of pleasures to offer, but claims that

Although it can be enjoyed on a purely superficial level as a rollicking
adventure yarn with some nifty special effects and a cast of attractive heroes and evil villains, there are deeper levels in which the main
elements and characters of the show cast historical and mythical shadows and deeper levels still in which the overall story arc is essentially a
massive replication of Jung's theories of the mind.[22]

The Dream of Interactivity

JMS is happy to engage with his fellow sci-fi fans in the discussion of his work, its meaning, and the development of the story arc. This approachability is a feature of sci-fi writing,[23] but only the Internet has allowed the kind of interactivity JMS embraces. He posts very regularly on rec.arts.st.tv.babylon5.moderated, a Usenet group. In one month, for example, the topics of his comments range from the availability of director's cuts of *B5* (27 February 2000), to discussions with fans about potential conversations in the B5 universe (23 February 2000), and his opinion on Star Trek conventions (14 February 2000).

As the main writer on the series, he sits in on the editing process and has control over a wide range of aspects of production, so he has been in a position to let discussions on the Web sites influence the program's content. Well-publicized (for example, through episode guides and sci-fi magazines), these instances of interactivity and audience input have become widely known in the fan community.[24] This interweaving of the inter- and extratextual worlds can become quite complex: in one episode a character was called "Julie Masante" to honor "a fan who helped raise money to reimburse Michael O'Hare, after money due to him for a convention he attended was not paid."[25]

JMS's own publicized view of his fans stresses the similarity between their expertise and his own credentials as a sci-fi fan and writer: "I've found a lot of *Babylon 5* fans to be very bright, very detail-orientated, and a very friendly bunch. They're simply behind the story!"[26] These alignments with fans through the various Internet organs, convention appearances, and publicity interviews create a form of audience engagement that parallels the mixed inter/intra-textual signifiers of quality discussed earlier. *B5* is about metatextuality, its production apparatus and text forming a discursive whole. John Ellis characterized this form of viewer engagement as distinguishing television from film:

> Far from wanting to disguise its discourse as story, television seems to want to foreground its discursive status. . . . Television's foremost illusion is that it is an *interactive medium,* not that we are peering into a self-enclosed diegetic space.[27]

The fans' delight in interactivity and metatextual discussions stands in interesting tension with the quality discourses of the sole creator and the predetermined story arc. As the previous quotes have shown, JMS is open to discussing creative processes, meanings, and analyses, clearly understanding the B5 universe as a mixture of pop culture and high art concerns, and of the bricolage work of both writer and consumer:

> One of the things really lacking in American culture, I think, is a sense of *myth*. So the story of *Babylon 5* has a very mythic kind of struc-ture . . . Which is why a lot of the elements I draw on aren't traditional television devices . . . literature, poetry, religion, hard SF, metafiction, Jungian symbology. . . . There are an awful lot of ingredients in this particular pie, culled from the less likely aisles in the supermarket.[28]

The B5 pie does, however, contain some traditional television ingre-dients. Many sci-fi cult series relate character development to an unre-solvable dilemma, supporting Ellis's assertion that "the series implies the form of the dilemma rather than that of resolution and closure."[29] In *Star Trek: Deep Space Nine*, for example, plots often entailed ex-ploration of the tension between Odo's human and Dominion traits, or Captain Sisko's religious and scientific impulses. Ongoing unresolved sexual tension between Captain Jean-Luc Picard and Chief Medical Officer Beverly Crusher or between First Officer William Riker and Ship's Counselor Deanna Troi provided plots for *Star Trek: The Next Generation*. Outside the Star Trek universe, the conflict between con-trol and weakness comically haunts the central character of *Lexx,* and familiarity and strangeness are the poles at work in *The Prisoner*. B5 has its fair share of these character-based dilemmas: the struggle be-tween the ridiculous and the sublime in Londo Molari, or the relation-ships between the Alien/Vorlon/Telepath and human aspects of the character of Lyta Alexander. But the resonance between the characters' growth (through meditations on dilemmas) and the overall narrative (based on conflict and resolution) differentiates *B5* from other cult sci-fi shows. For example, the complex historical narrative woven around Delenn over the years (involving previous Minbari leaders, time travel, love complications, and human/Minbari genetics) magnifies the im-portance of the enigmatic comments and slowly accruing information concerning the tension between her Minbari and human sides, which epitomizes larger narrative conflicts between human and other and be-tween group (B5 politics) and gray council (Minbari politics).

But, contra Ellis, resolution and closure also figure importantly in *B5*'s narrational format. The overthrowing of Earth government, the termination of the war against the Shadows, and the loss of the Vorlons, another ancient alien race, are all foreshadowed and anticipated narra-tive events clearly worked toward in the so-called arc episodes.

As important as these dilemma- or conflict/resolution-driven aspects of B5 narratives are, however, a self-conscious referentiality encompasses not only the arc structure itself (as in Londo Molari's dreams or the time-travel scenarios) but also the act of fan viewing. Many of B5's episodes employ mediality (the processing of "life" through discursive patterns employed by contemporary media) or mediation (of narratives through character viewpoints). An instance of the latter ("View from the Gallery," season 5) entails two dockworkers, Bob and Mack, ambling through the station while going about their duties. Their perceptions of the B5 "bigwig" story unfolding around them can be seen as mirroring the relationship between fans and JMS. They comment comically "from below" on the actions of the "big shots," gloss the series' structure ("something new happens every week," "people come, people go"), give their approval (to the captain: "you're OK in my book, ma'am"), learn how hard the main cast's lives are (as they find Dr. Franklin attending to alien wounded and dead after an attack), and are astonished that the "big shots" might just possibly remember their name (as Delenn does). They are aware of clichés and narrative devices, and can make knowing comments ("The cavalry is here" about the appearance of the White Star ships). Both ironic and appealing, these maintenance workers are appreciated, even if normally invisible. The episode shows that the B5 universe embraces all its maintenance crew—cast, production team, and fan culture—in its metatextual universe, its family of readers and writers. The relationship between science fiction fan and science fiction writer is reproduced in a familiar, comfortable, self-reflective way, supporting Jane Feuer's comment that "the 'implied spectator' for television is not the isolated, immobilized pre-Oedipal individual described by Metz and Baudry in their metapsychology of cinema, but rather a post-Oedipal, fully socialized family member."[30]

Several episodes use television reports and news items as important plot features, while some episodes are made up entirely of these mediations of the normal fictional world of B5. The episode "The Deconstruction of Falling Stars" (season 4) consists of televised history debates, with different historians analyzing President Sheridan's actions one hundred years after the end of the fictional time span of the B5 series. The episode then jumps four hundred years into the future, one thousand years, and finally one million years, showing the fictional event's continued resonance in humanity's future. JMS sees these episodes as part of the risk-taking, serious aspect of B5:

> One of the things I always do is look for ways to turn the series format on its head and show us characters from other perspectives, since

perspective is so much at the heart of the show. . . . Whether that's jumping forward in time or an ISN documentary or seeing everything through the eyes of a third party (or two), it's always a risk because it's never what one expects to see, and a lot of people like to see what they expect to see.[31]

This essay argues that *B5* can take these derivations from the conventional series format since the B5 universe employs a form of intertextuality that already uses multiple viewpoints, identifications, and viewing strategies.

The implied interactivity of media format, viewing practice, and viewpoint also extends itself into the creation of fan-authored materials. Like most cult work, *B5* has engendered spin-offs not only from "sanctioned" sources (which include various novelizations and TV films), but also fans' own writing, which often shows an understanding of the workings of the series' format. While some fan writing takes a pseudoscholarly form, such as Lane's critical commentary or comparisons between B5 and other fictional universes, other fans write in a more humorous vein. The two episodes discussed above appear in this format on a Bogus B5 episode guide Web site:

The Extirpation of Falling Warts
Sheridan's infamous misdoings as a dermatologist, and the effects those had on people, are reviewed by a historian from the future.

A Viet from the Galley
A Vietnamese oarsman and a friend of his tour the station, visiting its most interesting places. They even get to see the fireworks show in the Sanctuary.[32]

These sarcastic and knowing rewrites show a clear appreciation of the "use" of the particular episode within the B5 arc. They also merge the B5 frame with topoi from MUDs[33] (in some of these, toads, warts, oarsmen, whales, mazes, spiders, and other "medieval" topics that appear in Miguel's list have a certain currency), again pointing to the media literacy of this fan community. Comments mocking full textual engagement and identification with the B5 universe can also be found in other genre-parody Web sites. These include joke sites with Koshisms and spoof song texts, such as this rendering of YMCA:

Stayin' Alive Here on Babylon 5
Stayin' Alive Here on Babylon 5

They fought the Psi Corps, Shadows, and Clark's police
They're our very last, best chance for peace[34]

The "knowingness" of B5 fans also manifests itself in the discourses surrounding legality, copyright, and so on. One B5 fan signs his site "© 2000 by Gary Henderson, all rights reserved, and all that legal nonsense. Don't copy it, blah blah blah. Don't run with scissors, yadda yadda yadda. And like that."[35] The metadiscourse of fandom, studio control, and JMS's own monitoring of his creation clearly influences this and other sign-offs parodying legal discourse.

Conclusion

"Who are you?" As this chapter has shown, both inter- and intratextual discourses interpellate B5 fans as participants in a wide-ranging metatextual environment. Fans can engage in an immersive world that takes genre history, author discourse, and quality writing procedure as well as formulaic production methods, other cult universes, narrational analysis, and production background into consideration. This discursive construction of B5 as metatext offers a number of different modes of audience address. Similar to contemporary texts such as the Scream horror film series with its self-referentiality and genre jokes, the discourse allows for "knowing winks" and interesting and innovative plays with form deriving from the fans' Internet and media literacy. At the same time, aspects of the discourse hark back to conventional, literary-based markers of quality and authorship. In the fictional universe as well as in the intertextual framework, interactivity and authorship exist in productive tension, between the discourses of literary merit and hypertextual openness. Internet Web sites together with more numerous and less expensive niche publications lead to widely enlarged fan communities wanting to interact with each other and their authors. This interactivity influences the publicity strategies of media corporations and the visions of contemporary sci-fi writers and TV producers. Aware of the commercial framing of their discourses, fans humorously negotiate texts, intertexts, intratexts, and metatexts. As a B5 fan and a critic of popular culture, I believe that space stations will spin on as long as science fiction pays attention to new and old forms of viewer (and reader) literacy.

When I started in this business one of the things that was a goal was to do a pretty cool piece of science fiction, and I think this is a pretty cool piece of science fiction.[36]

Notes

1. At the time of writing, the Sci Fi Channel is well into its third round of screening the whole *B5* in a more compact format, but even with one show a night, some narrative developments take a long time to conclude.

2. This article focuses solely on the five-year original *B5* plus material generated directly in relation to this period. Due to the success and cult status of *B5*, television movies and a new spin-off series have been developed and screened, but their publication package is more conventional, and they are not discussed here.

3. *SFX,* February 1996, 18.

4. Stuart Banks, "Shadowy Tales: Understanding J. Michael Straczynski," *Starburst* 214 (June 1996): 50.

5. J. Michael Straczynski, "Approaching Babylon," *Foundation* (1995), reprinted in Andy Lane, *The Babylon File: The Definitive Unauthorized Guide to J. Michael Straczynski's Babylon 5* (London: Virgin, 1997), 9.

6. Ibid., 10.

7. Ibid., 10–11.

8. Banks, "Shadowy Tales," 52.

9. The material surrounding *B5* and JMS points out the obsessional qualities of this control—again, qualities that have been associated with the idiosyncratic production methods of "artists" and "authors," and less with the demands of industrial production machineries.

10. Gary Westfahl, "Beyond Logic and Literacy: The Strange Case of Space Opera," *Extrapolation 35,* no. 3 (fall 1994): 177.

11. Ibid., 177.

12. David Richardson, Stephen Payne, and Paul Warbrick, "John Copeland: And Now for a World," *Starburst* 215 (July 1996): 34.

13. Joe Nazzaro, "Harlan Ellison on Babylon 5," *Starburst* 215 (July 1996): 26.

14. Ibid., 27.

15. Michael O'Hare, quoted in Stuart Banks, "Michael O'Hare: Still in Command," *Starburst Yearbook,* December 1995, 34.

16. Matt Bielby, "The World according to J. Michael Straczynski," *SFX,* February 1996, 18–19.

17. Steve Holland, "Powerplayers 1996," *SFX,* August 1996, 49.

18. Lane, *The Babylon File,* 71.

19. Airyn, "We are all Kosh," at http://home.intranet.org/~airyn/b5/theone.html, last accessed January 2001.

20. Lane, *The Babylon File,* 28–29.

21. Ibid., 37–38.

22. Ibid., 38.

23. Many science fiction authors include their personal address as well as the publisher's address in their publications, and many fans turned authors in the Star Trek spin-off publications quote from and react to fans' responses to

previous publications in the sometimes lengthy preambles to the text proper. Places for metawriting on sci-fi have long been provided in science fiction journals and small press publications. In the UK, the small press publication *Zine* only publishes reviews of other journals and discourse about the nature of genre writing and no "creative writing" at all.

24. One particular case of this is highly interesting in its negotiation of JMS as auteur, his personal quirkiness, and his and the fans' awareness of industrial production methods, copyright issues, and suing practices: one episode, "Passing through Gethsemane," has a plotline that is similar to one suggested by a fan on an Internet discussion group in 1994. JMS delayed his writing until the fan sent him a legal statement that allowed him to continue with the plot.

25. Lane, *The Babylon File*, 276.

26. Bielby, "The World according to J. Michael Straczynski," 29.

27. Emphasis in original; John Ellis, *Visible Fictions* (London: Routledge and Kegan Paul, 1982), 104.

28. Lane, *The Babylon File*, 38.

29. Ellis, *Visible Fictions*, 104.

30. Jane Feuer, "Narrative from American Network Television," in *High Theory/Low Culture: Analysing Popular Television and Film*, ed. Colin MacCabe (Manchester: Manchester University Press, 1986), 103.

31. Jane Killick, *Babylon 5: The Wheel of Fire* (London and Basingstoke: Boxtree, 1998), 58–59.

32. Miguel Farah, "The Babylon 5 Bogus Episode List: Part of Sector 83x9x12," at http://www.webhost.cl/~miguel/Sector83/index_eng.html, last modified 23 October 1999.

33. MUDs are Multiple User Dungeons (or, in some usages, Multiple User Dimensions), interactive text-based role-play games lodged on one server that players can access from different sites. Many MUDs create fantasy worlds filled with pseudo-medieval references, although there are many different conventions and forms. Within a MUD, a player takes on an identity and interacts via typed commands and dialogue with other players.

34. Arthur Levesque, "Back Slash's Babylon 5 Page: The Third Page of Mankind," at http://users.erols.com/backslash/b5.html, accessed April 2000.

35. Gary Henderson, at http://pebkac.trippy.org/~kaa/babylon5.htm, accessed March 2000, now off-line.

36. Killick, *Babylon 5*, 7.

4

"Bright Particular Star": Patrick Stewart, Jean-Luc Picard, and Cult Television

Roberta E. Pearson

Were it all to end tomorrow, in most people's minds
[I would be] Jean-Luc Picard and nothing else at all.
—*Patrick Stewart*

■ In December 1999 Patrick Stewart appeared as Ebeneezer Scrooge in Hallmark Entertainment's version of Dickens's *A Christmas Carol*, which aired several times over the holidays on satellite superstation TNT in the United States. *Variety* commented that Stewart was such "a perfect piece of casting that it will be hard to imagine anyone else as the sour ol' tightwad in years to come."[1] But other critics wondered whether the man who had portrayed starship captain Jean-Luc Picard for seven years could persuade audiences to accept him as Dickens's (in)famous miser. Critic Michael E. Hill, writing in the *Washington Post,* said that the adaptation would rise or fall on the casting of the central character. "In the end, the production may be judged most heavily by Stewart's well-practiced portrayal. Can Stewart, so familiar to TV audiences as *Star Trek*'s Captain Picard, be convincing as Scrooge?"[2] John Levesque's *Seattle Post-Intelligencer* review inadvertently responded to Hill's question, saying that Stewart "plays Scrooge with a snarl and a growl so convincing that one wonders how the charming and suave Jean-Luc Picard could have emerged from the same person."[3] But John Carman, of the *San Francisco Chronicle,* was not persuaded. "As surely as Scrooge is haunted by the ghost of Jacob Marley . . . Stewart is haunted by the ghost of Jean-Luc Picard. It's just that Stewart is bound to project the same qualities he put into Picard—the sense that he's a chilly but nevertheless humane intellectual. The essential meanness of the early Scrooge is missing."[4] Carman could not separate the actor Patrick Stewart from the character Jean-Luc Picard, ascribing the same qualities—chilliness, humaneness, intellect—to both.

According to John Ellis, television may encourage this conflation of actor and character far more than the cinema.

> The television performer appears regularly for a series which itself is constituted on the basis of the repetition of a particular character and/or situation. The television performer appears in subsidiary forms of circulation (newspapers, magazines) mostly during the time that the series of performances is being broadcast. The result is a drastic reduction in the distance between the circulated image and the performance. The two become very much entangled, so that the performer's image is equated with that of the fictional role (and vice versa).[5]

Ellis argues that such entanglement or equation happens to most actors in television drama. Refining Ellis's hypothesis of the television actor/character relationship, I want to suggest that cult television may equate or entangle actor and character even more than other television fictions.[6] Ellis asserts that television tends to produce personalities rather than stars, but the featured actors of cult television programs meet his "basic definition of a star," which is "a performer in a particular medium whose figure enters into subsidiary forms of circulation and then feeds back into future performances."[7] But paradoxically, the very process that turns cult television program actors into stars also makes it difficult for the actors to escape the characters they embody. The subsidiary forms of circulation of cult television stars privilege the character over the actor, whereas the subsidiary forms of circulation of film stars privilege the actor over the character. With film stars, Ellis says, "The fictional figure is 'to one side' of the star's general image. . . . Certain elements of the publicly circulated star image complex are used by the film, other elements are refused, other elements are added." With cult television stars, the fictional figure overlaps the star's general image, which makes it difficult for subsequent texts to refuse or add elements. If Patrick Stewart played Jean-Luc Picard as a chilly but humane intellectual, some viewers, or at least one viewer, believe that he can play Ebeneezer Scrooge in no other fashion. An anecdote Stewart relates about his performing Prospero in the New York Shakespeare Festival's *The Tempest* further illustrates this overlapping of actor and character: "I made the mistake of tugging on the front of my doublet. There was an instantaneous burst of laughter. I was very careful never to do that again."[8] The laughter came from Star Trek fans, amused by Stewart's inadvertent rendition of the "Picard maneuver," the affectionate nickname given to the actor's habit of pulling down on the front of his uniform tunic. Stewart's tugging on his doublet caused some audience members to briefly replace Prospero with Picard. Stewart was very careful never to repeat the move, banishing Picard from Prospero's magical isle or, in other words, denying that Stewart, Picard, and Prospero were coterminous.

Yet Patrick Stewart's long-term association with *Star Trek* has made him one of the central icons of perhaps *the* central cult television phenomenon, *Star Trek*. Stewart has played Jean-Luc Picard, captain of the United Federation of Planets' flagship USS *Enterprise,* in 178 episodes of *Star Trek: The Next Generation (TNG)* (1987–1994), and in four feature films (*Star Trek: Generations* [1994], *Star Trek: First Contact* [1996], *Star Trek: Insurrection* [1998], and *Star Trek: Nemesis* [2002]). The modes of production, distribution, and reception characteristic of cult television ensure that Patrick Stewart is, to most people, Jean-Luc Picard and nothing else at all. Paramount-Viacom, *Star Trek*'s production company, uses its flagship franchise to maximize profits across all divisions. Paramount's publishing subsidiary Simon and Schuster has published literally hundreds of Star Trek novels, with Jean-Luc Picard, a k a Patrick Stewart, appearing on cover after cover. Paramount also publishes or authorizes the publication of Star Trek magazines that frequently contain pictures of Picard/Stewart, interviews with Stewart about Picard and *Star Trek,* and updates about the actor's non–Star Trek activities—the implicit assumption, of course, that the reader's interest in Stewart stems primarily from his *Star Trek* associations. Paramount licenses products ranging from mugs to T-shirts to calendars to action figures, many of which display the features of Picard/Stewart. These commodities are targeted at the fans, but the most high profile of all Star Trek commodities, the feature films, reach a much wider audience. Despite continued good ratings, Paramount ended the television run of *TNG* in 1994, rushing the cast onto the big screen to replace the by-now geriatric crew of the original series. The prerelease publicity for each of the four *TNG* films reinforces Stewart's identification as Picard: the actor appears on talk shows and does press interviews to hype the film while the rest of the entertainment media assists Paramount with extensive coverage, much of which involves Stewart as Picard.

For non-fans, the *Star Trek* films mark the highest degree of entanglement between Stewart and Picard, but cult television's mode of distribution constantly bolsters the connection. Cult programs recycle endlessly: local stations and satellite channels strip the syndicated episodes and producers distribute videos for rental and sell-through. At the present moment in the United Kingdom, Sky shows three episodes of *Star Trek: The Next Generation* each Sunday afternoon, and another episode on weekdays at five, repeated at midnight. In New York City, Channel Eleven, WPIX, has been rerunning *TNG* late on Sunday nights for years; the continuous showing of the series is common among local stations around the country. *TNG* videos are readily obtainable both in specialized video shops and in the local supermarket. Such ubiquity ensures that most viewers will at some point have encountered Patrick Stewart as Jean-Luc Picard, at least to the extent of recognizing him as "that bald guy on *Star Trek*." As Stewart himself says,

> *The Next Generation* was there every Saturday night and it continues now. They will always be running *TNG*. Although *Moby Dick* [in which he appeared as Ahab] was tremendously successful on USA Cable that cannot possibly have the lasting impact of something which is seen every night of the week for the last twelve years. There's probably a difference in places like New York where I've done a lot of stage work so I'm primarily known there as a stage actor and also here in London too. But behind that there's still the silhouette of *Star Trek* and that will remain for the rest of my career.[9]

The mode of reception also conflates actor and character. Cult television programs approximate what Roland Barthes dubbed "readerly texts," creating complex alternative realities and encouraging an intense, imaginative engagement with the fictional world that results in devoted fans producing their own, homemade products, ranging from videos to short stories to Web sites.[10] The vast majority of fan products focus on the characters rather than the actors, with fan fiction being emblematic in this regard. Star Trek Web sites and newsgroups provide access to literally thousands of stories starring Jean-Luc Picard, starship captain, but rarely ones starring Patrick Stewart, actor. These few stories tend to be parodic in nature, affectionately contrasting what is seen as the "real" actor with his fictional alter ego. For example, in Melanie Miller-Fletcher's "Revisiting a Visit to a Weird Planet Revisited; or, 'Patrick, I Don't Think We're in L.A. Anymore,'" a transporter malfunction switches Stewart, Jonathan Frakes, and Brent Spiner to the "real" *Enterprise,* and their respective Starfleet counterparts, Picard, Riker, and Data, to the Paramount lot; Stewart, playing Picard "for real," must face down the hostile Romulans.[11] The rarity of actor-centered fan fiction stems in part from the realist writing mode practiced by most fan writers. The best of the character-centered stories display a full knowledge of the protagonists' inner lives, predicated on the accumulated data of the entire run of a series.[12] Such detailed information concerning the actors' inner lives is simply not available, perhaps one reason for the conflation of actor with character.

Patrick Stewart's identification with Jean-Luc Picard is a prime exemplar of the extreme entanglement between actor and character produced by cult television programs, yet in Stewart's case this entanglement has not precluded a very active and successful post–*Star Trek* career. Stewart stated that he "was absolutely determined to be in a state of preparedness . . . to move on after ST:TNG went off the air,"[13] a goal he achieved by playing off and against the Picard character in film, television, and the theater. Stewart deliberately selected his first post–*Star Trek* role (that of Sterling, the flamboyantly camp interior designer in *Jeffrey,* a film about the vicissitudes of gay life and love in New York City under the shadow of AIDS) to take him "as far away as possible from Captain Picard, science fiction and ships of any kind."[14] Stewart used some of his post–*Star Trek* television appearances to work against his associations with the repressed, slightly stuffy Captain Picard. The actor hosted a top-rated episode of *Saturday Night Live* in which his opening monologue parodied *Star Trek,* "guest-voiced" on *The Simpsons,* and did a segment for *Sesame Street.* Other post–*Star Trek* television work has been undertaken for Hallmark Productions: *The Canterville Ghost* (1995), *Moby Dick* (1997), *A Christmas Carol* (1999), and an updating of *King Lear,* called *King of Texas,* seen on American television in 2002.

In addition to establishing himself as an actor in "quality" television, Stewart has ascended rapidly to the upper echelons of American theatrical actors since *The Next Generation* ceased production in 1994. Stewart returned to the theater in a one-man rendition of Dickens's *A Christmas Carol* undertaken during breaks in *TNG*'s shooting schedule. Stewart's first post–*Star Trek* theatrical venture was the New York Shakespeare Festival's *The Tempest,* which transferred to Broadway for an extended run. Next he starred as Othello, in a "photo-negative" reconceptualization of the play that cast him as a white British mercenary opposite a company of African-American actors. More recently, Stewart appeared as the central figure in the New York City premiere of Arthur Miller's *The Ride Down Mt. Morgan* and reprised it on Broadway during the spring and summer of 2000. In 1998, the magazine *GQ* recognized Stewart's increasing centrality to the American theatrical scene by selecting him as its man of the year in the theater, tellingly not film or television. And in 1999 the American theatrical establishment officially embraced Stewart as one of its own: the American Theatre Wing, an eighty-year-old nonprofit charitable organization best known as the founder and copresenter of the Antoinette Perry "Tony" Awards, included him as one of its "Men for All Seasons" (together with Americans Ossie Davies, Kevin Kline, Jason Robards, and Sam Waterston) at its annual honors luncheon.

Such an active and cross-media career is quite unusual for an actor who achieved fame in a cult television show. Some television actors, e.g., George Clooney, manage to parlay their small-screen stardom into large-screen stardom, but many more try and fail, e.g., David Caruso (of *NYPD Blue*) and Jimmy Smits (of *LA Law* and *NYPD Blue*). And each of these actors has the advantage of association with "quality television" rather than with the somewhat down-market science fiction genre. It is even rarer for actors in cult television programs to forge successful post-cult careers. The most famous Star Trek captain of all, William Shatner (Captain Kirk in the original series) had, prior to donning Starfleet uniform, done a considerable amount of theater in his native Canada as well as appearing in American film and television, and his subsequent non–*Star Trek* work has included television, theater, and film. But the verdict is in: William Shatner will forever and always be Captain James T. Kirk and nothing else at all. In recent years, Shatner has exploited his Star Trek association in knowing and postmodern fashion, appearing, for example, as The Big Giant Head in *Third Rock from the Sun* and as himself in the American indie *Free Enterprise*. But a better comparison with Stewart might be Diana Rigg who, after playing Mrs. Peel in the British program *The Avengers* in the 1960s, went on to other television, film, and theater work, eventually becoming literally a grand dame of the British theatre. Like Stewart, Rigg trained as a classical actor in one of Britain's premiere drama schools (the Royal Academy of Dramatic Arts in her case) and spent a number of years with the Royal Shakespeare Company before performing in a popular television program.[15] But the analogy then breaks down. Rigg appeared in *The Avengers* at a much younger age than Stewart did in *Star Trek: The Next Generation;* the former program, despite its popularity, has had nothing like the global impact of the latter; the actor played Mrs. Peel for a relatively short time (two seasons) and achieved her subsequent success primarily in the United Kingdom. In fact, my American friends tell me that for them, Diana Rigg is Mrs. Peel and nothing else at all.

Yet, while Patrick Stewart may be Jean-Luc Picard to many Americans, he is to many others Scrooge, Ahab, Othello, Prospero, and Professor Charles Xavier, leader of the X-Men. Ellis's analysis of television stardom may help us to understand how Stewart has managed to some extent to break free of Picard. Ellis believes that the "creation of stars is impossible in broadcast TV (which fosters personalities)."[16] Television stardom is impossible because the medium's actors do not maintain that tension between ordinariness and extraordinariness first discussed by Richard Dyer in his pioneering book, *Stars*. Dyer postulated that film stars are simultaneously ordinary and special. "Are they just like you and me, or do consumption and success transform them into (or reflect) something different?"[17] Ellis postulates that the television performer is just like you and me, since she or he "exists . . . in the same space as the television audience, as a known and familiar person rather than a paradoxical figure, both ordinary and extraordinary."[18] David Marshall is in basic agreement with Ellis's analysis: "Whereas the film celebrity plays with aura through the construction of distance, the television celebrity is configured around conceptions of familiarity."[19] Marshall argues that three factors reduce the aura of the television celebrity: the domestic nature of television viewing, the close affinity of the celebrity with the organization and perpetuation of consumer capitalism, and "the shattering of continuity and integrity of character that takes place through the interspersal of commercials in any program."[20] But Patrick Stewart is in several respects neither ordinary nor familiar in the context of American television. It was extraordinary for a British actor to be given the central role in an American television program, for a long-term member of the prestigious Royal Shakespeare Company, unfamiliar to all but a fraction of the television audience, to play the lead in a science fiction series, and for a bald, middle-aged man to become a sex symbol lusted after by countless women (and not a few men). The rest of this essay explores Stewart's extraordinariness in the context of American television in the hope that this particular case study might more generally illuminate the processes of cult television stardom.

Gene Roddenberry, legendary producer of the original series, and Rick Berman, who eventually succeeded him as *Star Trek*'s executive producer, took a considerable risk in choosing Stewart to play their captain. Says Stewart, "It still even today after twelve years, strikes me as being absolutely bizarre. I have no explanation for it at all."[21] Why cast a middle-aged English actor as Captain Jean-Luc Picard, a key role on which the success of the program may well have depended?[22] American television producers generally rely on American actors with American television experience: among Stewart's *Enterprise* crewmates were Jonathan Frakes (Commander Will Riker), with a decade's small-screen work behind him; LeVar Burton (Lieutenant Geordi Laforge), another old television hand, best known for his role as Kunta Kinte in the hit miniseries *Roots;* and Michael Dorn (the Klingon, Lieutenant Worf), a regular on both *The Mary Tyler Moore Show* and *Chips.*[23] Many watching the show's pilot may well have identified the familiar faces of Frakes, Burton, and Dorn (well, perhaps not the last, hidden by all that Klingon makeup), but relatively few would have recognized Stewart, whose theatrical and television work had been limited to the United Kingdom. Stewart came to *Star Trek* from a lengthy career on the British stage, where he had played a wide variety of Shakespearean and other roles. In the 1970s, he began to work in cinema and television, appearing in several relatively minor films as well as the occasional more prestigious films such as *Excalibur* (John Boorman, 1981) and *Dune* (David Lynch, 1984) and performing in various British television productions, most notable among the latter his portrayal of the evil Sejanus, the commander of the Roman Emperor's Praetorian Guard in the BBC's *I, Claudius.* Among American television viewers Stewart's recognition factor would have been primarily limited to *Masterpiece Theater* fans familiar with *I, Claudius* and those who might have seen the actor on stage in Stratford or London on their European travels.

While Stewart's nationality strongly militated against his being cast as *The Next Generation*'s captain, the actor's Englishness, which constitutes a highly salient element of his star image, may have aided his attempts to break free of Picard. In the 1992 Turner documentary about MGM Studio, *When the Lion Roars,* Stewart's beautifully tailored faux period garb, props such as champagne glasses and a silver cigarette case, and his perfectly enunciated diction created an image of suave sophistication that resonates with the conventional American conception of the classy English actor. Stewart has starred in three productions for Hallmark Entertainment, a subsidiary of Hallmark Cards Inc., which distributes the Hallmark Hall of Fame programs (the one survivor from American television's golden age of weekly, one-off dramatic shows) and specializes in prestigious, high-production value miniseries based on classic literary sources (e.g., *The Odyssey, Gulliver's Travels,* and *Merlin*).[24] Stewart's work for Hallmark draws heavily on the quality connotations of the actor's well-known associations with the British stage in general and the Royal Shakespeare Company in particular. Stewart portrayed a deceased English aristocrat (and recited several Shakespeare sonnets) in *The Canterville Ghost* (1995), based on a short story by Oscar Wilde, which presented a very American vision of an England of stately homes, noble families, and comic faithful retainers. In a return to ships, if not science fiction, Stewart starred as a captain whose iconic status perhaps outstrips even that of Jean-Luc Picard, *Moby Dick*'s Ahab. And, as already noted, Stewart starred in Hallmark's production of Dickens's *A Christmas Carol*. Stewart's appearance on the seventy-first Academy Awards presentations in 1999 also accented his Englishness, as he introduced clips from *Elizabeth* and *Shakespeare in Love,* two films that dealt with the very English subjects of Elizabeth I and Shakespeare and that were heavily publicized in the United States as British imports.

For Americans, Stewart's nationality, as signaled by his accent, distinguishes him from other performers, thereby expanding the range of roles for which he is suitable. "You can't get much more British than Patrick Stewart," said a contributor to a rec.arts.movies thread concerning the most "British" actors and actresses.[25] Stewart, who began life with a Yorkshire "dialect" that "was much more than an accent" and spent "a period . . . struggling toward standard pronunciation" in drama school, believes that speaking Received Pronunciation English provides him "with a neutral base."[26] This might be so in Britain, where listeners recognize the actor's drama school inflections as well as the occasional Yorkshire undertone, but in the United States his accent carries distinct connotations, identifying the speaker as "cultured" and "upper-class." As a poster to the newsgroup rec.art.startrek.current commented, "[Britons] have great accents that sound cultured and sophisticated, not like the way Americans abuse the spoken word with our terrible accents and pronunciations."[27] Stewart's accent reinforces his cultural cachet, a product branding that might benefit the actor in an American market that still values British imports. It also creates a rather unusual tension between actor and character. *Star Trek* fans often speculate as to why the supposedly French Jean-Luc Picard speaks like a tony Brit. Stewart offers a pragmatic explanation. "Just think how tiresome it would have been listening to me for 178 episodes speaking with a French accent. It would have driven everyone crazy. You should hear my French accent. We did do it, we actually rehearsed with a French accent for about two minutes and everybody decided what a terrible idea it was and we abandoned it."[28]

As demonstrated in threads on Star Trek newsgroups, however, fans continue to find the disjunction between Picard's nationality and accent intriguing. Some seek an explanation within the Star Trek universe: Picard went to school in England or had an English tutor. My favorite theory mixes the diegetic with the nondiegetic. "Everyone in Star

Fleet speaks English. English has been explicitly referred to on-screen several times. The young Picard, already wanting to join Star Fleet and already a fan of Shakespeare learnt a lot of English by watching videos (or whatever) from the Royal Shakespeare Company, and was influenced by the accents he heard there. (In particular an actor from the late twentieth century called Patrick Stewart.)"[29] Harder-headed fans insisted on the extratextual explanation, as in the following. "You also need to remember, Star Trek is not real!!!! Picard has an English accent because Patrick Stewart is originally from England!"[30] Klingons or androids with American accents did not strike American viewers as inappropriate; they may even have accepted a Frenchman with an American accent, but Stewart's English accent foregrounded the actor embodying the fictional character. Perhaps cognizant of this discrepancy, the *Star Trek* producers requested Stewart to adopt certain American speech forms. "I Americanized what I said all the time. We had a deal . . . on all technical terms, all overtly different pronunciations."[31] Despite this "Americanization," the clash between the textual signifiers that marked Picard as French (name, hometown, and so forth) and the performance signifier (accent) that marked him as English inadvertently approximated Brecht's "Verfremdungseffeckt," creating a gap between performer and role. The captain speaks with an English accent because he is played by an Englishman, Patrick Stewart, who is not completely synonymous with the Frenchman, Jean-Luc Picard.

Stewart's Englishness relates to another very salient aspect of his star image, the fact that he was an associate artist of the Royal Shakespeare Company for more than two decades before transferring to Starfleet. From the very first, *Star Trek* made much of its star's Shakespearean background, both in publicity and in the primary text itself. During the first season, a sign on Stewart's Paramount trailer read "unknown Shakespearean actor," and Stewart has often spoken of connections between Shakespeare and *Star Trek*. "In the early years of the series, it was perpetually suggested to me that I might be slumming or selling out by coming to Hollywood to do this television series—that in some way, I was betraying my Royal Shakespeare Company past. . . . All the time I spent sitting around on the thrones of England as various Shakespearean kings was nothing but a preparation for sitting in the captain's chair on the Enterprise."[32] Captain Picard kept a copy of the Globe Shakespeare on permanent display in his ready room and traded Shakespearean quotes with the omnipotent entity Q in the episode "Hide and Q." *The Next Generation*'s Shakespearean references served diegetic and nondiegetic functions. In the fictional world, they helped define the character of Jean-Luc Picard as a cultured and civilized man, the apotheosis of *Star Trek*'s humanist philosophy. In the "real" world they reinforced an aspect of the star's image, reminding viewers that the actor, despite appearing in what many in the industry considered "that syndicated kids' science fiction show,"[33] still retained the cachet of a higher cultural form, much like the diva who releases a compact disc of popular show tunes but then returns to the Met.

Paradoxically, the very characteristics of cult television that create such tremendous overlap between character and actor also permitted Stewart to foreground the Shakespearean associations that would prove crucial in his post–*Star Trek* career. Television producers wish to retain their lead actors throughout the run of a program, since the viewers' strong identification with the characters is crucial to the success of a series. Miss Ellie in *Dallas* and Darrin in *Bewitched* were both famously portrayed by more than one actor, but the conflation of actor/character in cult television would militate against such substitution. The fans may care more about the character than the actor, but it is the actor who establishes the character's physical characteristics and mannerisms. For example, *Avenger*'s fans reacted with horror to the big-screen version of their favorite program, considering it a rank travesty for anyone other than Patrick Macnee or Diana Rigg to pretend to be Steed and Mrs. Peel.[34] Such strong viewer identification gives a certain power to the lead actors in cult television programs. Producers, realizing that these actors face the potentially stultifying boredom of playing the same role week after endless week and begin to look for ways not "to fall asleep or go crazy or something," grant them a degree of control over both story lines and dialogue. According to Stewart, "leading actors in series have [changed dialogue] a lot. They can do it because they have the power to do it. . . . It meant that from time to time I could expand on themes that interested me." Stewart talked "every day to [executive producer] Rick Berman about the scripts. I don't think a day passed that he and I didn't have some conversation about the current script. And he was always tremendously supportive of what I was trying to do, encouraging." Stewart's involvement in the production process meant that "any scene of any substance that I played throughout the seven years would somewhere in it [have] some tweakings or fine tunings from me."[35] One example of this fine-tuning occurred in the third-season episode "Menage a Troi," in which Picard must persuade a Ferengi captain who has kidnapped Lwaxanna Troi (Counselor Deanna Troi's mother) that he is madly jealous and willing to destroy the Ferengis' ship to win her back. Picard does so by reciting a mélange of lines from the sonnets, Stewart performing Shakespeare in the over-the-top manner of a nineteenth-century matinee idol. Stewart recalled doing this extempore. "We did that on the set. I'd been thinking about it and then I remember saying, 'Listen, why don't you just keep rolling the camera.' So I just quickly thought of a few things and put them in. It was rare that that happened but that actually was an instance."[36]

The holodeck, the virtual reality computer program, gave Stewart the chance to lecture about Shakespeare to millions of viewers who might never attend a theatrical performance. A third-season episode, "The Defector," begins with a holodeck sequence in which Captain Picard acts as drama coach to the android Data as he rehearses the "little touch of Harry in the night" scene from *Henry V*. In dialogue undoubtedly tweaked by Stewart, Picard and Data discuss the play after exiting the holodeck. Data tells Picard that he intends to study the interpretations of "Olivier, Branagh, Schapiro, and Kolnak." Picard responds, "You're here to learn about the human condition and there is no better way of doing that than by embracing Shakespeare. But you must discover it through your own performance, not by imitating others." Data then asks, "Why should a king wish to pass as a commoner? If he is the leader should he not lead?" Picard replies, "Listen to what Shakespeare is telling you about the man, Data. A king who has true feelings for his soldiers would wish to share their fears with them on the eve of battle." Picard rejects postmodernity's endless string of signifiers, urging that Data return to the original text and enjoy the privileged encounter between author and reader celebrated by traditional literary studies. This is in keeping with the textualist tradition of the British stage that Stewart himself espouses. When asked whether it is easier to work with a "great text," Stewart responded,

> The constant revelation of a great text is something which occurs every day whether it's Ibsen or Shakespeare. . . . All you have to do is open your eyes and pay attention. That's not as easy as it sounds but it's there, it exists to be mined, the depth of a major Shakespearean character . . . ranging from as crude as the character's actions through to the character's imagery and specific use of language.[37]

In other words, "Listen to what Shakespeare is telling you about the man."

The seventh-season episode "Emergence" opened with yet another Shakespeare holodeck sequence in which Picard/Stewart gives a donnish lecture. This time Data plays Prospero in *The Tempest*. After delivering the famous act 5, scene 1 soliloquy in which Prospero abjures his "rough magic," Data seeks advice from the captain:

> DATA: I am not certain I fully understand this Prospero character. I would appreciate any insight you might have that would improve my performance.
>
> PICARD: Shakespeare was writing at the end of the Renaissance and the start of the modern era. And Prospero found himself in a world where his powers were no longer needed. We see him here about to perform one final creative act before giving up his art forever.
>
> DATA: There is certainly a tragic aspect to the character.
>
> PICARD: Yes, but there's a certain expectancy, too, a hopefulness about the future. You see, Shakespeare enjoyed mixing opposites, the past and the future, hope and despair.[38]

A little more than a year after filming this episode, Stewart himself appeared as Prospero in the New York Shakespeare Festival's *The Tempest,* the laughter resulting from his inadvertent performance of the "Picard maneuver" attesting to the actor's permanent association with his twenty-fourth-century alter ego. But might Stewart's very presence on that Central Park stage have been due to his cult television fame and to the opportunities that *Star Trek* afforded him for the reinforcement of his Shakespearean actor image?

As we have seen, "Englishness" and "Shakespeareanness" form key elements of Patrick Stewart's star image, both making him extraordinary relative to other performers in American cult television, but from the actor's own perspective the most extraordinary element of his image may be his widely discussed sex appeal. Stewart has "been named The Most Bodacious Man on TV by the readers of *TV Guide* (1992), one of the 10 Sexiest Men by *Playgirl* (1995), and one of the 50 Most Beautiful People by *People Magazine* (1995)."[39] Asked how he felt about *TV Guide*'s readers voting him "The Most Bodacious Man on TV," Stewart replied, "It still astonishes me. It is truly incomprehensible to this day. But it's very pleasant."[40] Journalists regularly mention Stewart's unlikely combination of baldness and sex appeal, dubbing him the "follically challenged sex symbol"[41] or the "bald sex symbol."[42] *GQ* referred to the actor as "a man who can heat up grandmothers and DiCaprio teen queens alike,"[43] while an interview in the British newspaper the *Independent* included a reference to "his Internet fan club" that "is called 'The Patrick Stewart Estrogen Brigade [PSEB].'"[44] The Internet provides copious evidence of Stewart's sex appeal aside from

the Web page of the PSEB. In the course of a debate on Stewart's acting abilities in the high-toned Shakespeare newsgroup humanities.lit.
authors.shakespeare, an interesting gender difference arose. A male
poster complained, "All I see are a bunch of women who are mesmer-
ized by an authoritarian figure." A female poster denied this, humorously remonstrating, "We adore Mr. Stewart because his riding breeches
fit rather well."[45] Later, in another thread, the same poster discoursed
at greater length about Stewart's attractiveness. "I admire Mr. Stewart
greatly—I believe he is a wonderful actor, possesses a marvelous voice
with the range and subtlety of tone coloration of a fine Spanish guitar
in the hands of a master, and is so madly attractive that the mere sight
of him sends quantities of hormones surging through my bloodstream
sufficient to inhibit all higher brain functions."[46] Posters to other newsgroups share this opinion: "Patrick is God's gift to women";[47] "Patrick
Stewart is just one hunka hunka";[48] "one of the hottest men ever to
grace television, stage, or screen (his voice makes me melt)";[49] "Patrick Stewart, <big dreamy sigh>";[50] "the man is just PURE sex in a
package";[51]and "Patrick Stewart . . . is the sexiest man alive."[52] One
woman, posting to a thread on "TV's Hunkiest Men," responded: "A
partial list . . . I'll finish it later: (1) Patrick Stewart, (2) Patrick Stewart,
(3) Patrick Stewart, (4) Patrick Stewart, (5) Patrick Stewart, (6) Patrick
Stewart, (7) Patrick Stewart, (8) Patrick Stewart, (9) Patrick Stewart,
and, of course, there's always (10) Patrick Stewart."[53] Stewart may be
somewhat bemused by his sex symbol status but acknowledges that
it is useful to his career. As Stewart told *TV Guide,* this perception
of him has "opened up an area of work for me I'm delighted with
because I never anticipated romantic roles would be accessible" (*TV
Guide,* 1994).[54]

Ellis says, "[T]he star is at once ordinary and extraordinary, available for desire and unobtainable," but argues that television reduces
"the extraordinariness of its performers, and their status as figures of
an equivocal attraction and identification by viewers both male and female."[55] On the above evidence, television hasn't reduced Patrick Stewart's "extraordinariness": he functions as a figure of equivocal attraction for viewers both male and female—desirable but beyond the reach
of the ordinary fan.[56] A post about Stewart nicely catches the equivoca-
tion between attraction and identification of which Ellis speaks: "From
those who have met him, he's also a very NICE person. Not pretentious
or arrogant or anything that would be a negative. His choices in chari-
ties are commendable and he's an all around nice guy from all reports.
If I met him in person (as one of my friends did) I would (as she did)

become completely tongue-tied and swoon."[57] The poster's expectation of becoming tongue-tied and swooning contradicts Ellis's and Marshall's assertions that the domestic nature of television renders its stars familiar and ordinary. A poster who did encounter Stewart in person provides further evidence of the extraordinary effect he can have on his fans. The poster had arranged to meet her friend at the Ambassador Theatre prior to seeing *The Ride Down Mt. Morgan*:

> I was just hanging out right smack next to the stage door, which I didn't realize was the stage door. There were also about 6 people in a group standing there on the sidewalk. Next thing I know, there is Patrick Stewart, greeting them, being really friendly and animated and signing all their Captain Picard 8x10's. . . . I stood there and stared, in awe, I swear to god it was an out-of-body experience, I was transfixed on this scene. Next thing, he turns and goes to the stage door and buzzes to be let in. He turns and looks me right in the eye and smiles, I was 3 feet away, leaning against the building! I already had a frozen smile on my face . . . so I hope he took that as me smiling back because I was speechless. . . . When my girlfriend found me 15 minutes later, she says I looked like I was in a coma holding up the building, that I had this really far-off look on my face! Well, shit, yeah! I had just come face to face with GOD!!!![58]

Conclusion

This essay has sought to show:

1. Cult television's modes of production, distribution, and reception have conflated actor Patrick Stewart with character Jean-Luc Picard to a greater degree than usual even on television.
2. Nonetheless, Stewart has managed to some extent to free himself from Picard.
3. It is Stewart's extraordinariness in the realm of American television with regard to his Englishness, Shakespeareanness, and sexiness that has opened up a distance between him and his fictional alter ego.

Therefore, contra both Ellis and Marshall, ordinariness and familiarity does not, in all cases at least, account for television's conflation of actor and character. Patrick Stewart is both conflated with his character and extraordinary. What then accounts for the conflation? The logic of capitalism is always a good starting point. In the last two months of

1998, disparate and conflicting representations of Stewart circulated simultaneously. *The Ride Down Mt. Morgan* approached the end of its initial off-Broadway run, while Dreamworks Studios and Paramount shifted their respective publicity machines into high gear for two major film releases, *The Prince of Egypt,* in which Stewart voices the Pharaoh Seti, and *Star Trek: Insurrection,* in which, of course, the actor once more donned what he refers to as his "spacesuit." Both *In Theater: The Weekly Magazine of Broadway and Beyond* and *Time Out: New York* featured Stewart on their covers. The former promulgated the image of the serious thespian with an in-depth interview that focused primarily on the Miller play. The latter gave an overview of Stewart's post–*Star Trek* career, but tellingly remarked that his enactment of the lead in *The Ride Down Mt. Morgan* made him "the first Brit to star in a New York production of a work by America's greatest living playwright."[59] The Dreamworks publicity invoked the British actor image since *The Prince of Egypt* followed a long-standing tradition of casting Brits as the bad guys in historical films; Stewart, together with fellow Englishman Ralph Fiennes, played the evil Egyptians against the good Jews of Val Kilmer and other American actors.[60] But Paramount's intense publicity spotlighted Stewart's cult television connections, casting the other images into the shadows. The actor's picture graced the covers of such specialized magazines as *Starlog* and *Cinescape* while the man himself did the talk show rounds, appearing on *David Letterman, Rosie O'Donnell,* and several other New York–based programs to tout the merits of *Insurrection.* Meanwhile Insurrection paraphernalia flooded the stores: trading cards, action figures, books, and magazines, many prominently featuring an image of Stewart/Picard. Paramount's publicity and marketing juggernaut ensured that during late 1998 at least, Patrick Stewart was, if not Jean-Luc Picard and nothing else at all, primarily Jean-Luc Picard.

Notes

Many thanks to Patrick Stewart for a lengthy interview and for a positive and encouraging response to an earlier version of this paper, as well as for all his subsequent help with various Trek-related research. And thanks also to Karen Backstein for her constructive criticism of that same earlier version. Thanks also to my colleagues Máire Messenger Davies and Matt Hills for further suggestions.

1. Michael Speier, "TNT revives Dickens' 'Carol,'" *Variety,* at http://dailynews.yahoo.com/h/nm/19991201/en/review-televisioncarol_1.html, accessed 4 December 1999.

2. Michael E. Hill, "A Scrooge Straight Out of Dickens," *Washington Post,* 4 December 1999, at http://www.bergen.com:80/yourtime/scrooge1999 12042.htm.

3. John Levesque, "The Richness of Scrooge's Nastiness Makes TNT's 'Christmas Carol' Sing," *Seattle Post-Intelligencer,* 4 December 1999, at http://www.seattlep-i.com:80/tv/scrg04.shtml.

4. John Carman, "Lemmon's at His Best in 'Morrie.'" *San Francisco Chronicle,* 3 December 1999, at http://www.sfgate.com:80/cgi-in/article.cgi?file=/chronicle/archive/1999/12/03/DD91106.DTL.

5. John Ellis, *Visible Fictions: Cinema, Television, Video* (London: Routledge, 1992), 106.

6. Sara Gwenllian-Jones argues that specific characteristics of cult television forge such a strong bond between actor and character that "the performer's star image is not so much 'entangled' or 'equated' with the fictional character as exceeded by it." In the case of *Xena: Warrior Princess,* says Gwenllian-Jones, "it is Xena, not [Lucy] Lawless, who is the focus of fans' engagement with the series and who is the main object of their fascination and fantasies" ("Starring Lucy Lawless?" *Continuum* 14, no. 1 (spring 2000): 12.

7. Ellis, *Visible Fictions,* 91.

8. Jeff Craig, "Rebel with a Cause" *SFX,* February 1999, 27.

9. Personal interview with Patrick Stewart, Ealing Studios, London, 16 March 1999 (hereafter "Stewart interview"). This interview was conducted with my colleague, Máire Messenger Davies. Together, we are writing a book titled *Small Screen, Big Universe: Star Trek as Television Studies* (Berkeley: University of California Press, forthcoming).

10. For detailed discussions of Star Trek fandom, see Camille Bacon-Smith, *Enterprising Women: Television Fandom and the Creation of Popular Myth* (Philadelphia: University of Pennsylvania Press, 1992); Henry Jenkins, *Textual Poachers: Television Fans and Participatory Culture* (New York: Routledge, 1992); and John Tulloch and Henry Jenkins, *Science Fiction Audiences: Watching Doctor Who and Star Trek* (London: Routledge, 1995); as well as Jeffrey Sconce in this volume.

11. The story is a homage to one of the most famous of original series' fan fiction stories in which Captain Kirk, Mr. Spock, and Dr. McCoy switch places with William Shatner, Leonard Nimoy, and DeForrest Kelly.

12. As Sara Gwenllian-Jones notes of actress Lucy Lawless, "I have yet to find a single example of a fan fiction story which invokes Lawless as herself, or indeed even mentions her. It is Xena, not Lawless, who is the focus of fans' engagement with the series and who is the main object of their fascination and fantasies (whether erotic or otherwise)." See Jones, "Starring Lucy Lawless?" 12.

13. Ian Spelling, "A Captain's Revenge," *Star Trek Monthly,* December 1996, 22.

14. Pamela Roller, "The Legacy of Captain Picard," *Star Trek Monthly,* March 1995, 54.

15. At http://www.mindspring.com/~jglane/riggbio.htm, accessed 3 March

2000. Stewart studied at the Bristol Old Vic, another of the country's leading drama schools. Of course, Rigg spent only five years with the Royal Shakespeare Company before *The Avengers,* while Stewart had been with the company for twenty-odd years before *Star Trek.*

16. Ellis, *Visible Fictions,* 91.

17. Richard Dyer, *Stars* (London: BFI, 1998) (first edition published 1979).

18. Ellis, *Visible Fictions,* 106.

19. P. David Marshall, *Celebrity and Power: Fame in Contemporary Culture* (Minneapolis: University of Minnesota Press, 1997), 119.

20. Ibid., 121.

21. Stewart interview.

22. The only precedent for casting a British actor as the star of an American television program that I can think of is Edward Woodward in *The Equalizer,* which ran from 1985 to 1989. Subsequent *Star Trek* series—*DS9, Voyager,* and the new *Enterprise*—have all cast their captains much more conventionally, the producers choosing American actors with American television experience, including, for the new series, Scott Bakula, well-known as the star of the fantasy cult television program *Quantum Leap.*

23. And also, of course, on American actors with little or no television experience. Neither David Duchovny nor Gillian Anderson had worked in television prior to starring in *The X-Files.*

24. See http://www.buybroadway.com/shows/sound-music/bio-team-hallmark.htm, accessed 17 March, 2000.

25. Lore69 (lore69@aol.com), "The Most *British* Actors/Actresses?" posted to rec.arts.movies, 10 April 1995.

26. Stewart interview.

27. Greg Bryant (gbryant@kent.kent.edu), "Why is Picard's accent English if he's French?" posted to rec.arts.startrek.current, 27 May 1997.

28. Stewart interview.

29. Steve Pugh (mafb90@dial.pipex.com), "Why is Picard's accent English if he's French?" posted to rec.arts.startrek.fandom, 19 May 1997.

30. Chris Morris (chrism@sprintmail.com) "Why is Picard's accent English if he's French?" posted to rec.arts.startrek.fandom, 27 May 1997.

31. Stewart interview. It's interesting to note that New Zealander Lucy Lawless, Xena, Warrior Princess, played her role with a Californian American accent rather than her native Kiwi. Television producers apparently consider a slightly Americanized English accent suitable for an American market but not a New Zealand accent.

32. See http://www.efr.hw.ac.uk/EDC/StarTrek/picard.html, accessed 16 March 2000.

33. Patrick Stewart interview, at http://www.scifitalk.com/page3.htm, accessed 15 March 2000.

34. See David Black's chapter in this volume.

35. Stewart interview.

36. Stewart interview.

37. Stewart interview.

38. I am almost certain that Stewart wrote this dialogue, but when I asked him about this scene he said that he had absolutely no memory of filming it. "If you'd asked me if we'd ever made any reference to *The Tempest* in the series I would have said no."

39. See http://www.primenet.com/~jbedford/PSEB/PS-FAQ.html, accessed 15 March 2000.

40. Stewart interview.

41. Ed Tahaney, "Stewart Keeps On Trekkin'," *New York Daily News,* 10 December 1998, at http://www.nydailynews.com/1998-12-10/New_York_Now/Movies/a-13277.asp.

42. Roger Moore, "Patrick Stewart Interview, No. 2," *Journal Arts,* 10 August 1997, at www.lustchip.com.

43. Andrew Corsello, "Men of the Year: Theatre," *GQ,* November 1998, 415.

44. James Mottram, "Boldly Going Back to His Roots," *The Independent,* 5 June 1998, Eye on Friday section, 9.

45. CCarter756 (ccarter756@aol.com), posted to humanities.lit.authors.shakespeare, 11 October 1998.

46. CCarter756 (ccarter756@aol.com), "Re: Where's the Patrick Stewart Quote," posted to humanities.lit.authors.shakespeare, 23 April 1998.

47. Debby Traywick (debbytraywick@ussvoyager.com), "Best Actor of ALL TIME?" posted to alt.tv.star-trek.voyager, 21 April 1999.

48. Marcy Scott (marcys@umr.edu), "OLDER HEARTTHROBS," posted to bit.listserv.rra-l, 5 May 1995.

49. naishaat (naishaat@aol.com), "Patrick Stewart is CTD fan!" posted to alt.music.ct-dummies, 25 November 1996.

50. Shirley Liu (shliu@ucsd.edu), "OLDER HEARTTHROBS," posted to bit.listserv.rra, 5 May 1995.

51. Goddess (goddess@peak.org), "You might be a feminazi if . . . ," posted to alt.feminism. soc.men, 18 July 2001.

52. Tom Vavasour (tomkris@ihug.co.nz), "Same sex couples," posted to nz.soc.religion, 5 January 2000. This post from a man shows that Stewart's appeal is not limited to one gender.

53. Joan Fechter (jfechter@freenet.columbus.oh.us), "TV's Hunkiest Men Now/All Time," posted to rec.arts.tv, 6 September 1995.

54. At http://www.primenet.com/~jbedford/PSEB/PS-FAQ.html, accessed 15 March 2000.

55. Ellis, *Visible Fictions,* 91, 105.

56. Two caveats here: First, there are those who fail to see Stewart's appeal and find it baffling that others find him sexy. Second, the posters' language of desire, if you will, exactly parallels that about other supposedly sexy cult

television figures, e.g., David Duchovny. As Karen Backstein put it to me, "The discourse is remarkably repetitive; only the names change."

57. Goddess (goddess@peak.org), "You might be a feminazi if . . . ," posted to alt.feminism, 19 July 2001.

58. Shammie (shamtrek@aol.comharemgrl), "Mean Things To Do On The Enterprise," posted to alt.tv.star-trek.next-gen, 16 July 2001. The reference here to coming face-to-face with God reminds us of the religious connotations of the cult in cult television, but there isn't room in this essay to explore them. I refer the reader to John Frow, "Is Elvis a God? Cult, Culture, Questions of Method," *International Journal of Cultural Studies* 1, no. 2 (August 1998): 197–210; and Matthew Hills, "Media Fandom, Neoreligiosity, and Cult(ural) Studies," *Velvet Light Trap* 46 (fall 2000): 73–84.

59. Robert Kolker, "Vocal Hero," *Time Out: New York*, 26 November–3 December 1998, 10.

60. The *Guardian*'s review noted, "The old toga-movie clichés rule. The Egyptians speak in bossy English accents—Pharaoh Seti is Patrick Stewart in fruity James Mason mode, while Rameses is Ralph Fiennes at his most lip-curlingly effete. The American voices are much less distinctive—Steve Martin and Martin Short barely register as the comedy priests, Val Kilmer is less than authoritative as Moses (Jonathan Romney, "Screen: Film of the Week: The Prince of Egypt: Pyramid Selling," *Guardian*, 18 December 1998, 8).

Part II
Fictions

Virtual Reality and Cult Television

Sara Gwenllian-Jones

I'm in Xena's world. I'm really here . . .

■ The desire to enter another reality is an old one. It has precedents in certain kinds of religious experience; in narcotic-induced hallucination; in our long fascination with dreams, visions, and madness; and in the experience of fiction in general—the notion of being lost in a book or movie. In the fantastic genres of science fiction, fantasy, horror, and speculative fiction, elaborate constructions of emphatically alternate realities are central narrative devices, meticulously imagined and described. In literature, the fantastic cosmologies of Mervyn Peake's Gormenghast, Ursula K. Le Guin's Hain universe, Gene Wolfe's Urth, and J. R. R. Tolkien's Middle Earth are not merely exotic backdrops to linear narrative events but vivid and dense semantic domains that saturate character, themes, action, and plot. In addition to furnishing atmosphere and the spatial dimensions that support the narrative, they also have dynamic functions, shaping characters' experiences, inflecting plotlines, and supporting intricate networks of cross-connections through which narrative events resonate. In this sense, the cosmologies of fantasy genre cult television series such as *Star Trek, Babylon 5, Farscape, The X-Files, Xena: Warrior Princess,* and *Buffy the Vampire Slayer* function in much the same way as their literary counterparts. They present exotic and ethereal fictional worlds to which the alchemy of textual data and imagination transports the reader, facilitating a pleasurable psychic sense of "being there" as the action unfolds.

Successful fictional worlds are a matter not only of textual surface but also of environmental *texture;* they create an impression of spatial presence and of a solid geography, of gravity, height, distance, terrain, climate, and so on. The blizzards of the fictional world must rage coldly against the skin; its cliffs must induce a dizzying fear of heights; its nights must amaze with stars; its silences drown out the noisy traffic of actuality. Immersive engagement with the fictional world depends on uniting what is conveyed by the text with the reader's own experiences and knowledge, facilitating a sense of vicarious presence in the imaginary environment. When we enter a fictional world, Janet H. Murray writes,

> We do not suspend belief so much as we actively *create belief.* Because
> of our desire to experience immersion, we focus our attention on the
> enveloping world and we use our intelligence to reinforce rather than to
> question the reality of the experience.[1]

Immersive experience is an alchemical effect of text and imagination, a species of willed hallucination that transports the reader into another realm. It is not a passive experience; the reader must play an active part in creating and sustaining its integrity, drawing on memory as well as imagination to reinforce its perceptual substance.

Immersion in a fictional world is a core concept of virtual reality. But "virtual reality" itself is an ambiguous term whose meaning, Marie-Laure Ryan observes, "stretches along an axis delimited by two poles." At one end of the axis stand the fake and the illusory, the simulated realities described by Baudrillard; at the other end stands virtuality as potential, as a construct of the implicit or latent aspects and possibilities of the text.[2] Mark Poster defines virtual reality in terms of a particular set of user experiences; it must present "images with depth, images which one can enter, explore, and perhaps most importantly, with which one can interact."[3] Virtual reality pioneer Jaron Lanier also emphasizes the interactive aspects of virtual reality technologies:

> You're not in retreat. You're not passive, you're not having an experi-
> ence wash over you. You have to be intentional. You get tired. It's a
> waking state activity. It's not like taking drugs; it's like going on a hike.
> Or, it's like going on a hike and being the sculptor of the mountain at
> the same time.[4]

Interactivity may entail some sort of physical action, as occurs in live action role-playing games (LARPs) and computer games (where the user uses a console or keyboard to direct the action). But interactivity can also describe certain kinds of cognitive process, an interaction of the user's imagination and the imaginative text that, to use Pierre Lévy's term, "deterritorializes"[5] the fiction in the process of actualizing it in the reader's imagination. This notion of a deterritorialized fiction is key to understanding the operations of cult television; it allows us to consider the myriad ways in which cult fictions extend themselves beyond the bounds of their primary texts, migrating across other media, morphing into countless versions, both official and unofficial, material and immaterial, that together constitute vast and incompletable metatexts. Cult television series already include processes and devices of deterritorialization within their primary texts, making exuberant use of intertextual, intratextual, and self-reflexive references, playing with fragmentation and excess and extending their fictions beyond the television text to a variety of other discourses and media incarnations. These characteristics function to dissolve, emphatically and explicitly, singular textual containments of the fiction, releasing it into virtuality. The cult fiction exceeds its primary textual expression (as television text) and, as virtuality, invites and supports intense imaginative viewer engagements that may be immersive or interactive or both.

Though the virtual reality installations of *Star Trek*'s holodeck and the direct mind-machine interfaces of William Gibson's cyberpunk futures remain science fictions, they constitute an ideal of total entertainment to which the culture industry, for obvious commercial reasons, has long aspired. The dream of a technology that will generate a sophisticated virtual world—a fictional world that the user somehow experiences as if it were a real environment—has been the impetus behind developments as diverse as the camera obscuras and panoramas that preceded the cinema, as well as theme parks, role-playing games, and Sensurround sound. IMAX movie theaters are promoted in terms of their facility for immersive experience: "With crystal clear images, ten times larger than traditional cinema format, the IMAX experience draws you in with pictures so real you want to touch them, so powerful you can feel them."[6] IMAX 3D attempts to take the immersive experience even further:

> Using state of the art electronic headsets, complete with infra red sensor to detect the left and right eye images, the IMAX 3D experience has brought 3D enjoyment a long way from the cardboard glasses of the 1950s.[7]

In their inspiration and effect, such technologies and applications approach the functions of the head-mounted displays of existing virtual reality systems. The object is to erode the boundary between spectator and text, saturating or replacing the material world with the visual and aural signs of the textual world and thereby facilitating a perceptual substitution of virtuality for actuality.

The technologies of cult television cannot furnish the overwhelming spectacles and cocooned environments of IMAX cinema or the holistic environmental experiences prophesied for computer-mediated virtual reality systems. Cult television's technologies of world building, narrative construction, and transmission do not facilitate *embodied* entry into the ethereal domains beyond the screen. Its virtual machines are not streamlined installation technologies but rather sprawling macrosystems that extend across a range of different media and objects. Like the "paperback, computer game, comic book, role-playing game, film and CD-ROM markets" described by Daniel Mackay, the cult television phenomenon is characterized by its trajectory toward

> *imaginary-entertainment environments:* fictional settings that change over time as if they were real places *and* that are published in a variety of mediums . . . each of them in communication with the others as they contribute toward the growth, history and status of the setting.[8]

Cult television fictions extend across a wide range of secondary media, untidy yet comprehensive, so that the multiple and various signs of the fictional world saturate the world of actuality from which it is imaginatively accessed. Fans are voracious consumers of spin-off texts and artifacts, surrounding themselves with signifiers of the desired virtual reality. In the process, they feed the lucrative merchandise industries that have evolved around cult television series and serialized, transmedial film franchises such as *Star Wars* and *The Crow*. Posters and photographs adorn walls; PCs display themed wallpaper, icons, and screensavers; dolls and models stand on desks; life-size cardboard cutouts of characters lurk in corners; series-related books fill shelves; CDs play sound tracks; countless screen snatches are downloaded from the Web and scrutinized; recorded episodes are repeatedly viewed and closely analyzed until they are indelibly embedded in memory. The consumption of such an array of spin-off products may bespeak a compulsion for collecting among fans, but a less pathological explanation is that they function, as I have argued elsewhere, as talismans of fantasy that serve as prompts to the imagination, synecdochically invoking the beloved fictional world.[9] In its totality, the transmedial metatext of a cult television series constitutes a macrosystem that recalls (without technologically constituting) Ryan's assertion that in "its ideal implementation, VR is not merely another step towards transparency, to be 'remediated' by future media, but a synthesis of all media that will represent the end of media history."[10]

The Worlds of Cult Television

The concept of virtual reality supposes the possibility of immersion in a fictional cosmology. It entails a spatial and populated dimension that supports narrative potential and affords users a strong sense of presence within the narrative world. In cult television series, such cosmologies are grounded in, without being limited to, primary narratives conveyed through image and sound (dialogue, sound effects, and the ambience of nondiegetic music). Seriality is an important and largely—though not exclusively—medium-specific factor; cult television series usually consist of scores of episodes that together constitute a hundred or more screen hours and that are played out across several years of production and distribution. Their fictional worlds are therefore vast and/or dense with detail and are further augmented by officially produced secondary texts (episode guides, novelizations, comics, computer games, and, in some instances, spin-off series and films) and fan-produced tertiary texts (fan fiction, fan art, cultural criticism, scratch videos, Web sites, screensavers, and so on). The formats through which cult television series present their worlds vary according to the premise used to trigger and condition narrative action. Four broad narrative formats may be identified (though these are not mutually exclusive categories): travelogue, nodal, combination, and portal.

Travelogue Formats

The protagonists of *Xena: Warrior Princess (XWP)* are rootless wanderers, always on the move and rarely spending more than a few diegetic days in a single location. The majority of episodes begin with Xena and Gabrielle traveling to some new and often unspecified location, where adventure awaits them, and concludes with them resuming their journey. Episode by episode, Xena's world expands and develops as her nomadic lifestyle takes her across a mythologized terrain of snowcapped mountains, lakes and rivers, forests, wind-scoured plains, deserts and dunes, gentle green hills, and miles of wild coastland. On this varied and evocative geography is inscribed a fantastical version of a pre-Christian world that spans Greece and its surrounds, the Roman Empire, China, Mongolia, India, North Africa, Celtic Britain, and Japan. Diverse populations of exotic peoples inhabit this fabulous topography. Each has its own distinctive character, its own culture and politics, its own dramas, its own histories, present circumstances, and possible futures.

Secondary characters come and go, each bearing traces of their own history—a suggested, but largely unrepresented, trail leading back to some previously unimagined origin that lies somewhere beyond the horizon they have crossed into the visible spaces of the diegesis. Empires rise and fall, kingdoms are rocked by wars and political intrigues, tribes battle with their neighbors, warlords and outlaws terrorize civilians, and peasants till the land and endure. Here, otherworldly realms (Tartarus, the Elysian Fields, the Dreamscape of Morpheus, the magical realm of Illusia) are as real as anywhere else. Mythical and supernatural beings inhabit the same specular space as ordinary mortals, constituting a fabulous bestiary of gods, centaurs, Cyclops, Titans, Bacchae, giants, apparitions, heroes, and villains with supernatural powers. The laws that govern this teeming cosmos are different from those of our own everyday reality, collapsing the boundaries between the natural and the supernatural, the historical and the mythological. Even the time frame is fluid, moving freely around several centuries of ancient history and taking occasional detours into the twentieth century.

This is the Xenaverse, a fictional cosmology mapped onto the real New Zealand landscape where *XWP* was filmed. It is the morphological dimension of the metatext accumulatively constructed by the travelogue structure of the series itself and further extended and embellished in secondary and tertiary texts. Its extensive use of characters, events, and places from history, mythology, and popular culture blurs the boundaries between fictional and actual worlds so that the Xenaverse continually opens out onto and interconnects with wider narrative possibilities.

Nodal Formats

The nodal narrative world consists of a single localized space at the heart of the fiction. This space is a stable, consistent location that also functions as an intersection through which pass a variety of transient characters. The wider cosmology that surrounds it is everywhere implied but rarely explicitly presented; viewers infer its existence and morphologies from characters and their cultures, story lines, and dialogue. In *Roswell,* explicit presentation of the nodal world of Roswell, New Mexico, is extended by the implied extraterrestrial origins of the series' central alien characters. In both *Babylon 5* and *Star Trek: Deep Space 9 (DS9),* nearly all the diegetic action takes place on a space station inhabited by permanent and semipermanent characters. *DS9*'s space station includes a variety of internal settings, such as Quark's Bar, the holosuites, the cargo bay, and the living quarters of major characters. Through this bounded zone pass emissaries from other worlds, each a metonym for a vaster unseen culture that usually (though not always) itself remains outside the diegesis. Thus the arrival of a Klingon character in *DS9* invokes, in the mind of the viewer, a sense of Klingon worlds beyond the represented spaces of the diegesis. Costume, customs, language, and references to Klingon history and mythology combine with story events to form an evidential foundation on which the viewer builds, in imagination, some part of the spectral, unrepresented architecture of a wider cosmology.

In the later generation *Star Trek* series *(Next Generation, DS9, Voyager, Enterprise),* the metatextual cosmology consists of the vast Star Trek universe and several centuries of diegetic Star Trek history, in which all the series are set and to which each contributes. Chris Gregory describes how *Star Trek*'s "parallel universe" constitutes "a symbolic landscape" where

> The complex history of alliances and conflicts between the major players in galactic politics—the Federation, the Klingons, the Cardassians, the Romulans, the Borg and the Dominion—now forms a constantly shifting political backdrop to the action, and often provides motivation for the stories.[11]

The microcosmic space station world of *DS9* resides inside the macrocosm of the aggregate Star Trek universe, sharing its histories, cultures, themes, structures, and logics and connecting intratextually with the narratives of the other *Star Trek* series as well as the *Star Trek* films and other secondary texts.

Combination Formats

Series such as *Star Trek* (the original series, *The Next Generation, Voyager,* and *Enterprise*), *Blake's 7, Farscape,* and *Andromeda,* in which the characters inhabit star ships traveling through populated universes, combine aspects of both the travelogue and nodal formats. In some episodes of these series, much or all of the action takes place within the bounded world of the starship; in others, the story lines follow characters that disembark and encounter alien civilizations on exotic worlds. The effect is one of a world within a world, the closed environment of the starship existing within, but distinct from, a vaster and more diverse exterior cosmology. The dynamic that drives most of the stories set in combination worlds is one of osmotic interactions between the stable microcosm and the ever-changing exterior universe through which the characters journey in the enclosed environment of their starship.

Portal Formats

The portal format is usually, but not always, a variation on the nodal format. Series such as *Buffy the Vampire Slayer, Angel, Beauty and the Beast,* and *Stargate SG-1* maintain a stable, contained setting at one level of reality but furnish within it some mechanism that opens the localized world onto an alternate reality. In *Beauty and the Beast,* the action moves between everyday contemporary New York and a quasi-medieval fairy-tale underground world that exists in the tunnels and caverns beneath the city. In *Buffy,* the small Californian town of Sunnydale is also the Hellmouth, an interdimensional portal through which fiends and monsters invade ordinary America. In *Stargate SG-1,* the Stargate itself is a portal, housed in a high-security underground military facility, which generates an artificial wormhole that gives access to any one of an infinite number of possible worlds.

The X-Files, on the other hand, combines the travelogue and portal formats. Mulder and Scully pursue cases the length and breadth of a stylized version of contemporary America that is forever rolling back reality to expose its dark supernatural and conspiratorial underside. The certainties of everyday actuality are stripped away; predatory horrors from folklore and mythology prowl urban and small-town America; ordinary social and political order is exposed as a charade disguising a range of sinister government and military activities, including pacts with hostile aliens, human genetic engineering experiments, political assassinations, covert military and intelligence operations, and a range of other staples from conspiracy theory's catalog of reasons to be fearful. As in series such as *Xena, Roswell,* and *Buffy,* the fantastic fictional world connects to the world of actuality at innumerable points, achieving a degree of apparent authenticity while extending itself into an expansive network of possibilities.

The allure of these fictional worlds lies in their invitation to and tolerance of immersive reader engagements in exotic cosmologies. For the avid reader or fan, the object is to so completely inhabit the fictional world that, in Janet H. Murray's words, it "takes over all our attention, our whole perceptual apparatus."[12] The distinctive narrative strategies of cult television series—their emphasis on fantastic subjects, their fascination with metaphysical conundrums, their textual devices of intertextuality and intratextuality, self-referentiality, semantic density, play of excess and fracture, bricolage and exoticism—require and cater to powerful imaginative engagements. They afford entry into fictional worlds of infinite suggestion and inexhaustible possibility, which reward close textual scrutiny, extrapolation, and speculation and exert their fascination not through the linear pull of story events but rather through their lateral resonance and connectivity. Crucially, they also provide rich materials and support for readers' imaginative interventions, constituting a macro-resource that consists of settings, characters, cultures, events; alien, humanoid, and/or mythological species; fauna and flora; costumes, technologies, themes, structures, and logics that can be disassembled, rearranged, and added to in order to create new stories and meanings. These elements, present in the text and learned by the reader, together compose an "encyclopedia" of the fictional world that forms, in cult television fandom, the basis for interaction with the deterritorialized fiction itself.

The Fictional World Encyclopedia and Interactivity

In Jorge Luis Borges's short story "Tlön, Uqbar, Orbis Tertius," the narrator discovers a volume of an encyclopedia that describes the fictional world of Tlön. Enthralled by this discovery, the narrator says,

> I now held in my hands a vast and systematic fragment of the entire history of an unknown planet, with its architectures and its playing cards, the horror of its mythologies and the murmur of its tongues, its emperors and its seas, its minerals and its birds and fishes, its algebra and its fire, its theological and metaphysical controversies—all joined, articulated, coherent, and with no visible doctrinal purpose or hint of parody.[13]

This single volume of the larger encyclopedia of Tlön provides detailed insight into another world—a world that is organized according to an alien logic, that presents its own exotic cultures and histories, that is driven by dynamics different from those of our own everyday actuality. From the perspective of Borges's narrator, Tlön has two realities. The first is textual and explicit: Tlön exists in the form of the data provided in the pages of the encyclopedia. The second reality is virtual and implicit, a complex planetary architecture suggested by the encyclopedia and actualized in the narrator's imagination (and in our own, as readers of the narrator's tale). Virtual Tlön owes its form and coherence not only to the explicit information presented in the encyclopedia, but also, in Marie-Laure Ryan's words, to "the import of information provided by internalised cognitive models, inferential mechanisms, real-life experience, and cultural knowledge, including knowledge derived from other texts."[14] In other words, virtual Tlön is the product of the explicit data and implicit potential of the text *and* the readers' internalized encyclopedia of the real world *and* the readers' imagination. Virtual Tlön is greater than its textual origin; it consists of *both* the explicit *and* the actualized implicit that exists in the reader's imagination, and it is limited to neither.

Fictional worlds, of necessity, always exceed the texts that describe them, relying in large part on the reader who must import exterior information to and imaginatively engage with the text in order to actualize its latent aspects. The recovery of the fictional world from its fragmented and partial textual presence is a dynamic cognitive process in which textual data, knowledge of the real world, and imagination are all marshaled. Lubomír Dolezel uses the metaphor of the encyclopedia to describe the compiled and cross-connected body of information about the fictional world—the only world that is available to and known by the characters that exist within it—that accumulates and actualizes in the mind of the reader:

> The immensely varied fictional encyclopaedias guide the recovery of implicit meaning in fictional texts. In order to reconstruct and interpret a fictional world, the reader has to reorient his cognitive stance to agree with the world's encyclopaedia. In other words, knowledge of the fictional encyclopaedia is absolutely necessary for the reader to comprehend a fictional world.[15]

For cult television fans engaging with the fictional worlds of their favorite series, every episode, spin-off (whether officially or unofficially produced), and intertextual pathway may contribute something to the fictional encyclopedia. The accumulation of knowledge about the fictional world is of central importance, and the meticulous gathering and mapping of textual and metatextual data is a characteristic activity of fans. Information gleaned from the metatext, in its many and various manifestations, is collected, cross-referenced, and often further elaborated on through reference to and investigations into related external texts and discourses (history, mythology, scientific, and so on). The implicit aspects of the fictional world are, in imagination, rendered explicit; gaps are filled in; inconsistencies are smoothed out by means of plausible explanations that are in keeping with the interior logics of the fictional world; creative interventions are made.

Fan cultures produce their own data banks and reference resources to further facilitate this process. For example, *The Illustrated Encyclopaedia Xenaica*—an extensive Web resource presenting a wide range of data relating to the fictional world of *Xena: Warrior Princess*—includes entries on both fictional and real-world phenomena. For example, the following entry, on "Boadicea," weaves together the actual history of the Icenian British queen and her fictional counterpart in the television series, making no clear distinction between the two:

> (bo-duh-cee'-a) Am. (bo-duh-cee'-r) N.Z. *n.* Correctly spelled "Boudicca," derived from the Celtic word for "victorious" *(Larousse Dictionary of Women; The Encyclopedia of Amazons).* "First Century A.D. British Warrior-Queen who led a great uprising against the Romans . . . was queen of the native tribe of Iceni (Norfolk, Suffolk and part of Cambridgeshire)." Her husband had been an ally of Rome but when he died, the Romans annexed the Iceni territory and pillaged it. "According to Tacitus, Boadicea was flogged and her daughters raped. The Iceni rose in fury and led by Boadicea, destroyed the Roman colony of Camuldunum (Colchester), sacked and burned Londinium (London), and razed Verulamium (St. Albans), killing up to 70,000 Romans" and temporarily liberating her people from the Roman yoke. "The earliest sources described her as tall of person, of a comely countenance . . . she stood a while surveying her army and, being regarded with a reverential silence, she addressed them an eloquent and impassioned speech." Boadicea was by no means the only woman on that battlefield. The Roman army was urged on with the observation that the Celtic Queen's forces included "more women than warriors" . . . for all such disparaging feelings toward an army consisting largely of women, the Romans were routed. In "The Deliverer," Xena joined forces with Boadicea and played a major role in winning this battle. Xena not only defeated Caesar, but humiliated him for his betrayal of her 11 years earlier. (See "Caesar" and "Destiny".) According to recorded history, the following year, "the Roman governor of Britain, Suetonius Paulinus, . . . gathered two legions and overwhelmed the Iceni in a bloody battle . . . Boadicea herself is said to have taken poison rather than surrender. One tradition, which has nothing of history about it, held that Stonehenge was her burial place." *Ref., Larousse Dictionary of Women,* Melanie Parry, Editor, 1996; *The Encyclopaedia of Amazons: Women Warriors from Antiquity to Modern Era,* Jessica Amanda Salmonson, 1991; LDCorrea.[16]

The function of this sort of fictional world encyclopedia—whether it is compiled in the minds of avid viewers or in textual form—is threefold. First, the encyclopedia serves to make the fictional world more "real" by fleshing it out. The more detail that is available about the world, the denser and more comprehensive it becomes. It assumes the familiar complexity of the material world, sharing its three-dimensional clutter and myriad connective possibilities.

Second, the interconnections between the encyclopedias of the fictional world and the real world furnish the fictional world with the gravity of apparent authenticity. It becomes a plausible extension of discourses and knowledge grounded in actuality. Thus, *XWP* fandom's re-actualizations of the Xenaverse in the form of, say, fan fiction or textual analysis can include filling in gaps in the historical record (gaps that can accommodate Xena) and the blurring together of myth, history, and fiction.[17] X-Files fandom and the official texts that cater to it demonstrate a profound interest in theories of the paranormal, the weird, and the ufological,[18] while those of *Star Trek* include a substantial body of work exploring the scientific feasibility of technologies such as teleportation, phasers, and warp drive.[19] Anchoring the fictional world to the everyday world of actuality and feasibility renders it not just fictional but *possible*. It assumes if not true authenticity then at least authentic potential, allowing readers to indulge in fantasies of how our world might once have been *(Xena: Warrior Princess, Hercules: The Legendary Journeys)*, or perhaps really is beneath the surface *(The X-Files, Beauty and the Beast)*, or may become one day in the far distant future *(Star Trek, Babylon 5)*. By grounding the imaginary in the actual, such connections and potentials diminish the threat of an unwelcome cognitive collapse into recognition of impossibilities—a collapse that would demolish immersive experience of the fictional world.

Third, the fictional world encyclopedia functions as a resource for the kinds of interactivity that fans engage in with the metatextual cult fiction. It deconstructs the fictional world to form a bank of raw information materials (substantial, structural, dynamic, and interconnected) that fans draw from in order to reconstruct the fictional world in imagination and to reactualize it in tertiary textual form (as fan fiction, scratch video, and so on). Broken down to its constituent elements yet retaining the substance and logic that give it coherence, the deterritorialized fiction exists as data and potential that is subject to all manner of interventions and reconfigurations. As Pierre Lévy says,

> while we fold the text in upon itself, thereby producing its self-referentiality, its autonomous existence, its semantic aura, we are also relating the text to other texts, other discourse, images, and affects, to the immense fluctuating storehouse of desires and signs that constitutes our being. It is no longer the meaning of the text that concerns us but the direction and elaboration of our thought, the accuracy of our image of the world, the fulfilment of our plans, the awakening of our pleasure, the thread of our dreams. This time the text is no longer crushed and

crumpled to a ball, but cut up, pulverized, distributed, evaluated in terms of an autoparturient subjectivity.[20]

This is a mode of interactivity. But it is not the interactivity proposed by the holodeck model of virtual reality, in which the user becomes a character in a story and performs her role in a fluid choreography of action and reaction. Nor is it the interactivity of the computer interface that enables the user to navigate a responsive avatar along forking narrative paths through a fictional environment. Rather, it is a kaleidoscopic manipulation of data and a process of imaginative intervention that reconstructs the fictional world and reactualizes its narrative possibilities according to the experiences, needs, wants, and creativity of the individual user. It constitutes the world of the cult fiction as a basis for what Murray terms a "multiform plot,"[21] the components of which can be rearranged to produce myriad narratives that, although immeasurably various in their detail, nevertheless retain the semantic and thematic consistency of their common origin.

"Interactivity," writes Marie-Laure Ryan, "is not merely the ability to navigate the virtual world, it is the power of the user to modify this environment."[22] Every imaginative intervention in the cult fiction is an interaction that transforms the deterritorialized fictional world and thereby reconfigures the fan's immersive experience. But, unlike the prophesized virtual realities of science fiction, these modes of engagement do not (and cannot) occur simultaneously anywhere outside the imagination. Fan interactivity entails creative interventions in the form of some sort of text production. Fans interact with the narrative world of the cult series by contributing to its deterritorialized fiction—the fiction in its virtual, rather than its textual, form—their own reformulations, in the forms of fan fiction, scratch video, cultural criticism essays, Web sites, poetry, music, art, and theater.

Conclusion

It is possible, perhaps even probable, that we will never produce a sophisticated technology such as the holodeck that will afford embodied entry into a fully interactive and fully convincing virtual reality. Nevertheless, the dream of such installations exerts a powerful hold on our imaginations, conditioning our cultural consumption and practices as well as the evolving technologies and marketing strategies of the culture industry. The trajectory toward provision of fully realized user experiences of imaginary worlds is evident throughout contemporary popular culture in the forms of role-playing games and theme parks, IMAX cinema technologies, video and computer games, and the eruption over the last four decades of so-called cult fictions such as *The Lord of the Rings, Star Trek,* and *Star Wars* across a full range of media and media-related artifacts. Though these transmedial and deterritorialized cult fictions are ramshackle and primitive technologies in comparison with the imaginary holodeck, they nevertheless strive toward and sustain an idea of a fully realized virtual reality as the telos of entertainment.

Notes

Epigraph is from Ogami, *Subtext,* at http://www.forevaxena.com/fanfictiondelights/fanfic/ogami/subtext.html.

1. Emphasis in original; Janet H. Murray, *Hamlet on the Holodeck: The Future of Narrative in Cyberspace* (Cambridge: MIT Press, 1999), 110.
2. Marie-Laure Ryan, *Narrative as Virtual Reality: Immersion and Interactivity in Literature and Electronic Media* (Baltimore: The Johns Hopkins University Press, 2001), 27.
3. Mark Poster, "Theorizing Virtual Reality," in *Cyberspace Textuality: Computer Technology and Literary Theory,* ed. Marie-Laure Ryan (Bloomington: Indiana University Press, 1999), 47.
4. Cited in Oliver Burkeman, "The Virtual Visionary," *Guardian Saturday Review,* 29 December 2001, 7.
5. Pierre Lévy, *Becoming Virtual: Reality in the Digital Age,* trans. Robert Bononno (New York: Plenum Trade, 1998), 29.
6. IMAX promotional statement, at http://www.imax.com.au/index.asp, accessed November 1, 2001.
7. At http://www.imax.com.au/experienceWhatssodifferent.asp, accessed November 1, 2001.
8. Daniel Mackay, *The Fantasy Role-Playing Game* (Jefferson, N.C.: McFarland, 2001), 29.
9. Sara Gwenllian-Jones, "The Sex Lives of Cult Television Characters," *Screen* 43, no. 1 (2002): 79–90.
10. Ryan, *Narrative as Virtual Reality,* 91.
11. Chris Gregory, *Star Trek: Parallel Narratives* (Basingstoke and London: Macmillan Press), 21.
12. Murray, *Hamlet on the Holodeck,* 98.
13. Jorge Luis Borges, *Fictions,* trans. Andrew Hurley (London: Penguin Books, 2000), 11–12.
14. Ryan, *Narrative as Virtual Reality,* 91.
15. Lubomír Dolezel, *Heterocosmica: Fiction and Possible Worlds* (Baltimore: The Johns Hopkins University Press, 1998), 181.
16. Ellipses in original; at http://pweb.jps.net/~mythology/B.html, accessed November 1, 2001.

17. See Sara Gwenllian-Jones, "Histories, Fictions, and *Xena: Warrior Princess*," *Journal of Television and New Media* 1, no. 4 (2000): 403–18.

18. See Ann Simon, *The Real Science behind the X-Files: Microbes, Meteorites, and Mutants* (London: Simon and Schuster, 1999).

19. For example, see Lawrence Krauss and Stephen Hawking, *The Physics of Star Trek* (London: Flamingo, 1997).

20. Lévy, *Becoming Virtual*, 48–49.

21. Murray, *Hamlet on the Holodeck*, 185–213.

22. Marie-Laure Ryan, "Immersion vs. Interactivity: Virtual Reality and Literary Theory," *Postmodern Culture* 5, no. 1 (1994), at http://www.humanities .uci.edu/mposter/syllabi/readings/ryan.html.

Charactor; or, The Strange Case of Uma Peel

David A. Black

Prologue: The Construction of Uma Peel

In the *Avengers* episode "Epic," crazed film director Z. Z. von Schnerk and his accomplices, quondam movie stars Damita Syn and Stewart Kirby (unwilling victims of contractual fine print, they would have us believe), kidnap Mrs. Peel and force her to star in a movie—a snuff film, yet—titled *The Destruction of Mrs. Emma Peel.* Thus Uma Thurman, star of the 1998 film *The Avengers,* cannot claim the distinction of having been the first woman cast in the role of Mrs. Peel in a feature film. That honor goes to Mrs. Peel herself.

Still (as interesting as "Epic" is, in point of reflexivity and self-conscious examination of the character of Mrs. Peel in the context of the show itself), the focus of this essay will be on the real-world, theatrically released film *The Avengers* and on the phenomenon of which it is a part—namely, the recent vogue for producing theatrically released feature films based on old television shows. The matter of character, specifically the phenomenon of representing in a film a character familiar from television, will be a thematic rallying point throughout the essay; the essay will also cast a wide enough net to include some observations about the TV-to-film phenomenon in general.

Many fans and critics deplored the performances of Uma Thurman and Ralph Fiennes as Mrs. Peel and Steed in the film. More radically, some rejected the very idea that *any* actors other than Diana Rigg and Patrick Macnee could in any meaningful sense be said to be playing the roles of Steed and Mrs. Peel. Out of the widespread unwillingness to accept Uma-as-Emma (whether due to Thurman's performance, and/or to a conviction of the impossibility of anyone other than Rigg playing Mrs. Peel) emerged the witticism "Uma Peel," a name designed to refer exclusively to Uma-as-Emma and to protect both Emma Peel and Diana Rigg from sacrilege.[1]

The plot of the Avengers movie has to do in part with the cloning of Mrs. Peel by the villain, Sir August de Wynter (Sean Connery). Predictably, there are moments when one or another character is uncertain which Mrs. Peel is present, the real/good or the fake/bad. One rather uncanny result of this plot device is that the issue of the identity and legitimacy of Mrs. Peel comes to the surface in the film itself, in a manner evocative of the extrafilmic Thurman/Rigg controversy. Uma Peel has to worry that others do not accept her as Emma Peel, and those other characters, like many of the film's viewers, puzzle over the question: is this being before us, in fact, Mrs. Emma Peel?

An intriguing case study in the role of character in fan culture, Uma Peel also offers an interesting glimpse at some wider and deeper issues. Understanding Uma Peel requires exploring at least two broader topics: first, *The Avengers* itself as a text and as a cult phenomenon (because the response to Uma Peel gains its meaning largely from its position in existing Avengers fan culture); and, second, the film-industry trend of which the Avengers movie is a part, namely, the trend toward releasing films based on television shows.

This essay will have something to say about both of these areas and about their intersection. The essay's exploration of the TV-to-film phenomenon may thus be understood as background to a deeper understanding of the significance for fan culture of Uma Peel; alternatively, the choice of Uma Peel as a case study may be understood as an occasion for a more expansive look at the phenomenon of TV-to-film and the position of character in fan culture.

Toward a Taxonomy of TV-to-Film Adaptation

Since the 1980s, an almost incredible number of television shows, mostly from the 1950s and 1960s, have reappeared as theatrically released feature films. Indeed, the TV-to-film process has taken on somewhat the quality of a reflex or involuntary function, such that virtually any show is fair game and some proportion of first-run movies at any given time will, in all likelihood, include at least one such adaptation. A partial list would include *Star Trek, The Fugitive, Sgt. Bilko, The Flintstones, The Mod Squad, The Addams Family, The Twilight Zone, The Brady Bunch, Wild Wild West,* and *Rocky and Bullwinkle.*[2]

As even this short list suggests, films based on television programs draw on a variety of television genres: sit-com, dramatic series, anthology series, Western, cartoon. Moreover, TV-to-film adaptation is only one of many types of filmic adaptation—and filmic adaptation itself is only one type of adaptation. There is not room here, of course, for anything like a comprehensive overview of the entire topic of adaptation. Still, a few remarks on TV-to-film adaptation in comparison with novel-to-film adaptation may help to put the former practice into higher relief.

A novel-to-film adaptation performs the singular act of leaping the hurdle of visual instantiation; that is, while the written text may have been extremely visually evocative, it was not per se a visual narrative, whereas the film is. A TV-to-film adaptation, on the other hand, *re-visualizes* the text.[3]

A novel-based film may not correspond to what a given reader had pictured when reading the book (and literally cannot correspond to what every reader pictured). To that extent, no adaptation is safe from the displeasure of fans of the source. But the TV-to-film transition, when unsuccessful, can inspire a particularly potent strain of displeasure. The inverse is also true: a TV-to-film adaptation can have a ready-made fan base, and embracing a film as an extension of a TV cult is in a sense an easier process than embracing a film as an extension of pleasure in a book. Here, the fact that TV and film are both already on the same side of the verbal/visual divide facilitates the merging of the cults. At the same time, TV-to-film adaptations can afford to alienate existing fans of the source TV show as long as the film also attracts new fans.[4]

TV-to-film adaptations do a number of different things with their source programs: they update the time frame (or not), alter the characters and/or the casting (or not), change from animation to live-action, renarrate familiar events, narrate new events, and so forth. The variety of source-to-film relations suggests the need for at least a preliminary critical apparatus or vocabulary for describing the practice. What follows, accordingly, is a kind of descriptive map, or at least a first approximation of one, of certain salient variables in the TV/film relationship:

- Internarrative ratios: retelling, in-filling, extending
- Incremental versus singular narratives
- Character/charactor

Character appears last in this sequence not because it is less important than the other categories, but because it is often the *most* central and contested thing and is thus somewhat easier to examine once something has been said about the other categories—which, though interesting in themselves, often operate in a manner subordinate to character.

The goal here is not to chronicle the industrial history of any significant number of such adaptations, nor to offer any final or predictive word on the forms that such adaptations may or may not take. Rather, the goal is to sketch out a set of descriptive and critical terms, useful for the analysis and, in particular, the case-to-case comparison of adaptations. This approach will take us to the threshold of a closer examination, in its historical and fan-cultural context, of *The Avengers*, the movie based on it, and in particular the issue of character and how character is handled in the transition from television to cinema.

Internarrative Ratios: Retelling, In-filling, Extending

A film based on a television show must establish some relation to the narrative space of the original show and must do so in a way that makes for a meaningful film on criteria of duration and temporal structure, whether or not it exactly duplicates the temporal structure of the show. This relation may take any of several forms.

To begin with, a film may *retell* specific events from one or more episodes of the TV show. Examples of this internarrative ratio include *The Fugitive*, the film version of which, though very different as to details, pacing, and style, retold events from the original show, particularly the escape from custody of the innocent Dr. Kimble (actually represented in the credit sequence of the show) and Kimble's eventual exoneration through the solving of his wife's murder. *Twilight Zone: The Movie* also retold specific events from the television show—in this case, by the technique of remaking three episodes.

A TV-based film may also engage in narrative *in-filling*—that is, it may insert events into the narrative space of the show that the original show did not include, taking place in narrative time that the show *did* include. A film based on a show with no narrative beginning—a show whose first and subsequent episodes all began in medias res—may nonetheless posit a "beginning"; this is, in fact, exactly what the Avengers movie did by representing the first meeting between Steed and Mrs. Peel.

This kind of in-filling, where the film presumes to tell us things that the show left implied or entirely mysterious, runs a particularly great risk of incurring the displeasure of fans of the original show, whose veneration of the text quite likely disallows this kind of tampering with narrative information. This certainly proved to be the case with *The Avengers*, where the very idea of depicting the first Steed-Peel meeting— let alone depicting it as having taken place in a steambath, with Steed naked—struck many fans as presumptuous.

A film may also *extend* the narrative space and information of the show on which it is based. This describes the behavior of the Star Trek films (and the post–original series TV shows), which do not retell specific events but, instead, add noncompetitively to the accumulated narrative. This approach to adapting a TV show for film offers perhaps the most open-ended and, not accidentally, sequel-rich permutation.[5]

Incremental versus Singular Narratives

In addition to establishing some kind of relation with the totality of the narrative space previously staked out by a television show, film adaptations of television shows have to come to terms with certain behaviors discernible in the shows' narrative organization and chronology, particularly as manifested in their handling of the relation between and among individual episodes. Television shows, in turn, exhibit quite a range of behaviors in these areas, though at the same time those behaviors tend to operate within fairly strict limits.

Considerable variation occurs along the axis of episode self-containment, that is, on the criterion of whether or not story lines are continued from one episode to the next. A strong tradition of self-contained episodes operates in American network prime-time television, though over the past twenty years or so the sway of that tradition has lessened considerably. (So-called nighttime soap operas, such as *Dallas* and *Falcon Crest,* represented one wave of prime-time continuing-story programming, as did *Hill Street Blues* and *St. Elsewhere,* and there have been others.) Some programming types, notably soap operas, employed the continuing story-line model all along.

What does *not* vary nearly as much is the tendency of commercial fiction television to structure its narratives incrementally and to avoid narrative singularities. Turn on a rerun of *Gilligan's Island* and you will not (unless you have deep knowledge of the show) be able to tell which season it comes from. But you *will* know that the Professor is not going to die. The same applies, at least to a considerable extent, to continuous-story shows. Such shows may have greater increments between episodes—ongoing plots may, at times, result in some degree of change in underlying situations—but truly singular, irreversible changes are relatively rare. When they do occur, their determinants are often either biological (actors die, young actors get older and their characters go to college) or contractual (an actor tires of the show and leaves).

Narrative singularity also sometimes emerges in the form of privileged first and/or last episodes, which set forth the show's premise or suggest how and why the show must end. Examples include *The Fugitive,* which ends with the capture of the elusive murderer of Dr. Kimble's wife, or *The Mary Tyler Moore Show,* the last episode of which chronicles the firing of all but one of the main characters from the TV news studio where they had worked throughout the show's run.

In some sense, each episode in an episodic series is a sequel to the one before it—or, ideally, to whichever one a given viewer happens to have most recently seen. By the same token, to describe the phenomenon of films with sequels one might borrow an image from television studies and say that such films are episodes and that a multisequel cycle of films emulates the episodic structure of television. The case of *Star Trek* offers a rather spectacular example of a series of films becoming so numerous that they function almost as episodes in a hyperproduced, cinematic TV series. The *Enterprise* does explode in one film—a singularity—but the ship is reconstituted in a subsequent film. The death of Mr. Spock, likewise, is subsequently reversed.

Things have not gone as far with other shows as they have with *Star Trek* (yet). Moreover, to associate the narrative form of the inconclusive episode too closely with television is to oversimplify its literary history. Still, the matter of the episodic and the singular is an important one in the study of television shows, and a useful area to map out in the study of the TV-show-to-film transition.

Many permutations can arise, and several have arisen. It is possible, for example, for a television series to represent certain singularities, such as the origins of the show, and for the movie (at least the first movie, if it turns out to be one of a series of them) also to represent those singularities. It is also possible, given a television show that consists of nonsequential or loosely sequential episodes, for the film to function more or less exactly as one of those episodes, simply starting in with the premise fully formed, just as a randomly chosen, mid-run TV episode would. These things can be combined, too; that is, a TV-based film may re-present originating or founding events from its TV program and then go on (even in that first film) to show what essentially amounts to a mid-run episode.

Most TV-derived films traffic in the episodic, rather than the singular. For example, a *Brady Bunch* film is unlikely to show family members dying or other such singular events. There are exceptions (such as the death of Captain Greer, a familiar character from the TV show, in the *Mod Squad* film), but this overall adherence to the episodic is not surprising, since it is conducive to the generation of sequels in a benign relationship to the narrative space of the original show.

Character/Charactor

The formal specifics of any TV-to-film transition have to do with degrees of abstraction. How detachable from a given enactment, or instantiation, is a given event? Does the show manifest a "world" that can, without change of underlying identity (at least by consensus), be boiled down to elements of style, setting, genre—and be injected into a film thirty years later?

Of course, these questions of a show's "essence" actually equate to questions of marketing. There is no guardian deity of adaptation standing watch, empowered to prevent the creation of essence-violating films. Still, it is fair to say that there have been, from the point of view of television connoisseurship, a few surprises. Evidently it was not essential to *The Flintstones* that it be animated. *The Mod Squad,* we now know (or are expected to think), could be transplanted from a sixties setting to a nineties setting and still be *The Mod Squad.* More predictably—but perhaps also more ironically, given his status as champion of indispensability in the *Star Trek* world—it did not have to be William Shatner looking out of the plane window in *Twilight Zone: The Movie* and seeing a gremlin on the wing.

Like other formal elements, character and casting in the TV-to-film transition have much to do with degrees of abstraction. Traditional theater roles do not adhere to particular actors; not even a great Hamlet can ever be the only Hamlet. Television shows, on the other hand, create a perhaps uniquely powerful identification of actor with role. Still, especially after the passage of significant amounts of time, actors cannot be expected to reprise their TV characters. A poor re-creation of a beloved television character or the perceived impossibility of re-creation (as in the cases of Steed and Mrs. Peel, for many fans) might result in a negative response to a film; however, such a film might nonetheless attract a new audience composed of younger viewers who do not hold the original program sacred and do not care how the film's performances compare with the originals.

As with setting and plot and style, when it comes to character there are ultimately no "essential" textual properties: given the right circumstances (and *pace* Star Trek fans), it would be perfectly *possible* to recast Captain Kirk, or Lucy Ricardo,[6] or even the Mary Tyler Moore character Mary Richards. Similarly, it is possible that when we see concretely that certain decisions have been made in this realm (such as the decision to recast Emma Peel), the decisions may or may not turn out to have been good ones, in the sense of being conducive to popularity and favorable critical reception.[7]

But if the whole thing is a function of the exigencies of production, rather than a function of any reality underlying the join between character and actor, that join can still be an extremely strong one in the fan and public imagination. The word "character" hardly conveys the cultural weight and position of a sustained television performance like Shatner as Kirk, Carroll O'Connor as Archie Bunker, or Ball as Lucy Ricardo. The point here is not to praise the skills of these actors, but to remark on the sometimes tremendous robustness of the character/actor join in television—something that, thanks to an orthographical felicity, we may refer to as the phenomenon of *charactor,* a character that is particularly resistant to abstraction from a given actor.

Charactor can certainly arise in media other than television, but the sheer quantity of text in a successful television run creates, at the very least, unusually favorable conditions for the charactor phenomenon. Moreover, until recently it was very unusual for the question of who should play a given television character to arise; one would not have thought of the role of Gilligan or Steve McGarrett as being up for grabs in the way that traditional theatrical roles are. There are some interesting exceptions to this, particularly in connection with mid-run replacements—for example, the two Darrins in *Bewitched*—but on the whole, and adaptations into film aside, traditional commercial television tends to associate actors uniquely with roles over long periods of time, thus providing an almost ideal breeding ground for charactor. Indeed, it is only when a challenge on the order of Uma Peel comes along that the contours of the original charactorization come fully into view.

We will continue to explore some of these issues as we turn to take a closer look at *The Avengers* in relation to the formal categories just sketched out.

The Avengers and Charact[eo]r

The Film and Its Reception

With diligent research, it is possible to scare up a few positive remarks about the Avengers film here and there. For many fans, the film had the considerable merit of rekindling interest in the original show, bringing in new fans, and making possible the successful release of remastered videotapes of *The Avengers* by the A&E network. Still, from the point of view of the making and marketing of commercial films, the Avengers film may be confidently characterized as an almost perfect failure at every level.

Critics not only hated the film but hated and saw portent in the fact that Warner Bros. took the extremely unusual step of not holding prerelease press screenings; according to one critic, the studio "is so uneasy about *The Avengers* that [it] doesn't want too much buzz about it before it opens. Moreover, the studio clearly prefers to delay critical appraisals until after the movie opens rather than face the customary Friday reviews."[8] Overall, critics seemed to take the position that the film deserved to be pitied rather than censured (though perhaps a bit of both). Ralph Fiennes's Steed, for example, impressed at least two critics as invisible—a nonperformance—rather than aggressively bad. "Fiennes underplays to the point of near invisibility" wrote David Ansen in *Newsweek*; while Mark Steyn, in the *Spectator,* suggested that "Fiennes underplays to the point where he's almost as invisible as Macnee's cameo."[9]

Lukewarm-to-hostile responses to Fiennes and the other principles were, to be sure, not the film's only problem. Audiences, particularly those composed of Avengers fans, took exception not only to the portrayal of the familiar roles of Steed and Mrs. Peel, but to the plot, the mood, the mise-en-scène, the music, the editing, the dialogue, and the inconsistent, seemingly haphazard dipping into the Avengers bag of tricks for a few disconnected elements (such as the characters of Mother and Father, or scattered allusions to specific episodes).[10]

In some respects, the negative reception of the film was so broad and so thoroughgoing that teasing it apart or trying to map it onto our general categories of TV-based film analysis may be projects of limited return; however, a certain amount of such scrutiny will help highlight some important aspects of the film, its relation to the original show, and its reception—particularly when we return to the matter of charact[eo]r.[11]

Internarrative Ratios

The Avengers film involves what I have called in-filling of narrative space, meaning that it narrates events that belong chronologically inside the familiar narrative space of the television series but were not actually represented in that series. In particular, the film vouchsafes to its viewers an enactment of the first meeting between Steed and Mrs. Peel, a famously hidden and completely unavailable moment in the original series.[12] The film also depicts an erotic kiss between Steed and Mrs. Peel, entirely short-circuiting the celebrated ambiguity of the relationship of the original characters.[13]

This contrasts with the entire Star Trek cycle—the several TV series and all the films. *Star Trek* traffics in *extending* narrative space and does so across the TV/film border; for example, the second Star Trek film, *Star Trek II: The Wrath of Khan,* reintroduced a villain who had already appeared in an episode of the original series. But this differs greatly, as a narratological matter, from the kind of in-filling represented by the Steed-Peel first encounter.

The Avengers film also indulges in a certain amount of retelling: that is, of presenting elements or events known from the TV series in a new way. The characters of Mother and Father are in a sense retold. To place Mother, and especially Father, in the Mrs. Peel narrative space—and to make Father a villain and kill her off—is to meddle in that narrative space in a paradoxical, nonadditive way.

To some extent, of course, this kind of scrutiny of the comparative statuses of the narrative worlds of television and movie Avengers is simply the pleasurable, familiar fan game of looking for inconsistencies and contradictions. But it is also distinctly unpleasurable and alienating— and it is not insignificant that the Star Trek cycle, for all its immensity, has none of this. Star Trek fans have a lot more text in their canon than Avengers fans, but they have never been called on to accept the kind of invasion of narrative space carried out by even the one Avengers movie.

Incremental versus Singular Narrative

When it comes to TV-based films, the episodic/singular distinction has to do primarily with the matter of sequels and with the question of whether a string of sequels might come to resemble a series of television episodes (as in the case of Star Trek). While the Avengers film was sequel-ready (that is, open-ended in such a way as to accommodate and even suggest sequels), it seems that there are to be no sequels (mercifully, in the general view).

Still, a couple of points of interest in the episodic/singular connection can be teased out, particularly with regard to the original show. In one related quirk of narrative fate, two Cathy Gale episodes were remade as Emma Peel episodes—which meant that a certain amount of retelling was going on between seasons of the show itself, putting an unusual spin on the common narrative economy of episodic television. (Somehow, fans manage to take this in stride, finding it amusing perhaps that Steed underwent the same experiences twice, with different partners, and did not seem to notice.)

The most significant singularity in the episodic cycle of the television show, however, came in the form of the abrupt departure of Mrs. Peel at the end of the second Rigg season. American fans, never having seen the pre-Peel episodes, understandably equated The Avengers with the Steed-Peel pairing. The first U.S. broadcast of "The Forget-Me-Knot" was quite a jolt to fans: suddenly Mrs. Peel, by that time a cult icon as well as simply the star of a favorite show, left and was replaced by the utterly un-Peel-like Tara King.

"The Forget-Me-Knot" was in some respects more of a singularity than an out-and-out final series episode would have been. Moreover, its full implications lay in the realm of character—or charactor—to which we next return.

Character/Charactor

Toby Miller introduces his book *The Avengers* with a very comprehensive, quite eye-opening survey of the spread and sprawl of the phenomenon. As Miller illustrates, the show was seen in many countries; was spun off into various products and projects; and has been endlessly referred to, quoted, parodied, and honored in an indeterminable number of texts.[14]

Miller's introduction charts what might, following Gerard Genette, be called the Avengers paratext: the noncanonical and/or unofficial fragments of text and allusion that seem to orbit about or spin away from a given work. In this way, Miller places *The Avengers* as a text with a kind of centrifugal force, a TV show that has become an idiom that, in turn, can turn up recognizably expressed in books, clothes, TV commercials, record albums, and all sorts of other material points.

At the same time—and for understandable reasons—Miller also takes a more centripetal, canonist's-eye view of the show, establishing a relatively focused scope:

> Other occasional helpers in the early years included Martin Rollason as Dr John King and Julie Stevens as Venus Smith. In later seasons, Steed sometimes had an on-screen superior. . . . But Blackman's Catherine Gale (1962–64) and Diana Rigg's Emma Peel (1965–67) were such strong personalities that the others had no place. . . . Most of what follows concentrates on Blackman, Rigg, and [Macnee].[15]

To focus on these three, somewhat at the expense of Linda Thorson's Tara King (and of the show's 1970s reincarnation, *The New Avengers*), is indeed a respectable decision, from the fan as well as the scholarly perspective. Still, the very fact that Miller uses character in this way as at least a preliminary organizing principle is revealing. The rest of the book is organized thematically (with chapters on "Sex," "Fashion," "Following," and so on), but character functions initially as a kind of principle of principles. Disapproval of the casting and/or performances of Thurman and Fiennes in the Avengers film has taken two forms, or operated at two levels. First is the level of dramatic connoisseurship—that is, the question of whether or not the two were "right" for the roles of Peel and Steed and played the roles well. Second is the level of character ontology: is it even possible or meaningful to speak of actors other than Rigg and Macnee "playing the roles" of Peel and Steed at all?

Both of these questions received attention in the Usenet group alt.tv.avengers—where, indeed, discussion on many aspects of the movie raged for weeks after its release and resurfaced periodically thereafter. In a message in the thread "Recasting the movie??" David Scott Lessenberry offered a succinct view of the second, ontological question:

> I have always supported the notion that the movie made the fatal mistake of featuring the Peel/Steed characters. Since Rigg/Macnee defined those roles, any casting decision seems doomed. I know this sounds corny, but maybe the movie should have utilized new characters with the old formula. Rigg, Macnee, Blackman, and Thorson could have then made cameo appearances as their original characters.[16]

To be sure, the "whom to cast" issue received a lot more attention from Usenet participants than the "is it meaningful?" question. (Suggestions for Steed included Hugh Grant, Pierce Brosnan, Alan Rickman, Rupert Everett, Liam Neeson, Sam Neil, and Anthony Stewart Head; Peel candidates included Elizabeth Hurley, Minnie Driver, Finola Hughes, Miranda Richardson, Andrea Parker, and Emma Thompson.) Even Lessenberry preceded his antirecasting remarks with some musings of his own about who would be best in the roles. Given that the film had already been made, it is not too surprising that categorical rejection of the possibility of new actors playing Steed and Peel was relatively rare in discussions of recasting; after all, the ontological argument is, in a sense, a dead end, while speculation about different casts offers opportunity for open-ended discussion and debate.

But if participation in such discussion, arguably, represents at least some degree of acceptance of the transferability of the Steed and Peel roles, nonetheless much of that participation included a palpable measure of protest. Recasting the movie comes across in Usenet discourse largely as a matter of finding a lesser evil, not a perfect solution:

> [Sam Neil is] the guy from Jurassic Park? That archeologist disliking children? In that case, a definite "No" from me. He's a good actor, but I just can't imagine him as Steed. I'd rather have Val Kilmer, and THAT one—although he's one of my favourites—I can't imagine as Stee[d], either.[17]

This "lesser evil" approach may not have the philosophical purity of an utter rejection of the notion that these roles are playable by new actors. However (and even aside from the fact that philosophical purity is not the goal of the discourse), this approach—this recasting-under-protest, so to speak—does put the roles of Steed and Peel in a different category from, say, Hamlet, or Blanche DuBois. Specifically, it puts them in the category of charactors, irreducibly character and actor at the same time.

Perhaps one lesson of the Usenet debates about recasting is that charactor is a qualified consubstantiality. Condemnation of the film was not universal, nor was rejection of the possibility of recasting Steed and Peel successfully. But the underlying pull is for consubstantiality: Steed and Peel come across fundamentally as charactors, not traditionally refillable roles, and the burden of proof is on those who would equivocate.

Of those fans who resist or entirely reject recasting, it may be said, if somewhat whimsically, that they have interpreted the Avengers movie as wearing the mantle not of *The Avengers,* but of von Schnerk's *Destruction of Mrs. Emma Peel,* with Steed thrown in for good measure.[18] On this construction, to treat "Steed" and "Mrs. Peel" as assignable roles, as abstractions that may admit of more than one legitimate embodiment, is to assault Steed and Mrs. Peel, even to destroy them.

Conclusion: The Abstraction of Mrs. Emma Peel

Mrs. Peel offers a rich study in charactor because of her celebrated uniqueness, her singularity. Yet in the end, that uniqueness is at least in large part a product of timing and accident. The revelation of Mrs. Peel to American audiences, in particular, was bracketed in such a way as to maximize the impression of unprecedentedness. On one end, Mrs. Peel benefited from the invisibility of her predecessor: the Cathy Gale (Honor Blackman) episodes were not shown in the United States until the 1990s, and even then were sneered at by some fans for their somewhat glitchy live-to-video production values. Gale and Peel were hardly identical. Still, once the Gale episodes started to circulate again, it became clear to many fans who had not previously realized it that Peel was a lot more like Gale than King was like Peel. Gale and Peel shared a predilection for leather, were masters of numerous academic subjects, and were martial arts experts. Familiarity with the figure of Cathy Gale makes Emma Peel seem a lot less like the causeless phenomenon ex nihilo she is often taken to be.

On the other end of her run, Mrs. Peel also benefited from the absurdity of the character who "replaced" her, the voluptuous, vacuous spy trainee Tara King. Indeed, the Peel/King transition itself was unprecedented for viewers in the United States and elsewhere who had not lived through Gale/Peel—and quite abrupt, for all viewers. For one thing, it happens in a tag scene, not, like Gale/Peel, between seasons: Mrs. Peel's husband, long presumed dead, turns out to be alive, and comes to pick her up outside Steed's flat. Tara mounts the stairs, exchanges a few words with the departing Mrs. Peel, and becomes Steed's new partner. Reaction to Tara King was extremely negative among fans, due in large part simply to the fact that she had replaced Mrs. Peel but also in part to the character of King herself. Long before critics were saying that Uma Thurman was no Emma Peel, fans were saying the same thing about Linda Thorson.

Avengers culture offers its participants an abstraction that, perhaps making a virtue of necessity, provides something of a framework for understanding and accepting the show's transitions: namely, the notion of the "Avengers girl" as a consistent entity, a role that *can* be filled again and again. Of course, the whole "Avengers girl" concept arose from the vagaries of production: had Honor Blackman stayed indefinitely, no such abstraction would have had to be embraced. But the term has been embraced and has enjoyed rather wide currency. (It is an index of the strength of the Rigg/Peel charactor that at no lower a level of abstraction than "Avengers girl" have fans and commentators been able to agree on a category to which both Rigg/Peel and Thorson/King belong.)

At first glance it appears that Uma Peel impinges on the Rigg/Peel charactor along a different axis, an axis of displacement, rather than of succession. But even as one displaces the character, one succeeds the actor, and the reverse. Uma Peel might as well be Linda Thurman; this is a consequence of the indivisibility that is, by definition, charactor. The singularity of the Rigg/Peel charactor may have something, or much, to do with historical contingency; but of historical record, too, is the culture of response that has asserted that singularity and has had to come to terms at more than one point with its vulnerability.

Notes

1. The origins of the name Uma Peel are unclear. I strongly suspect it is a case of simultaneous or near-simultaneous coinage by more than one person. The earliest use of the name I have been able to find is in a 1997 document on the Elan Avengers Web site, at http://www.animus-web.demon.co.uk/elan/nautumn.htm.

2. See Martin Connors and Jim Craddock, eds., *Video Hound's Golden Movie Retriever 2000* (Detroit: Visible Ink Press, 2000), 1199, for an extensive list of films based on television shows.

3. Some of what follows will, I hope, include a somewhat more nuanced, less monolithic treatment of the question of what "the text" consists of. For further theoretical exploration of the ontology and epistemology of multiple versions of stories and narratives, see Barbara Hernnstein Smith, "Narrative Versions, Narrative Theories," *Critical Inquiry* 7, no. 1 (autumn 1980): 213–36; and David A. Black, "Synopsis: A Theory of Symbolic Representation," *Yale Journal of Criticism* 10, no. 2 (fall 1997): 423–36.

4. There are cases where the audience for the film probably does not overlap very greatly with the audience for the original TV show. Writing about the film *The Fugitive* in a 1998 article on the subject of TV-to-film adaptations, Andrew O'Hehir suggests that "only viewers over 40 are likely to have seen the original 1963–67 David Janssen TV vehicle" ("Gleaning the Tube," *Sight and Sound* 8 [1998]: 16–19, 18)—but the film was very successful, perhaps because, as O'Hehir suggests, "if anything the air of Kafkaesque paranoia and mistrust of the judicial system has thickened in the subsequent quarter century and the plight of wrongfully convicted Dr. Richard Kimble has gained currency." This raises the question of whether, in at least some cases, the use of a circa 1960s television show's premise as a film's premise might be almost entirely a matter of creative timesaving, rather than part of the nostalgia industry. One is reminded of the way in which pieces of classical music, and even classic rock, get transformed into elevator music and similar genres: by the time, say, a Beethoven piano sonata or a Lennon-McCartney song has been turned "lite," the results bear so little resemblance to the original that the only purpose the original has really served is to save the "lite" composers the trouble of writing a melody.

5. Then again, the film version of *The Fugitive,* a classic case of the "retelling" ratio, spawned a sequel, *U.S. Marshals.* That sequel, however, was more along the lines of what would be called, in the television realm, a spin-off.

6. In the made-for-TV film *Lucy and Desi: Before the Laughter* (1991), part of the first episode of *I Love Lucy* was re-created; but this was by way of a novelty, and the principal thing going on was that someone was playing the role of Lucille Ball, not Lucy Ricardo.

7. It is important in this connection to differentiate between what is *possible* and what either has happened or is likely to happen or is going to happen. I would consider it safe to bet that no one will ever produce a film in which someone other than Mary Tyler Moore plays Mary Richards. However, that does not mean that producing such a film is an impossibility. As an Avengers fan, I can attest to the fact that the production of the Avengers movie changed my perspective on the question of the reportrayal of television characters. My instincts would have placed Steed and Peel squarely in the Lucy Ricardo/Spock/MTM category of unrecastables.

8. Bernard Weinraub, "'Avengers' Gets a Stealth Opening," *New York Times,* late edition (East Coast), 12 August 1998, E1.

9. David Ansen, "Champagne That's Lost Its Fizz," *Newsweek,* 24 August 1998, 59; Mark Steyn, "The Invisible Men," *Spectator,* 22 August 1998, 40.

10. Mother, played by Patrick Newell, was a regular character during the Tara King era, appearing for the first time in the Peel-to-King transition episode "The Forget-Me-Knot." Father (Iris Russell)—a blind woman in both TV show and film, but a villain only in the film—appears in one Tara King episode, "Stay Tuned," filling in as boss for Mother. Episodes more or less unambiguously alluded to in the film include "The House That Jack Built" (the malevolent, paradoxical mansion), "A Surfeit of H2O" (the weather-manipulating premise), and the various invisible man episodes.

11. I borrow the square-bracket notation from the world of computer programming, specifically the syntax of regular expressions. A regular expression specifies a pattern of letters and other characters, generally for the purpose of testing one or more text strings for conformity to the pattern. In most regular expression syntaxes, [eo] means: match one character that is either "e" or "o." Thus both "character" and "charactor" match the regular expression "charact[eo]r."

12. Tara King's introduction to Steed is, by contrast, fully enacted in the Peel-to-King transition episode "The Forget-Me-Knot."

13. To this day, debate rages among fans: do they or don't they? As puerile as this sounds, it is actually a credit to the show's subtlety that no consensus exists on this issue.

14. Toby Miller, *The Avengers* (London: British Film Institute, 1997), 1–6.

15. Ibid., 9–10.

16. From alt.tv.avengers, 15 June 1999; message id 7k4jvsbuq1@nnrp1.deja.com.

17. Birgit Schindlbeck, alt.tv.avengers, 17 June 1999; message id 3769B63A.16E9365B@ku-eichstaett.de.

18. Vigilant Avengers fans will of course remember that, on discovering that Steed had infiltrated the film studio, von Schnerk spontaneously retitles the film *The Destruction of Peel and Steed.*

Flexing Those Anthropological Muscles: *X-Files*, Cult TV, and the Representation of Race and Ethnicity

Karen Backstein

> Whenever you take a cultural archetype, whether
> it's Native American or Hassidic Jews, you are risk-
> ing certain clichés, and sometimes it's hard to ren-
> der the humanity in extreme groups. That's why . . .
> it's almost better to make up a group.
>> —*Howard Gordon,* X-Files *executive producer*
>> *and writer*

■ When *The X-Files* began in 1991, it was widely considered by network executives—and even by star David Duchovny—a sure-fire failure
in the making. Fox honchos focused all their energy on *The Adventures
of Brisco County Jr.,* another new series for which they had higher
hopes.[1] Although its first year's ratings appeared to bear out those
negative expectations, an unexpected Golden Globe win for best dramatic series, critical kudos, and a fiercely passionate audience gave
the show a buzz that ultimately made it, at least in the annals of the
then fledgling Fox network, golden. Eventually, *The X-Files* regularly
climbed into Nielsen's top ten, and when it came to drawing that prized
audience of eighteen- to thirty-five-year-old males, it proved even more
popular.[2]

In the process, the huge success of the series exploded and widened
the traditional idea of cult TV. The term that had once colloquially

and untheoretically referred to audience—specifically the fervent fans who championed a sometimes ratings-poor show—gradually evolved to encompass concepts of style and narrative. Despite the continued existence of the passionately involved "X-philes" who have established countless Internet sites, flock to conventions, purchase series-related goods, and create a wide body of fan fiction and other writings, the cult label has attached itself to *The X-Files* as much for its generic associations, darkly noir visuals, graphic and bizarre violence, and "out there" belief systems as for its viewer base. Because such science fiction, fantasy, and horror films (and literature) were, in the past, considered appealing only to a limited audience, they have retained the cult label, despite the growing and evolving interest in such texts triggered by social changes from New Age spiritualism to post-Watergate political paranoia.

Like many of these somewhat otherworldly "genre" texts, which did and still do compose the bulk of what falls into cultdom, *The X-Files* has a highly stylized and flexible structure that makes it ideal for dealing metaphorically with real-life concerns. It is stylized in the sense that filming often draws less on so-called realistic modes of representation than on ones already coded generically and instantly read in terms of particular narrative expectations (usually those in horror and science fiction texts). Furthermore, the treatments of these well-worn but hardy generic forms often lack postmodern irony; just as Mulder, in rather touching and deeply innocent fashion, searches hopefully for "the truth," something that today is often considered to exist only in relative terms, *The X-Files* poignantly retains its belief in a kind of old-fashioned storytelling and its pleasures.[3] Even the most seemingly postmodern episode of all, "José Chung's from Outer Space" (season 3), which unleashes a treasure trove of intertextual and self-referential jokes and citations, suddenly shifts modes and tone to end with one of the most breathtaking, heartfelt voice-overs in the show's history. And "José Chung's" final shot—a pan upward to a glittering starry sky—combines visual majesty and mystery with a metaphysical comment on human loneliness in the vast universe. Finally, *X-Files* posits an alternative "fantastic" world side by side with our own, populated by aliens and monsters, that's ripe for allegorical treatment—for, as most science fiction writers have cogently asserted, it has always been easier to deal with troublesome social issues when they're applied to some other universe or level of reality.[4]

The narrative flexibility emerges from the very idea of the "files," posited as cases that the FBI has failed to solve using conventional methods of investigation. Its broad range of murders, abductions, transformations, and other mysterious happenings constantly offer new opportunities to engage with almost any concept that touches both the paranormal and the extraterrestrial—as well as advanced scientific theories and more "human" (though no less unnerving) forms of governmental misbehavior. Plucking its storytelling and visual tropes from earlier periods, the series constructed a bricolage of, among other texts, traditional horror ("The Post-Modern Prometheus," season 5, a black-and-white episode that borrows heavily from the Universal/James Whale 1931 version of *Frankenstein*); 1950s B sci-fi ("Ice," a first-season episode based on Christian Nyby and Howard Hawks's *The Thing*); 1970s television (*Kojak, the Night Stalker,* Carter's stated inspiration) and conspiracy thrillers;[5] and early 1990s blockbusters (*The Silence of the Lambs,* whose dedicated, smart, vulnerable, and redheaded Clarice Starling provided an obvious model for agent Dana Scully). Another influence, perhaps in a sphere of its own, is TV's *Twin Peaks,* which also combined out-of-the-ordinary FBI investigators with bizarre crimes and paranormal weirdness.[6] Week after week, *The X-Files* simply switched genres and the styles associated with them, from pure science fiction and chilling horror to wacky postmodern comedy and romantic drama. Of course, to some extent almost all TV shows do this—as one of the most admired and humorous *Star Trek* episodes, "The Trouble with Tribbles," proved. But *The X-Files* makes generic change a regular and built-in part of the series' appeal; both writers and fans even have descriptive terms for each type, including "MOTW" (monster of the week).

In this age of multiculturalism, it is no surprise that *The X-Files* has repeatedly brought this thematic richness to bear on issues of race and ethnicity, frequently linking genuine alienation to "alien-ation" in the more allegorical sense. Jodi Dean notes that "the alien works as an icon that allows us to link into embedded fears of invasion, violation, mutation."[7] Indeed, *X-Files*' aliens embody a multitude of fears in this superscientific age—of genetic manipulation, altered humanity, rape, the loss of bodily control, even the end of the world as we know it—as well as a more positive hunger for spirituality and a "higher order" to enlighten us.[8]

As the show's "mythology"—the overarching conspiracy focused on a shadowy band of men out to manipulate the fate of the world—grew in complexity, an additional layer of meaning colored every racially and ethnically tinged episode: that of the Holocaust. An integral part of the show's continuing story, Nazism served as both the origins of the destructive "experiments" carried out by the Consortium and as a parallel to contemporary mischief. The World War II references link the fiction with factual horror and make the analogy between the alien plot to take over the world and Germany's National Socialist government all too abundantly clear—though the allusions to Third Reich scientists and their experiments are never explored or placed in any real historical context. Too often, the death camps of World War II, arguably recent history's most widespread and organized example of ethnic/religious intolerance and coldly state-sanctioned mass murder, become nothing more than a means of giving the viewer an extra frisson from the chill wind of "reality." Each mention of the Holocaust, therefore, simply injects an often-troublesome dose of thematic and moral weightiness into the mythological events. As such, the Nazis become generic villains, no more and no less than the Klingons in the original *Star Trek* or the Romulans and Cardassians in *The Next Generation* and *Deep Space 9.*[9]

Now, rather than the small group of more marginalized (and often more generically knowledgeable) spectators attracted to cult shows in the past, these serious issues are being presented to the more diverse and general public won by a top twenty series, as *X-Files* was. How has mainstream acceptance of *The X-Files,* as well as the show's historical birth in our multicultural era, altered and shaped what Daniel Leonard Bernardi called the "humanistic" and liberal ideology usually associated with such cult TV shows as *Star Trek?*[10] To answer this question, I will look closely at several episodes that deal with themes of racial, ethnic, and religious identity, examining their filming style, narrative organization, music, and in some cases fan response. Obviously, in the scope of a single essay, I cannot take on every such representation that has occurred in nine seasons' worth of *The X-Files.* I have therefore chosen to focus closely on two particular aspects of the series, though I will refer to others for comparative purposes: the dramatization of black culture, especially its more "African" aspects in which the show plunges into the "heart of darkness," and the portrayals of Native American themes, which alone of all the ethnic depictions has a regular place in the series' continuing mythology. These examples spotlight such subjects as Haitian Vodoun ("Fresh Bones," season 2), African folklore ("Teliko," season 4), and Indian religion and history ("Shapes," season 1; "Anasazi," season 2; "Blessing Way" and "Paper Clip," season 3; and several others).

With three exceptions ("Shapes," by Marilyn Osborne; "Hell Money," focused on Chinese immigrants, by Jeffrey Vlaming, season 3; and "The Unnatural," by series star David Duchovny, season 6), episodes delving into questions of ethnicity and race have come from the pens (or in the high-tech world of *The X-Files,* the laptops) of only three writers: Chris Carter, the series creator and executive producer, usually in charge of the Native American stories; Howard Gordon, author of many of the black entries (as well as the Jewish-themed "Kaddish," season 4), who served as Carter's second in command until his fourth-season departure; and John Shiban, who scribbled the much-despised Latino episodes.[11] A point perhaps worth considering: when *The X-Files* won its second Golden Globe, as Carter waited for a lengthy procession of men to wend their way on stage, he joked that "it takes a lot of people" to make the show. When his staff had fully assembled, it included only one person of color (fan favorite James Wong, of Chinese ethnicity, who works in partnership with Glen Morgan), and no woman at all (several had joined the writing staff, but none lasted more than a single season; in nine years, no woman ever directed an episode).[12] While one obviously doesn't have to belong to a particular culture, race, or gender to write about it—and, in my view, Howard Gordon's own Jewishness hardly led to a particularly sensitive or knowledgeable depiction of Orthodox Jews when he wrote about them in "Kaddish"—the staff's racial and sexual stratification is somewhat extreme even by American commercial TV's restrictive standards.

The special focus of this essay will be to see how what was the original *Star Trek*'s "infinite diversity in infinite combinations" has become reconceptualized in this post-network, postmodern world. Indeed, when one looks back at *Star Trek,* probably now considered the ur–cult show, the changes seem striking. *Star Trek* was notorious for taking on issues ranging from Vietnam to race relations and examining them in terms of alien planets and beings. Its location in the wilds of outer space meant that, for the most part, actual events on Planet Earth didn't require overt attention, although the "moral" at the end often explicitly referred to our world. As Bernardi correctly noted, the futuristic setting allowed the show to break certain contemporary racial taboos and to look back at our present-day problems from the wise perspective of those who had seen the battles fought and won, the cultural struggles calmed, justice the victor. Instead of black and white (no problem in the twenty-third century, attested to by the presence of the African-American Lieutenant Uhura),[13] in "Let That Be Your Last Battlefield," creatures from another world waged war because their skin patterning was different. Rather than the tumult of the 1960s, in "The Way to Eden" hippies from a time yet to come searched for paradise, regarded approvingly by Spock, who willingly joined them in music making.

Despite the weekly story shifts, *The X-Files,* just like *Star Trek* before it, places its protagonists within (primarily white) patriarchal organizations—the FBI for *The X-Files,* Starfleet for *Star Trek*—that set the rules for behavior and suggest a complex political history. But, in keeping with their different periods of production, the two series painted radically divergent portraits of the ruling powers that be. The fictional Starfleet (at least originally) was benevolent and idealistic, a group under which a multicultural crew could work together harmoniously to journey into alien worlds for peaceful purposes. Eventually *The Next Generation* and *Deep Space 9*[14] would deconstruct and darken Starfleet's utopian image, positing the existence of evil conspiracies beneath the romantically optimistic policies. Notably, however, *Next Generation* overlapped with *The X-Files,* and its move toward pessimism may have been influenced by the latter's popularity and "buzz." *Deep Space 9,* on the other hand, began airing well after *The X-Files* had become the taste du jour, and almost certainly fell under its influence—as did a range of other would-be cult TV shows.[15]

By contrast, *The X-Files'* FBI, drawing from real recent history, was suspect from the start, rotten to the core, and rife with underhanded doings stretching back decades—and very much connected to the WASP power structure that reigned during J. Edgar Hoover's years of governance. Only two black characters—X, Mulder's secret informant for a single season, and the quasi-evil Deputy Director Kersh, introduced in season 6 and promoted to prominence at the start of the eighth year—served as regulars. The FBI, in this depiction, is totally bereft of Latinos and Asians, and, with a couple of notable exceptions, few persons of color played major roles in the weekly episodes unless they centered specifically on racial issues.[16] Though Mulder himself had the appropriate ethnic credentials, he remained an outsider, a "company" joke, because of his personal ideology.[17] Every "standard issue" agent becomes a background against which Mulder's differences shine all the more. Never was this clearer than when Duchovny's decision to go part-time necessitated his replacement. Agent John Dogget, played by Robert Patrick, embodies the traditional, by-the-book detective: not only does this former New York City cop eschew Mulder's flippant break-the-rules attitude, but Patrick's chiseled, hard features—used to great effect as the ever-melting villain in *Terminator 2*—contrast mightily with Duchovny's softer look.[18]

Crucially, Mulder served as the spectators' guide, and (with Scully) as the primary figure of identification whose point of view oriented us on how to see the Other and his "foreign" rituals. As we will see, spectators are meant to share either his admiration for or hostility toward a cultural group, for his assumptions are not only right but also linked to a kind of primal intuition. In *The X-Files,* generic conventions have always affected the representation of race: as they shift, week by week, to fit the new story line, so does the meaning of Mulder's journey during that particular episode. First, in line with the show's "monster of the week," scare-the-pants-off-the-audience philosophy, the practices of racial others became a frightening unknown, a form of weirdness meant to creep out spectators. Second, the science fiction angle, with its focus on alien kidnappings, genetic testing, and the creation of engineered beings containing both alien and human DNA, provides a modern twist on miscegenation and rape narratives. (Scully, abducted, seen with mysterious machines boring into her bloated belly, given cancer, and then temporarily rendered sterile, becomes a sterling example of violated white womanhood. Her body—symbolic of most of the female abductees—becomes the dramatic locus on which issues of violation and physical abuse play out.) Third, episodes exploring New Age values portray alternative spiritual paths and grant Mulder access to "magic" shamanic powers that he himself does not possess. Significantly, most of these "spiritual" narratives focus on Native American rituals (rather than on black or Latino bodies) and eschew terror, tying into a longtime history of celebrating "civilized" Indian culture in opposition to more "primitive" African-based rites.[19] In many cases, these particular episodes affirm Mulder's heroic stature in contrast to the "normal" members of the FBI who have alienated and angered these noble others. And finally, these episodes often raised and addressed sociopolitical issues, although leaving them either in a disturbingly unresolved state or rife with contradictory messages.

Here, I must make what I see as a necessary distinction between political correctness—which I would define as adherence to a socially imposed set of rules about language and behavior in order to maintain the outward appearance of racial and ethnic tolerance—and genuine multiculturalism, based on a depth of knowledge and genuine respect for cultural and historical differences between peoples. As Robert Stam and Ella Shohat insist:

> The very word "correctness" comes with a bad odor. . . . The phrase "political correctness" (PC) evokes not only the neoconservative caricature of socialist, feminist, gay, lesbian, and multiculturalist politics, but also a real tendency within the left—whence the effectiveness.[20]

Frequently, it is the first that operates in *The X-Files.* In overtly "concerned" language and literary voice-overs, characters address such issues as fear of the outsider and the Other, as well as ethnic prejudice and violence. But this verbal discourse is like a soft buzzing against the louder, more insistent action that tells another, more conflicting story.

Abetting this ideological confusion is the series' vaunted and award-winning cinematography and editing, always functioning to unsettle the viewer: high contrast chiaroscuro; shadowy, uncertain spaces or out-and-out darkness (perhaps cut with a blinding burst of a high-tech flashlight); nerve-wracking camera movements; and point-of-view shots that selectively foster identification or fear all have their own language that speak as loud (or louder) than many of the words in the script. Rather than show a paranormal creature directly, a shaky, almost hand-held, track mirrors its movements as it heads toward a potential victim. Alien abductees get trapped in high-speed trembling and shuddering, almost turning into a blur as they rise into the air—while, for their part, extraterrestrials shape-shift via computer morphing in an effort to hide their identities from agents Mulder and Scully and the rest of the world.

From the weird green light that bathes the bodies of alien-human hybrids sleeping in "fishtanks" to pustules vividly exploding from leprosy-like diseases,[21] the show has exhibited a visual (and aural) care that has earned it a plethora of "tech" Emmys. As the *X-Files Official Magazine* trumpeted:

> even after 7 years, *The X-Files* still manages to set the standard for small screen brilliance. The series' consistently feature-like production values have made it one of the most award-winning shows in television history.[22]

How these winning strategies work in relationship to the various ethnic/racial groups says volumes about how the audience should imagine them.

Native American Spirits

From *Star Trek* to beyond, Native Americans have attained both a privileged and a troubled position in the world of cult. Unlike African-Americans, who from the start have interacted with whites—an ironic fallout from the structure of slavery—Indians' real-life continued presence on reservations has led to an attendant lack of contact with mainstream society. In addition, the ongoing destruction of their culture frequently raises unquenchable feelings of guilt. The stereotype of the "noble savage" (a trope Bernardi focuses on in his analysis of the *Star Trek* episode "The Paradise Syndrome")[23] persists, although now with the added element of New Age admiration for their "magic" and co-optation of their rituals.[24]

A quick examination of cult shows' representational strategies reveals these shifts: a look at the various versions of *Star Trek* alone would begin with the formerly mentioned "The Paradise Syndrome," in which Kirk, suffering from amnesia, marries an Indian maiden only to realize, once he returns to normal, that he can never fit into that "simpler" world. Then, *The Next Generation*'s "Journey's End" placed Captain Jean-Luc Picard in the uneasy position of atoning for his ancestor's past slaughter of Indians when Starfleet forces him to resettle another tribe so that Cardassians can have their planet; throughout, historical themes resonate as both Picard and the tribe members allude to the U.S. government's genocide of Native Americans.[25] Finally, *Star Trek: Voyager* actually features an Indian leading character, Commander Chakotay: he takes spirit voyages, has an animal totem, and, significantly, entered the show as a member of the Maquis, a guerrilla group fighting Starfleet. Here, difference is respected and the "outsider" ultimately becomes fully integrated into what is the most racially mixed cast yet—all under a female captain. At the same time, Chakotay embodies all the current attributes of Indian spirituality—just as did the spiritually advanced native peoples in "Journey's End."

Besides *Star Trek*, both *Buffy the Vampire Slayer* and *Roswell* have devoted episodes to Native Americans. *Buffy*, in a surprising move given today's worshipful (but essentializing) climate, had a negative view of Indians in "Pangs," a Thanksgiving tale dealing with the Chumash—a tribe of hunter-gatherers native to Southern California, renowned for their rock art and generally considered "peaceful."[26] These "native inhabitants of Sunnydale" magically return to life on Thanksgiving, with lead warrior Hus bent on vengeance for past wrongs. Unlike the other cult series, with their sympathetic if stereotypical attitudes, the no-nonsense slayer takes matters into her own hands, fighting and defeating the warriors. Although Buffy's friend Willow does refer constantly to the "genocidal history" of the holiday and her "watcher" Giles relates in extensive detail the terrible things done to the Chumash, by the end both must admit that Buffy has no choice but to kill Hus. The imagery validates that decision, with its close-ups of Hus brutally slicing throats, cutting off ears, and hanging victims by the neck: all the murdered are portrayed as "innocents," suggesting perhaps a political backlash against contemporary efforts by both Native Americans and African-Americans to receive reparations for history's injustices.

Roswell has both a *Star Trek* and *X-Files* connection through executive producer and sometime director Jonathan Frakes (who played Commander William Riker on *The Next Generation*) and director David Nutter (a director of many *X-Files* episodes and a former producer on that show). Unsurprisingly, the series takes a similar perspective to *X-Files* when tackling Indian themes. The episode "River Dog," directed by Frakes himself, focuses on a pendant with mystical powers that only a wise old Native American man can interpret; a "test" that one could liken to a vision quest; cave paintings that foretell the future; and dusty, dark filming of the isolated reservation that places it outside of time and history. Even more important, it shares *The X-Files'* use of portentous close-ups of the Indian characters and a tendency to have Native Americans speak in "meaningful" yet allusive epigrams rather than in real speech.

The X-Files introduced Indian stories in its very first season with the episode "Shapes" (aired 1 April 1994), a Manitou or werewolf legend that departs from Bernardi's "noble savage" syndrome in a few ways: it brings in history, does not place the tribe "out of time," and does directly raise the specter of racism. According to the *Official Guide,* the story was prompted by the Fox network's suggestion that the series try a "more conventional" monster show; producers/writers James Wong and Glen Morgan came up with the story, "a slightly different approach to werewolves, designed to serve fans of the genre while still feeling distinctive in *The X-Files* fashion."[27]

> Some say it's an ancient myth—"Each victim was ripped to shreds"—
> but this Friday the legend returns to kill.[28]

At the center of the "Shapes'" mystery is the shooting of an Indian by a rancher: did the white man, as claimed, believe he was firing at an animal mauling his cattle or did he deliberately murder a young Native American male? Mulder immediately links these events to the earliest extant X-file begun by FBI founder J. Edgar Hoover himself. It thus stands as a form of "originary myth," contrasting the "first people" with the "first file."

Reality rears its ugly head, however, when the agents and Indians meet, and the Native American characters in the show angrily refer to the FBI's violence during the seventy-one-day takeover of Wounded Knee by the Sioux Nation and AIM (the American Indian Movement) in 1973. Mulder and Scully encounter open hostility when they step on the reservation; much of the episode involves Mulder trying to earn their trust. Sarah Stegall, respected *X-Files* fan and Chris Carter's favorite cyber-reviewer, even comments, "Mulder didn't have much to do beyond being politically correct in the first half."[29] The soon-recurrent paradigm emerges in which Mulder, initially regarded with suspicion by "the Others," eventually wins their trust, not least through his willingness to dispense with "Western" scientific and rational belief systems that clash with values rooted in magic, ritual, and folklore. These beleaguered peoples serve to justify and elevate him, to set him apart as something special. In "Shapes," Mulder is immediately accepted by Ish, the character most in touch with traditional Indian culture— immediately distinguishing him from agents of the past.

Importantly, the difficult racial issues are tidily resolved both through the elders' acceptance of Mulder, in some ways suggesting a different and newly emergent FBI, and the episode's conclusion that, in fact, the initial killing was not a "hate crime" but a justified attack on a supernatural creature. "Shapes," in spite of its political allusions, remains little more than an atmospheric werewolf tale with Native American trappings. More crucial to the series as a whole are the episodes and Indian characters tied into the series' ongoing mythology.

Beginning with "Anasazi," which ended the second season with a (literal) bang, and continuing through "Blessing Way" and "Paper Clip," the third season "double-feature" openers, these stories mix fact and fiction to weave an elaborate narrative that encompasses Nazi evil and American duplicity, detached scientific research and political power plays, an ancient tribe of Indians and visitors from the skies.[30] "Anasazi" opens on a reservation in New Mexico, with tribal elder Albert Hosteen (Floyd "Red Crow" Westerman) telling his grandson Eric to "leave the snakes alone today." Then, in Navajo, he reveals to his son, "The Earth has a secret it needs to tell." The secret turns out to be a boxcar filled with the dead bodies of what appear to be aliens. In what Sarah Stegall points out is one of the episode's biggest cultural blunders, Albert, with several men, stands over the exhumed skeletons:

> There is only one real goof in "Anasazi." A rabbi will eat pork during Passover before a Navajo elder will approach a dead body, even the corpse of an alien. . . . Observance of so deeply ingrained a social imperative has nothing to do with education or superstition, it has to do with respect for one's religion and one's traditions.[31]

This "goof," in fact, raised the hackles of many Native American experts, and led a penitent Carter to spend considerable time doing research for episodes that (temporarily) resolved the story: as reported in several sci-fi periodicals, the official guide for that year, and in the introduction to

the episode on the video release, he attended an actual Diné "blessing way" ceremony and hired Indian artists to do the sand drawings
needed for his re-creation.

The construction of Albert, a central character in this narrative
thread—and one destined to reappear later in the series—reveals much
about the show's viewpoint on Native Americans. Played with dignity
by actor Floyd "Red Crow" Westerman, Albert features several singular and defining characteristics in his language and personality: first,
shifting between Diné and English, he speaks in deliberately "meaningful," yet indirect phrases, rich with a quasi-religious portent. Second,
in keeping with the Navajo oral traditions, he literally embodies his
people's culture, most obviously in the ancient rituals that he conducts,
but also in his unerring moral sense. And third, he has foresight, the almost magical ability to perceive and decipher future events: he can feel
when the world is about to turn upside down, when something earth-
shattering will occur, when a "special visitor" (such as Mulder) will
arrive to fulfill his assigned role in fate's unfolding.

Albert's own being extends like a blanket over the representation of
the entire Navajo nation, encompassing and defining them. Just as he is
a translator of words and wisdom, with mystical knowledge unavailable
to most, the Navajo encryption used during World War II was "the only
code the Japanese couldn't break." Already on the "anti-Nazi" side of
the battle, the Navajos maintain a vital trinity of powers: language, culture, and magic. It is they who possess the single tongue that can never
be "corrupted" or "understood" by the enemy. And throughout this
and the other two episodes in the trilogy, the Native Americans, with
their nobility and spiritual knowledge, forge a link with Mulder (and
secondarily, Scully)—and this acceptance equally signifies the agents'
moral certitude.

Visually, too, the presentation of Mulder and Scully in "Anasazi"
particularly links them to the Native American world: unlike almost
any other landscape to date in X-Files, "Anasazi" burns red and bright,
colors that capture the heat of the New Mexico desert and rocks. This
red light frequently bathes the agents in its glow—even off the reservation, as if that special space is already calling to them.

Rooted in precisely "that respect for tradition" Stegall mentions,
the Native Americans alone boast a social structure with enough force
to confront and defeat both technology and evil. At the end of "Paper
Clip," with the disk and its printout stolen; with Mulder's father and
Scully's sister shot and killed by Consortium assassins; and with Mulder,
Scully, and their boss Assistant Director Skinner in mortal danger, they

must depend on Navajo culture to rescue them. When Mulder's nemesis, Cigarette Smoking Man, refuses to bargain with Skinner for the agents' safety, Skinner opens a door in his office to reveal Albert standing there, waiting. Telling the figure popularly known to all fans as CSM to "pucker up and kiss my ass," Skinner triumphantly announces that Albert has translated the document and, in accordance with Navajo tradition, has told twenty other men in his tribe—and each of those twenty will do the same. "So unless you're going to kill the entire Navajo nation . . . Welcome to the world of high technology."

In the series' overall initial dichotomy, which posits Mulder as a correct believer in "more than is known to your philosophy," and Scully as the more limited soul who depends on science, the Native Americans firmly fall on the side of the extraterrestrial in the largest sense of the world.

African [American] Visions

Throughout *The X-Files* premiere season, the stories remained almost resolutely white in nature. It was almost as if, to make the show's weirdness even scarier, the action had to unfold in spaces traditionally represented as bastions of normality, such as the upstanding military, the high echelons of government and lawmaking, or (usually) sleepy small towns that signified the "true heart" of America. In choosing these locales, *X-Files* continued the practice of classic 1950s B and genre films, which both disfigured the familiar, safe spaces of everyday life and excised blacks from the picture. By the second season, however, things slowly began to change, and the first episode to feature a black lead aired on 7 October 1994—the fourth entry of that year. Written by Howard Gordon (his first script without cowriter Alex Gansa, who had left the series), the powerful "Sleepless" explored issues of governmental misconduct and lies during the Vietnam War.

"Sleepless" centers around a series of unexplainable deaths, all somehow linked to a special marine unit that served in Southeast Asia. In each case, the evidence unearthed by Mulder and Scully suggests seemingly irreconcilable facts. For example, although the first victim, Dr. Saul Grissom, reported a fire in his home and his internal organs were burned, neither his flesh nor the apartment shows any sign of charring. As the investigation continues, two facts emerge. First, the killer appears to be a black veteran named Augustus Cole. Second, Mulder unearths information leading him to believe that the men in Cole's unit all underwent secret military experimentation—in this case, experiments conducted by Grissom, a sleep specialist. The goal was to produce more aggressive, fearless soldiers who would require absolutely no rest. Additionally, Cole seems to have the ability to impose hallucinatory images on others, making them see and physically experience whatever he chooses.

The lengths to which nations will go to produce the perfect human fighting machine has long been a staple of science fiction literature (such as Orson Scott Card's magnificently multilayered *Ender's Game*) and television. Even *Star Trek: The Next Generation* had an episode, called "The Hunted," in which genetically engineered soldiers rebel against a repressive government that, in peacetime, no longer wants any part of the monsters it created. But here, the question of the United States' willingness to treat (covertly) its often poor and minority recruits as guinea pigs has a powerful real-life referent that ties smoothly into *The X-Files'* overarching sense of paranoia: the use of Agent Orange in Vietnam and later, the unidentified chemicals that produced Gulf War syndrome.

In fact, it turns out that Cole and his fellow soldiers have not slept in twenty-four years, ever since they ran amok and massacred villagers in a Vietnamese hamlet. Cole has set out on a mission of vengeance for the group's actions, and he uses his powers to force the other marines to visualize such threats as a Viet Cong aiming a gun at them, just as a shell-shocked soldier might imagine on his own. The visuals enhance the effect by placing the audience in the victims' positions, seeing the same images they do; at no point does any cinematic punctuation indicate that we are inside a mind rather than watching a "true" event. This strategy independently validates the existence of an "X-file" and of Cole's paranormal capabilities.

Whether intentionally or not, making Cole African-American cannot help but allude to the significant role played in Vietnam by black soldiers, who at the time were less able than whites to enjoy access to legal exemptions (including educational deferments) from service.[32]

> [D]uring the Vietnam War . . . African Americans faced a new problem—rather than being excluded from combat, they now found themselves inevitably condemned to it. . . . as military historian Michael Lee Lanning observed [they] "were 13.5 percent of the military age population [and] 10.6 percent of the total force of the war zone . . . [but were] 20 percent of U.S. battlefield casualties." It was, as one black soldier remarked, "the kind of integration that could kill you."[33]

Furthermore, as Wallace Terry pointedly remarks in his introduction to *Bloods: An Oral History of the Vietnam War by Black Veterans,* black draftees were

just steps removed from marching in the Civil Rights Movement or
rioting in the rebellions that swept the urban ghettos from Harlem
to Watts. All were filled with a new sense of pride and purpose. They
spoke loudest against the discrimination they encountered on the battlefield, in decorations, promotions and duty assignments. They chose not
to overlook the racial insults, confederate flags, and cross burnings of
their white comrades.[34]

As such, it is important that Cole's actions, rather than being evil, come
from his own victimization; no killer he, but avenging angel. Physically,
he is large and silent, rich in mystery and strength, and his lack of emotionalism (until the very end) makes him a figure of pure justice. Cole
also embodies the war's pain and guilt, and his final "suicide" through
dream projection marks the end of nearly a quarter century of agony
due to guilt and sleeplessness literally inflicted on him by the government, military, and science.

Early in the third season, *The X-Files* featured a heavily black cast
in another setting known in the real world for its disproportionate
number of African-Americans: the prison system. Titled "The List,"
it takes on the cruelty administered by prison officials and guards,
and, like "Sleepless," it thematically deals with redemption and justice.
Here, inmate Napoleon "Neech" Manley, after dying in the electric
chair, seems to be reaching out from beyond the grave to get back at his
tormenters—especially the penitentiary's warden and guard. However,
in the end, his more political raison d'être for the vengeful murders
shifts into the personal: the payback becomes directed toward Manley's
wife and her new lover, a guard named Parmelly. Both the casting and
the dramatization of the prison routine implicitly acknowledge the racial composition of America's jails and the mistreatment that frequently
occurs by officials.[35]

But it is not in these episodes that the most explicit examination of
the place of society's Others really occurs; for that one must look to the
stories that go beyond the shores of the United States—to Africa and
the more "African" side of the diaspora, in Haiti. These are the *X-Files'*
true humanoid aliens, and as Jodi Dean points out in her history of extraterrestrial sightings, most "looked like white humans, with some described as tall, attractive and Aryan";[36] following society's prejudices,
lightness goes along with "positive" qualities. The more paranormal
and religious focus of the *X-Files'* Africanized stories, however, operate
very differently.

Because the abductions and mythology stories have pretty much
become the province of Chris [Carter] and Frank [Spotnitz], they

are really no longer stories I can tell. So I've been exercising my anthropological muscles.[37]

Some of the scripts freak me out. . . . The one about voodoo! I don't even want to talk about it.[38]

What kind of barbaric religion would desecrate a grave?[39]

"Fresh Bones" aired right in the middle of *The X-Files'* second season, on 3 February 1995. For most fans and critics—as well as for Chris Carter[40]—it remains, with the crucial exception of the mythology shows, one of the best of the racially inflected tales (at least in terms of effective storytelling). It also topped the series' ratings for that year. Rich in creepiness and beautifully directed by the much-admired regular Rob Bowman, it employs a wide range of visual techniques to fill the atmosphere with fear.[41] And, like most of the others of its ilk, it sends mixed and contradictory messages both in words and images. Not only does the narrative focus on Vodoun,[42] but more politically on the role played by the U.S. military in Haiti's affairs and on the status of Haitian refugees fleeing to America to escape oppression and death squads.

Howard Gordon, inspired by news clippings, penned the episode in a fairly speedy fashion.[43] As he put it, he "decided to explore the mysterious world of voodoo," with an eye on ethnobotanist Wade Davis's well-known book *Serpent and the Rainbow,* itself made into a film (1988, Wes Craven).[44] Director Bowman was firm about trying to avoid the stereotypes associated with Haitian religion: "The goal was to keep this voodoo storyline from becoming silly, filled with bloody chickens and all of the things we've seen before. We wanted to create a very believable scenario."[45] Bowman's point is well taken: Vodoun evokes in the popular imagination such timeworn images as dolls with pins stuck in them and zombies, the walking dead. A question arises about horror's tendency to dig deep into the psyche until it reaches our "everyday" primal fears. Isn't it one thing to defamiliarize the well-known and comfortable (as many 1950s science fiction films did) and quite another to render strange the already frightening? In the case of Vodoun—a misunderstood religion whose practitioners have suffered untold injustices—does that not tap into prejudice rather than offer emotional catharsis?

Set on a military base, where so many *X-Files* episodes had unfolded in the first season, the teaser for "Fresh Bones" shows a tense and argumentative family headed by a marine clearly in the midst of a meltdown. A point-of-view shot captures his perception of cereal turning into maggots—a sight that causes him to flee his house, leap into his car, and, crazed with terror, drive at top speed into a tree. The camera then moves slowly around the tree, in an act of narration, until it stops on a *vever,* a Vodoun symbol normally associated with a particular god and drawn in chalk on the ground of the *houngan,* or temple. The slow pace of the camera's track immediately creates a sense of nervous dread about what it will find at the end, and when it comes to a stop, the symbol instantly suggests the cause of the marine's madness and death. This conclusion is reinforced later when Mulder informs Scully that the marine's wife refuses to accept the ruling of suicide. "If he didn't kill himself, what did?" she asks, and the camera, rather than Mulder, answers her by ominously cutting back to the marked tree as threatening music plays on the sound track. Never, despite the series' usual tendency to pile on explanatory background, does the script actually define the precise nature of the *vever,* which the police simply label graffiti and Scully refers to only as "some sort of a ritual symbol." (At one point, the sign is associated with the crossroads, which would link it to Ghede, the *loa,* or spirit, who opens up the path for the other gods to arrive.)

Throughout, in ways both small and large, racial and political issues permeate the atmosphere: the white marine is an "All-American" boy who believes in football and the honor of the U.S. military; Manuel Gutierrez, another soldier who suffered a strange death, is defined as Puerto Rican; and, of course, the Haitian masses huddled in the compound in hopes of freedom are both black and foreign. When Mulder and Scully enter the military complex, they and the camera are uncomfortably aware of the refugees (watched over by armed soldiers) staring angrily at the agents with resentful eyes. The sound track, enhanced with muttering voices and pulsing, unnerving music, adds to the tense mood. And the least threatening figure of all, the one comrade they have as they walk through, is a ten-year-old boy named Chester who befriends Scully—and who, unlike the adult men, is set up to be appealing. (He also turns out to be dead, an innocent from beyond the grave clearly come back to protect the agents.)

The issue of how to define the camp also raises, through denial, the specter of analogous injustices and violence: "Nobody said this is a hotel . . . but this isn't a concentration camp," insists the colonel in charge, which, of course, automatically suggests exactly the opposite. In fact, the script for "Fresh Bones" stands as a paradigm of *The X-Files'* contradictory mix of racial liberalism and demonism, where words professing sympathy for the Other clash with narratives depicting their evil. Though the text voices sympathy for the plight of the would-be immigrants, caught in what Gordon himself refers to as a no-man's-land,[46] ironically the "kind" solution that Mulder suggests—and the one that Bauvais, a pivotal Haitian character, dearly wants—is repatriation. For many of the real-world counterparts these figures are meant to represent, such an act would have meant death.

The very filming of "African" bodies becomes an issue: as Mulder and Scully interview Bauvais, who is charged with masterminding the murders of the G.I.s, he literally remains "in the dark," almost invisible in the gloom, his slow, unnerving voice emerging from the cell's black hole. In contrast, a bright spot illuminates Mulder, turning him into a figure of light, knowledge, and goodness. That he stands as the white opposite of the vicious Colonel Wharton, who administers beatings to the refugees, further lionizes him. Mulder serves as the voice of reasonable, concerned liberal rhetoric, as heard in his protesting words when he meets with X, his informant.

> X: These people have no rights. . . .
> MULDER: Why are they making these people invisible?
> X: In case you haven't noticed, Mulder, the Statue of Liberty is on vacation. The new mandate says if you're not a citizen, you'd better keep out.

Ultimately, however, as Scully nearly falls victim to a "voodoo spell"—and the Colonel, who has appropriated the religion for his own nefarious ends, actually does perish—it would be impossible to see this African-based creed as anything but spooky and evil, primarily dedicated to destruction.

Folkloric Monsters and Whitened Bodies

> But what science may never be able to explain is our ineffable fear of the alien among us—a fear which often drives us not to search for understanding but to deceive, inveigle, and obfuscate, to obscure the truth not only from others, but from ourselves." (Agent Dana Scully in the episode "Teliko," season 4)

Going yet deeper into "darkest Africa," "Teliko," also written by Howard Gordon, presents a folkloric spirit from Burkina Faso who, tellingly, lacks melanin. In order to survive, he must therefore steal it from living humans—preferably darker-skinned beings whose bodies possess more of the pigment needed to feed this quasi-albino creature. As he sucks his victims dry, their skins turn ashy white and their eyes become blue, prompting a puzzled Mulder, gazing at a palely colored cadaver, to say, "I thought the victim was black."

The case reaches Scully first, thanks to her medical expertise, for the Center of Disease Control fears it might have an epidemic on its hands. However, since the Teliko has specifically targeted young African-American men, the agency (understandably, given its history) also worries about taking heat for its inability to find the perpetrator.

The episode's narrative is clearly highly loaded and explosive. Not only does it deal with the high rate of violence among young black males and the seeming lack of concern among law enforcement, it also plays with metaphors of "whitening." Then it further adds the question of immigration and "foreign diseases" to the potent mix. Gordon himself admitted, "In a way, I feel a little guilty because of the xenophobic possibilities it presents," but then went on to say, "I think we dodged them by making the victims black as well."[47] In fact, as we will see, given the episode's themes, having black victims doesn't quite eliminate the xenophobic qualities of the story; it simply creates different issues.

The Teliko—who looks human and is passing under the name Samuel Aboah—is attempting to negotiate the INS (Immigration and Naturalization Services) with the assistance of Marcus Duff, a sympathetic West Indian lawyer who specializes in assisting illegals to receive their papers and to bring in their families, too: "I can help you bring in every brother, sister, aunt, uncle, cousin." He attempts to block Mulder at every turn, viewing him with suspicion. But he becomes the well-meaning "setup," designed to prove Mulder's legitimacy. At one point, after Mulder and Scully have succeeded in arresting a fleeing Aboah, Mulder and Marcus have a heated exchange about the Teliko's motivations:

MULDER: We only arrested him because he ran when we tried to question him and I want to know why. . . .

MARCUS: Sir, if you had ever been beaten by the police, or had your home burned to the ground for no other reason than being born, then maybe you'd understand why he ran, and why you would run too.

MULDER: That man ran because he was hiding something.

Here we can see how the episode attempts to encompass a number of wide-ranging and complex issues only to end up weaving a tangled web of ideas: every statement butts up against its contradiction, every over-arching politically correct observation meets its narrative opposite. Though we are indeed supposed to react sympathetically to Marcus's comment about the political violence many African immigrants have suffered, Mulder's angry retort turns out to be the correct view of the

Teliko's actions. Though perhaps subjected to human cruelty and mis-understanding, the Teliko has never suffered state repression. He holds no political view that renders him a victim. And Marcus's naïve outlook nearly costs him his life, as a "starving" Teliko eventually attacks even his benefactor. Only Mulder's timely arrival stops the assault. Given these events, Marcus's dedication to the "law-abiding" immigrants he so lovingly assists also must come in for skepticism, thus in some way confirming the idea that these "foreigners" cannot be trusted.

In looking at the violence suffered by young black men, "Teliko" paints a similarly confused picture—as opposed to Gordon's happy belief that featuring African-American victims lessens the potential for xenophobia. First, it raises the specter of FBI and police indifference (and even contribution) to their victimization. For example, Mulder ini-tially reacts skeptically to the CDC's diagnosis of an epidemic: "Scully, has it occurred to you that this might just be a little PR exercise . . . [t]o divert attention from the fact that young black men are dying and nobody seems to be able to bring in a suspect, the perception being that nobody cares?" But in this instance, the creature doing the killing is actually African, thus deflecting the guilt from the government, white society, and even the social conditions that contribute to real black-on-black violence in the inner city.

Added to this, the troubling question of "whitening" runs through the episode—at one point Mulder sarcastically says, "There's a Michael Jackson joke here somewhere, but I can't quite find it"—and it is also laid at the doorstep of Africa, rather than attributed to the effects of power and hegemonic definitions of beauty. (One black cop even com-ments, as they canvass a neighborhood in search of a victim, "Aboah? What the hell kind of name is that?" shaking his head and laughing.) As in "Fresh Bones," the dichotomous meanings arise from the clash of direct spoken discourse and performed narrative: every statement of compassion for the oppressed eventually meets its mitigating dramatic action. Both the visuals and the music add to the force of fearfulness attached to "darkest Africa"; the Teliko's spaces remain shrouded and scary, and the images very effectively convey the terror of his attacks. In one sequence, we watch as the creature leans back, opens his voracious mouth wide, and slowly pulls from his throat a long vine with narcotic seeds attached. These seeds are what he shoots into his prey, inducing paralysis while the immobilized victim remains all too aware of his im-pending death.

The lengthiest scene of an attack, and the only one showing the victim over an extended period of time, provides a clear vision of how sound and image overlay their own meaning onto the events. The sequence actually begins with a happy white couple in front of a touristic sign of the sphinx (itself redolent with the aroma of exoticism and mystery); then the camera continues moving till it reaches the interior of a bus shelter, where a teenaged black male—later identified as Alfred Kettle—sits on a bench, waiting. Suddenly, Alfred flinches and reaches for his neck, and a close-up reveals a spot of blood surrounding a strange-looking seed. He pulls it out, and eerie African chanting—thematically associated with the Teliko's assault—begins, mingled with the sound of the victim's labored breathing. The bus arrives, seen from the teen's now blurred and skewed point of view; the white driver, stereotypically fat and with a "working guy" accent, yells out, "Hey, I got a schedule. Getting in or not? What's your problem? You on drugs or something? Ah, the hell with you," before pulling away. (When queried later by Mulder on whether he thought to call for help, the driver very defensively cites the schedule once again as justification for his lack of involvement.) Throughout the tirade, the visuals crosscut between Alfred, lips occasionally opening slightly in a desperate attempt to speak, and a nightmarish, out-of-focus image of the shouting driver. Only after the bus leaves, freeing the vista, do we see the Teliko in long shot, standing across the street, waiting. The music then grows louder, more pronounced and throbbing, with drums added, and the camera cuts to a close-up of the Teliko from an unnervingly low angle before tilting upward and looking directly into his face. A reaction shot of Alfred's eye's widening in fear follows.

Except for the bus driver's words—which owe much of their effectiveness to dynamics (the harshness and loudness of the sound in the otherwise quiet night)—the scene lacks language, conveying its various shades of emotion both through visual distortion (fuzziness, double vision, canted frames) and culturally coded ideas of "primitive" music. The victim's youthful, frightened face, seen in close-up, is the primary figure of sympathy, as he becomes the pawn of both the bus driver's indifference and prejudices ("You on drugs . . .?") and the Teliko's insatiable hunger.

A central moment of "Teliko," and one that defines it narratively, occurs when Mulder visits the embassy of Burkina Faso and finally learns the nature of the creature he's fighting. Told in the form of a folk story by a minister (played by the esteemed South African actor Zakes Mokae), it begins with the words, "Even if I tell you what I know, you would never believe it," to which Mulder dryly responds, "You'd be surprised at what I'd believe, sir." What the minister furnishes is an almost "once upon a time" narration that in the American context must necessarily emphasize the idea of oral culture, superstition, and the otherworldly (affirmed in the minister's description of *telikos* as "spirits of the air"). It perhaps even has a touch of the childlikeness that Western culture has too often ascribed to such age-old stories. In fact, when Mulder later tells Scully what the minister said, she scornfully replies, "So you're basing the theory on a folktale."

Only one other *X-Files* episode uses, and takes further, such a narrative approach: the Mexican-themed "El Mundo Gira" (best translated "As the World Turns," the name of the long-running American soap opera), from season 4. That episode begins with a woman surrounded by a circle of people—almost like a story time for youngsters—as she tantalizes them with a tale about the mythological *chupacabra,* a creature who is half man and half goat. And once again, the drama deals with questions of immigration and the mistreatment of an embattled people whom mainstream society refuses to acknowledge. Attempting to present a sympathetic portrait of migrant workers and illegals, it links the legend of the chupacabra to modern-day pollutants, attributing the creature's existence and the humans' physical alteration to harmful chemicals.[48] Shunting aside the show's usual realistic performances and settings (which heighten the horror by basing it in an everyday context), here the actors perform melodramatically, while the reflexive, somewhat postmodern narrative alludes to the popular Mexican telenovelas. Yet, in the context, everything seems overwrought, a reaffirmation of stereotypical Latin emotionalism. The idea of social invisibility butts up against the chupacabra's outlandish and impossible-to-ignore physical image—which could not help but catch the gaze of anyone who came in its path.

The Alien League

> They're all aliens—all the great ones. See, all of the great ones don't fit in. Not in this world, not in any other world. (Arthur Dales, "The Unnatural," season 6)

Among the stories directly highlighting race, the richest and most complex is "The Unnatural," written and directed by David Duchovny. As in "Teliko" and "El Mundo Gira," the process of storytelling takes center stage, but in the form of a nostalgic first-person narration (and revelation) by Arthur Dales,[49] a former policeman who in 1947 had accompanied the Negro League baseball team known as the Roswell Grays.[50]

His job: to protect the Grays' brilliant batter, Josh "Ex" Exley, from Klansmen intent on upholding baseball's "purity" and "whiteness."

The flashback begins in the show's teaser, where, on a starry summer night, in a makeshift isolated field, two teams enjoy a game. Implicit in their sense of fun, the old-fashioned outfits, and the improvised ballpark is an idea of baseball as it once was, the American sport, played only for pleasure and free of modern-day commercialism. The tinkling sweet music, with just a touch of gospel, enhances the sense of loveliness. "You gonna be famous," the white catcher grins at Exley. "I don't want to be no famous man. I just want to be a man," Josh replies, smiling—a line whose meaning becomes clear only later, when we learn his "unnatural" identity. He then takes a swing at the ball and it soars upward, seeming to lodge in the heavens.

Suddenly, firelight replaces the starlight, and from the distance Klansmen come riding in on white horses. Thanks to the white pitcher, who knocks the enemy down with fastballs, the players succeed in disarming the white-sheeted invaders. When the manager pulls the hood off the Grand Dragon, however, he's in for a shock: he sees the face of an alien.

Throughout the episode, the blacks are equated with aliens, these "Others" never allowed to fit in or to feel safe. A particular image encapsulates the sense that under such conditions one must maintain both a public and a hidden identity: Arthur Dales, after napping on the team bus, wakes and glances back at the sleeping Exley. To his shock, Ex's reflection in the window shows not a man but an alien visage. Dales approaches slowly, peering closely at the glass, when Exley wakes. "What's wrong? You've never seen a black man before?" he asks, in a tone that clearly implies Dales should back off. The strange, pale vision in the window contrasts strongly with the handsome, serious, tense, and softly lighted face of actor Jesse L. Martin, who plays Exley.

When Dales finally learns the truth, after bursting into Exley's room while the alien has reverted to his true body, the cop faints: "I'm trying not to be insulted by your reaction to my real form. Would it be easier if I looked like this?" Ex says, his alien figure morphing into a beautiful, blonde woman who promptly sits on Dales's lap. Later the player affirms, "My people guard their privacy zealously. They don't want our people to intermingle with your people." Exley himself refuses this imposed segregation from outer space, while at the same time choosing to become one of the victims of human apartheid. On the one hand, blackness assures his invisibility, making it easier to keep his alien identity secret; on the other, it also saves him from becoming one of the perpetrators of earthly intolerance. The Negro spiritual "Come and Go with Me to That Land," a music theme throughout the episode, further enhances the idea of a human chain that links us all. "We'll all be together in that land," Exley and the other players sing, of some imaginary future beyond this world.

As the line "I just want to be a man" suggests, Exley hungers for warmth, laughter, *humanity*—and it is through baseball, or rather the passion and love that it signifies, that he finds it. Fatally stabbed by an alien executioner (significantly, the Nazi-like shapeshifter from earlier episodes), he warns Dales to stay away because his body fluids are poisonous to humans. "It's just blood, Exley, it's just blood," Dales says. Exley looks at his bloodstained hands, and, indeed, rather than the toxic green goo the aliens leak, he bleeds just like an ordinary person.

After Exley's death, as the spiritual plays quietly on the sound track, the camera cranes upward, looking down on the young Arthur Dales holding the body in his arms; it then cuts to the exact same angle pointing downward on his older self, sitting next to Mulder. Dales's face exudes anguish as he remembers. And the point of the story is not lost on Mulder, a man with his own finely cultivated form of alienation. At show's end, he has his arms wrapped around a laughing Scully as he teaches her how to swing the bat and connect with the ball—which goes flying off into the night, to take its place among the stars.

Ironically, the *X-Files* episode that looks most radically at ideas of Otherness has nothing overtly to do with race or ethnicity at all. Yet it succeeds by thoroughly deconstructing ideas of normality, beauty, power, and stereotypes. "Humbug" (season 2), a product of the unique imagination of writer Darin Morgan (an Emmy award winner and fan favorite), unfolds in a Florida freak show, where Mulder and Scully have come to investigate the death of one of the performers. In this world turned upside down, it is the conventionally attractive (the two agents) who eventually become strange and grotesque, while those with "deviate" bodies seem most human.

The very first scene shatters the audience's expectations: two little boys splash happily in a pool as we see, through crosscuts, a menacing shadow of a manlike figure diving beneath the water and swimming toward the children. When the tattooed creature emerges and grabs the youngsters, they scream—in joy. He is their father and has simply surprised them. Instead of the violence the images had prepared us for, we see hugs. We have learned that we cannot trust our eyes and our prejudices, and the lesson continues as every "inferential path"—to use

Umberto Eco's term—we take about the murder closes down. In the end, Dr. Blockhead, a sideshow performer capable of bearing the most extreme forms of pain (including having nails hammered into his flesh), states the episode's philosophy: Because of genetic engineering, the kinds of abnormalities that make his fellow "freaks" special will disappear. Instead, he notes disparagingly, gazing off-screen, they will all look like *that*—and he points to Mulder, standing in the distance, posing like a model, and appearing thoroughly silly in his handsomeness. By questioning the very nature of "normal," "Humbug" does more to deflate "white power" than any of *The X-Files'* direct attempts to deal with society's disenfranchised—who inevitably remain the other whose truth stays "out there."

Notes

I dedicate this to the great ladies of the Mulder and Skinner bulletin boards, who shared fun and discussion with me in the heyday of "X." Your "Natasha" offers heartfelt thanks for your insight, jokes, and friendship.

1. See *Trust No One: The Official Third Season Guide to The X Files,* ed. Brian Lowry (New York: HarperCollins, 1996), pp. 3–4, for information on the network's perspective, and p. 15 for Duchovny's view.

2. Ibid.

3. See Alison Graham, "Are You Now or Have You Ever Been? Conspiracy and *The X-Files,*" in *Deny All Knowledge: Reading the X-Files,* ed. David Lavery, Angela Hague, and Marla Cartwright (Syracuse, N.Y.: Syracuse University Press, 1996).

4. See, among others, Vivian Sobchack's *Screening Space: The American Science Fiction Film* (New Brunswick, N.J.: Rutgers University Press, 1986); Per Schelde, *Androids, Humanoids, and Other Science Fiction Monsters: Science and Soul in Science Fiction Films* (New York: New York University Press, 1993); Daniel Bernardi, *Star Trek and History: Race-ing toward a White Future* (New Brunswick, N.J.: Rutgers University Press, 1998). Even one of the classics of speculative fiction—H. G. Wells's *The War of the Worlds*—was inspired by contemporary events: at the height of British imperialism, Wells's brother Frank looked up at the sky and wondered what would happen if aliens came down to colonize us "the same way that we colonized Tasmania."

5. See Graham, "Are You Now or Have You Ever Been?" in *Deny All Knowledge,* ed. Lavery et al.

6. Many of the essays in *Deny All Knowledge* stress similarities between the two series (not surprising, as editor Lavery also compiled a collection of essays on *Twin Peaks*). In addition, the Twin Peaks cult magazine *Wrapped in Plastic* regularly features a section on *The X-Files,* indicating that fans certainly see a connection. Of course, another common factor between *The X-Files* and *Twin*

Peaks is David Duchovny, who played the latter show's transvestite FBI agent Dennis/Denise.

7. Jodi Dean, "The Truth Is Out There: Aliens and the Fugitivity of Modern Truth," *Camera Obscura,* no. 40–41, "Angels, Dinosaurs, Aliens" (May 1997): 45.

8. See John Mack's *Abductions: Human Encounters with Aliens* (New York: Ballantine Books, 1997). The "abductees" interviewed there frequently report that the aliens issue warnings about humanity despoiling the earth.

9. Not only *The X-Files* but another "X"—the recent film version of *The X-Men* comic book—uses the Holocaust as an important theme and narrative motivation.

10. See Bernardi's *Star Trek and History* for a complete discussion of race and ethnic representation on the various *Star Trek* series.

11. This comment is based on many years of participation in the official X-Files Web site, reading viewer responses posted there, and my own personal discussions with fans over the years. Shiban himself alluded to the harsh criticisms when he appeared at one of the fan conventions.

12. There are and always have been women as lower-end producers. It is also worth noting that James Wong was not on staff when "Hell Money," the Chinese-themed episode, aired. Also see "Boy's Club," Paula Vitaris's interview with Sara Charno, for a brief time one of the few female staff writers, in *Cinefantastique,* double issue, October 1995, 88.

13. See Bernardi, *Star Trek and History,* for a complete analysis of how *Star Trek* (and the network) dealt with the character of Uhura.

14. *Star Trek: Voyager* is somewhat of an exception in this respect. Because the ship was lost in space and out of contact with the Federation, episodes rarely focused on the hierarchy back home.

15. Among the many paranoia and alien-filled series that began life in *The X-Files'* wake were the short-lived *Dark Skies* and *Nowhere Man,* as well as the more recent *Roswell.* See the article "The Triumph of Evil" by Douglas Perry and Edward Gross on the subject in *Cinescape,* January 1996, 27–36.

16. Two exceptions: Actress CCH Pounder played Agent Kazdin in the seminal mythological episode "Duane Barry," season 2. She received an Emmy nomination for Best Guest Actress in a Drama Series, and later went on to become a semiregular in Chris Carter's second series, *Millennium.* In neither case was the character's race an issue. Notably, Pounder has amassed a résumé of roles in which she plays crisply efficient, no-nonsense authority figures—including a recurring role as a surgeon on the popular *ER.* And an eighth-season episode titled "Redrum" featured African-American actor Joe Morton as prosecutor Martin Wells who wakes up in jail, confused as to just how he got there. He finds that he has lost three days—and that he has apparently murdered his wife. The tale then goes "backward" one day at a time as he retraces the events that led him to prison. It explored no racially specific issues, but interestingly the real murderer is a Latino known as Cesar Ocampo whose motive was re-

venge: Wells had withheld evidence that could have exonerated Cesar's brother Hector on a drug charge. Instead, Hector went to jail, where he hanged himself. The episode ends with Cesar killed by agents Doggett and Scully—and Wells back in jail, this time for his own transgression. Of course, blacks and Latinos have played many bit parts, for example, used as local cops, and so on.

17. The question of Mulder's ethnicity was a matter of interest and debate from early on, when actor David Duchovny commented in an interview, "Until further notice, [he would] consider Mulder Jewish." This statement flew in the face of the first season's fourth episode, "Conduit," when Mulder sat crying in a church, holding a picture of his abducted sister. His family's New England breeding, plus Mulder's father's position in the State Department at a point when Jews were hardly welcome there, also seemed to cast doubt on Mulder's Jewishness. However, in "Kaddish," an anti-Semitic character suspiciously questioned Mulder's religion and Mulder did not answer directly; this temporarily burst the issue wide open again. Finally, the season 8 episode "DeadAlive" should settle the question: it begins with a funeral for the supposedly dead Mulder—a clearly Christian funeral. Duchovny himself has never elaborated on why he made his initial comment, though I might speculate on two potential reasons: given the actor's propensity to do such things as put a wedding ring on Mulder's finger right after his own marriage, the first is Duchovny's own half-Jewish background. Another might be that Mulder has a rather Talmudic approach to the "files," deconstructing potential cases the way a Jewish scholar works on religious texts.

18. An example of the kind of acronym used to describe David Duchovny's "puppy dog" appearance include: "C&C: Confused and Cute: refers to Mulder's condition when he looks as though he just woke up and has that look on his face that says, 'Huh?'" See http://www.geocities.com/Area51/Cavern/2812/xterm.html for series' acronym lists.

19. See chapter 3 from my own unpublished dissertation, "Dancing Images: Choreography, the Camera, and Culture" (New York University, 1996), for a look at some of the implications of different representational strategies for African- and Native Americans.

20. Robert Stam and Ella Shohat, *Unthinking Eurocentrism: Multiculturalism and the Media* (New York: Routledge, 1994), 11.

21. This frequently used gross-out tactic was amusingly mocked on one of *The X-Files* "gag reels," compiled at the end of every season. To the familiar strains of the *1812 Overture*'s cannon bursts, pustules rhythmically explode like fireworks.

22. *The X-Files Official Magazine* 4, no. 5 (winter 2000): 15. In more detail, the show has won several Emmys, among them John Bartley for Cinematography (for "Grotesque," season 3); Steve Cantamessa for Best Sound Mixing in a Dramatic Series; as well as many for makeup, special effects, music, and even its opening credits. The tech staff has also won individual guild awards and nominations. While Chris Carter has received several writing and directing

nominations (both for Emmys and from the Director's Guild of America), the sole *X-Files* screenwriter actually to take home the statue is the offbeat Darin Morgan, for "Clyde Bruckman's Final Repose," season 3, about an insurance salesman cursed with the ability to see into the future.

23. See Bernardi, *Star Trek and History,* 44–49.

24. See Wendy Rose, "The Great Pretenders: Further Reflections on White-shamanism," in *The State of Native America: Genocide, Colonization, and Resistance,* ed. M. Annette Jaimes (Boston: South End Press, 1992).

25. An additional problem with "Journey's End": The Indians' situation seems at least partly an excuse to explore the emotional quandaries of young, white ensign Wesley Crusher, who embarks on a Native American spirit journey to become evolved beyond their imaginings—and also to walk away from their problems, which had formerly concerned him.

26. See Stam and Shot, *Unthinking Eurocentrism,* 66–67, on historical and cinematic representations of "peaceful" versus "warlike" Indians.

27. Lowry, *Trust No One,* 144.

28. Teaser from "Shapes."

29. Sarah Stegall, "Shapes Review," 1994, at http://www.munchkyn.com/xf-rvws/shapes.html.

30. The twists and turns of this enormously complex trilogy are too convoluted to relate in detail, but, in brief:

"Anasazi": This second season-ender primarily focuses on three issues. First, an illegally downloaded document, encrypted in Navajo, falls into Mulder's possession. It contains the entire history of the Consortium's activities from World War II on. Second, Mulder learns that his father, Bill, once played a central role in a massive government conspiracy to engage in alien/human experimentation; during the course of the episode, Krycek, a Consortium assassin, murders Bill Mulder—and frames Fox for the deed. And third, a young Navajo boy named Eric discovers, on his reservation, a railway car full of dead bodies. These various strands come together when Mulder and Scully arrive at the reservation to meet with Albert Hosteen, Eric's grandfather and an original wartime "code talker" capable of translating the document. As Albert works on the papers, Eric takes Mulder to see the skeletons in the boxcar. The show ends with a literal bang, when Cigarette Smoking Man, Mulder's nemesis, bombs the boxcar with Mulder still inside, apparently killed. One fact does come to light: Scully's name is mentioned in the encrypted document, along with some other "merchandise."

"Blessing Way": During most of this episode, Mulder lies unconscious, his survival uncertain. The Navajos who have recovered his body try to save him by performing the traditional Native American ritual that gives the episode its title. While on this spiritual journey, caught between our world and the afterlife, Mulder speaks to his dead father as well as to Deep Throat, his informant and mentor from the first season (and also a victim of the Consortium's killers). Intercut with these events are Scully's interrogation by the FBI honchos and her subsequent suspension, the discovery that something metallic has been embedded in her neck, her vision of Mulder still alive, and a meeting with a mysterious gentleman (known as The Well-Manicured Man) who provides her with additional information on the conspiracy and warns her that someone will try to kill her. The attempted murder will either be done by a paid assassin or be the work of someone she trusts. Scully instantly focuses on Assistant Director Skinner, generally an ally to her and Mulder, but now behaving strangely. However, as Scully busies herself shadowing Skinner, the real murderers—including Krycek—mistakenly shoot her sister Melissa instead. The episode climaxes in a Ringo Lam/Quentin Tarantino-like standoff between Scully and Skinner in Mulder's apartment: each is holding a gun on the other, when they hear a sound at the door. . . .

"Paper Clip": Mulder bursts in, and now *he* grabs his gun, for a three-way holdup. Quick explanations establish Skinner's innocence—and a reunited Mulder and Scully go off to pursue their investigation. Acting on The Well-Manicured Man's leads, they visit a former Nazi scientist, recruited by the U.S. government after the war, and learn about a cache of secret files. The agents follow this up and enter a hidden, cave-like structure where they discover cabinet after cabinet lined against the wall—"lots and lots of files," as Scully notes. Organized by year, each one contains a person's name and a DNA sample taken during what were routine smallpox inoculations. First, they look at Scully's file; then Mulder runs to find his sister Samantha's folder. He notices that there's a paper clip holding her name tag on the file, and as he peels the label off, he realizes that his name was originally there. Apparently he, and not Samantha, was intended to be the original kidnapping victim. The two narrowly escape out a back exit as agents burst into the facility. By now, it is clear that the Consortium is ready to hunt down Mulder and Scully unless they turn over the disk with the document. And when Scully learns that Melissa is in a coma at the hospital, she is ready to make a deal. Mulder accedes to Scully's wishes, and Skinner hands over the tape to Cigarette Smoking Man. But Skinner has an ace up his sleeve: Albert Hosteen. The assistant director informs Cigarette Smoking Man that, in accordance with Navajo tradition, Hosteen has told twenty other men what was in the document, and if anything should happen to Mulder, Scully, or himself, they are authorized to reveal its contents. "Paper Clip" ends with Mulder comforting Scully beside what was Melissa's hospital bed; she has died from her wounds.

31. Sarah Stegall, "An Ancient Enemy," 1995, at http://www.munchkyn.com/xf-rvws/anasazi.html.

32. There was a follow-up episode to this several seasons later, but it was generally considered less effective and had a white protagonist who evoked decidedly less sympathy.

33. "Blacks in the American Military," at http://www.africana.com/research/Encarta/tt_235.asp, 5 May 2001.

34. Wallace Terry, *Bloods: An Oral History of the Vietnam War by Black Veterans* (New York: Ballantine Books, 1984), xiv.

35. According to writer/director Carter, although the casting did reflect the

real racial composition of America's prison population, that was not his focus because "it was so obvious." See the interview with Carter, "The List," by Paula Vitaris, *Cinetantastique* 28, no. 3 (October 1996). In addition, prior to the episode's airing, Carter warned that the show "should create a lot of discussion because it involves black men on death row . . . very loaded subject." See "It's in His Hands," an interview with Chris Carter by Sarah Stegall, in *The X-Files Magazine Official Collector's Edition,* no. 1 (winter 1996): 26.

36. Dean, "The Truth Is Out There," 47. As John Mack's study also makes clear, "the grays," or darker aliens, are often singled out as crueler, more terrifying beings.

37. Writer Howard Gordon, cited in Joe Nazzaro, "The Agony and the Ecstasy," *Starlog,* no. 239 (June 1997): 44.

38. Gillian Anderson, cited in "Occult Leader," by Tom Gliatto, *People* magazine, 13 March 1995, 97–98.

39. Colonel Wharton in the episode "Fresh Bones," season 2.

40. Carter, quoted in "X-Files Episode Guide: Season Two," in Cinescape's *1995 Science Fiction Television Yearbook,* 18.

41. According to the official episode guide, *The Truth Is Out There,* writer Gordon praised Bowman, who "'did a great job' mining his script for chills" (Lowry, *Trust No One,* 197). Additionally, Paula Vitaris, who wrote frequently on *The X-Files* for sci-fi magazines, called "Fresh Bones" "a solid, scary episode that appropriately respects Voodoo as the legitimate religion it is," a position with which I obviously disagree. See Vitaris's episode review in *Cinefantastique*'s special double issue (26, no. 6/27, no. 1 [October 1995]: 82) for more discussion on this episode and additional comments by writer Howard Gordon. Also see the episode guide in Cinescape's *Science Fiction Television Yearbook,* fall 1995, 18, for more observations by director Rob Bowman.

42. Note that the entire X staff chooses to use the Americanized and pejorative term "voodoo" rather than the properly Haitian "Vodoun."

43. See discussion of that particular episode in Brian Lowry's *The Truth Is Out There: The Official Guide to the X-Files* (New York: HarperPrism, 1995).

44. Nazzaro, "The Agony and the Ecstasy," 49.

45. Bowman, quoted in "X-Files Episode Guide: Season Two," 18.

46. Nazzaro, "The Agony and the Ecstasy," 49.

47. Joe Nazzaro, "Truth and Consequences," *Starlog,* no. 40 (July 1977): 74.

48. The idea of evolution and pollution was also tackled, more interestingly, in the second-season episode "The Host," which featured a giant wormlike beast called the "Flukeman," a product of the nuclear waste from Chernobyl.

49. The character of Arthur Dales had already appeared on *The X-Files* in the fifth-season episode "Travelers." But the role, originally played by Darren McGavin (former star of *Kolchak: The Night Stalker,* one of Chris Carter's inspirations), was taken on by M. Emmet Walsh at the last minute when McGavin had to pull out. So the character was turned into his brother—but with the same name.

50. The name of the team is a reference both to the town of Roswell, a center of UFO interest since 1947, when an alien vessel is alleged to have crashed, and to the grays, a species of alien identified by presumed abductees. The title of the episode itself, of course, comes from Bernard Malamud's baseball novel, "The Natural," filmed in 1984 with Robert Redford.

8

Monsters and Metaphors: *Buffy the Vampire Slayer* and the Old World

Mary Hammond

■ Ken Gelder has described Fran Rubel Kazui's 1992 film *Buffy the Vampire Slayer* as standing alone among late twentieth-century vampire narratives in several important respects. For him, the film remains in every way "resolutely local," while

> we have seen other vampire narratives use local scenarios for their
> action—Stephen King's *Salem's Lot*, for example . . . *Buffy* refuses to
> enlarge itself in the ways already noted in relation to King: [that is] to
> mythologise its community as American . . . or to monumentalise itself
> as part of a "classical" literary tradition (as Coppola's film [also 1992]
> monumentalises itself in relation to a tradition of cinema)—or to push
> itself towards the status of a blockbuster. . . . This is a film which places
> clear limits on its scope in order to underline the force of its relatively
> modest project, namely the mobilization of a Californian suburban girl.[1]

This 1994 reading of the film provides me with two imperatives. First, it describes the film as a teen movie concerned with Buffy's empowerment as a woman. It stresses the value of this approach by contrasting Buffy (who resists being "carried away by vampires") with Coppola's "swooning" Mina (who doesn't),[2] but it fails to acknowledge the film's mediocre reception both at home and abroad. The film may have deliberately resisted blockbuster status, but it was—less deliberately—only a very minor cult success. Clearly, the "mobilization of a Californian suburban girl" in the form of a martial arts battle between a camp vampire and a cheerleader was an insufficiently interesting premise for an audience that already had access to numerous films dealing with gender issues, horror, and the supernatural with far more sophisticated thrills and special effects and often better jokes: the early nineties saw the box office success not only of Coppola's *Dracula* but also of *Thelma and Louise* (USA, 1991), *The Crying Game* (Great Britain, 1992), *Barton Fink* (USA, 1991), and *Alien 3* (USA, 1992). Second, this reading predates an unusual related phenomenon—the production four years after the movie of a low-budget spin-off TV series that defied all predictions and became so successful that it went almost immediately into syndication, nearly single-handedly put the fledgling WB network on the map, and spawned a spin-off series of its own.

In this chapter I will suggest that the success of the series is not a mere accident of timing, but a result of the enormous differences in casting and scripting as well as form between the two versions. Far from being "resolutely local" in any sense, the new serialized world of Buffy encompasses alternate futures and a vast prehistory, explores "good" and "bad" Europeanness, and enables the creation of a vision of American teenagers in which female empowerment—though crucial—is only part of the picture. In the series, I want to argue, the small town of Sunnydale, California (the "Hellmouth"), is the embodied nightmare vision of a world power beset by anxieties about faith, morality, and the future and in need of a reinterpretation of its immigrant past. Sunnydale, in a nutshell, is a place in which the local, endangered, but disengaged American adolescence portrayed in the film is allowed to mature into a globally aware and morally forearmed but distinctly liberal young adulthood patently absent from it. This new politicization is a crucial factor in the series' success.[3]

Both versions were the brainchild of screenwriter/director/producer Joss Whedon *(Alien Resurrection, Toy Story, Roseanne)*. The original concept as described by Nancy Holder, coauthor of the *Buffy* novels and *Watcher's Guides,* is very close to Whedon's heart: "Joss doesn't think he'll ever do anything this personal again—because there isn't anything this personal."[4] It is also described by George Snyder, the show's head of development and one who has been with the project since the beginning, as to some extent rooted in Whedon's own history, a result, in some ways, of a combination of a difficult high school experience in England (where his English teacher mother sent him to protect him from poor California high schools) and his early avid interest in horror comics and B movies.[5] Whedon himself cites *Tomb of Dracula, Blade, Lost Boys, Near Dark, Night of the Comet, The Blob,* and the comic art of Gene Colan as powerful influences.[6] There was a crucial shift in Whedon's re-visioning of these influences, however. In the words of George Snyder, "Joss thought, why does the pretty girl always

go into the alley and get killed by the monster [in these narratives]?
What would happen if she went into the alley and beat the crap out of
it? Now *that* would be interesting."[7] This is a subversion of the laws of
early horror; it ignores the subversion already present in later horror
films in which, as Carol Clover has demonstrated, there is almost always a "final girl"[8] who does indeed "beat the crap" out of the monster.
Buffy's narrative raison d'être is manifestly as a perpetual "final girl,"
and she therefore owes much to the later slasher/horror films explored
by Clover. More, the concept as a whole obviously spans several other
genres including action-adventure and comedy. Nonetheless, its rooted-
ness in early American horror makes it appropriate, I think, to draw on
Robin Wood's much used but still valuable work on the American horror film tradition, particularly as I want to treat the *Buffy* phenomenon
in terms of its cultural significance, and for this I need a model of what
ideological work the screen monster might be doing at a given historical
moment.

In Wood's model, the horror film is a site where surplus repression—
the mechanism that makes us into "monogamous heterosexual bourgeois patriarchal capitalists"[9]—is embodied and dramatized in the
figure of the monster, be it a vampire, a shark, or an amorphous blob.
He suggests, "one might say that the true subject of the horror genre
is the struggle for recognition of all that our civilization *re*presses or
*op*presses: its re-emergence is dramatized, as in our nightmares, as an
object of horror, a matter for terror, the 'happy ending' (where it exists)
typically signifying the restoration of repression."[10] For Wood there is a
clear trajectory through this horror tradition that is simultaneously and
increasingly American and primarily centered on the family. Monsters
within this tradition range from the "foreign" threat of the 1930s and
1940s, through the domestic moral panic of the 1950s (particularly
where this centers on the teenager), to the psychological, satanic, family-
threatening monsters of the 1960s, 1970s, and 1980s.[11] In this model it
is possible to "read" the monster's "meaning" by the global, national,
and/or social history that surrounds its screen embodiment.

But here we come up against a limitation—or perhaps point to a
necessary emendation—of Wood's work. As we have seen, *Buffy* the series self-confessedly owes its existence to *all* these historical precedents.
Far from being a discrete narrative block that, like all of Wood's filmic
examples, exists as a universe unto itself (even allowing for sequels),
much of the *Buffy* series' success is predicated on a sharply knowing
comic intertextuality entirely missing from the film version; jokes, characters, visual styles, and even special effects consistently depend on a

vast range of popular culture references, both within and outside the horror genre. Further, if we take Wood's thesis to its suggested conclusion and read the horror film in terms of closure, either as a necessary annihilation and re-repression of the monster (the "reactionary" film) or as offering the possibility of social revolution (the "progressive" film) or—more likely—as an uneasy amalgam of the two,[12] then *Buffy* the TV show presents us with a problem because it represents an entirely different narrative structure and therefore entirely different sets of ideological possibilities. In *Buffy* the TV series the repressed that returns is polysemous, multifaceted, *serialized*. There is a new demon, a new development, and a new character in focus almost every week, coexisting alongside a slower-maturing narrative (usually Buffy's, but also her shadow monster's) across and between several episodes and/or an entire season, the whole framed by the sense of a school year passing. This seriality mobilizes a different kind of viewing experience from that available in narrative cinema, positing different types of closure or openendedness, and, perhaps, allowing for a more complex politics.

Buffy's form, its borrowings, its richly metaphoric return to a variety of monster types from a variety of periods, raises a new question. What is the contemporary cultural significance of a hugely successful show like this? Here the monsters are not just metaphors for Californian teenage sex angst whose successful resolution leads to "the mobilization of a Californian suburban girl." They are also rooted in the history of horror, a history that obsessively depicts U.S. anxieties about relations between the Old and New worlds, and they permit the audience to engage with a vast range of characters and/or cultural Others over a period of several years. In order to understand what makes this version of *Buffy* so successful and what that might be able to tell us about contemporary U.S. culture, it is necessary to evaluate the effects of differences in casting, scripting, and the serial form itself.

None of the original members of the cast of the film made it to the TV series (the one potential crossover was Seth Green, who plays a minor vampire in the film and an important, main character werewolf in the series, but was cut from the final version of the film).[13] In place of Kristy Swanson as Buffy, we have Sarah Michelle Gellar—equally blonde, equally pretty, equally dressed, made-up, and lit to emphasize her youth and Anglo-Saxon purity (she may wear miniskirts and strappy tops, but she sleeps in her bra). But unlike the statuesque Swanson, Gellar is tiny—towered over by demons and friends alike. This emphasizes the importance of the strength, resourcefulness, and athleticism that accompany her calling as Slayer and the extent to which that calling is a metaphor for girl power. The fact is acknowledged in the advertisements that accompany each product: posters for the film show Swanson, powerful thighs apart, occupying the full frame and dwarfing her male costar, while early posters accompanying the TV series emphasize the contrast between Gellar's frail, childlike, girly prettiness and the symbolism of the stake in her hand. It is also acknowledged diegetically: on being told that the end of the world is nigh in the season 1 finale "Prophecy Girl," techno-pagan computer science teacher Jenny Calendar takes the news phlegmatically, commenting, "the part that gets me, though, is where Buffy is the Slayer. She's so *little*." The idea has moved on, both narratively (episode 1 of the first season picks up where the film left off, with Buffy and her mother starting a new life in Sunnydale after Buffy's expulsion from the L.A. high school of the film) and conceptually (with the metaphor now occupying center stage). Now, as Snyder emphasizes, "the metaphor drives the show."[14]

Changed, too, is the position occupied by Buffy's "Watcher," the British scholar, part of a British Council of Watchers learned in monster lore and weaponry, who trains and supports her. In the film her Watcher was Merrick, played by Canadian Donald Sutherland eccentrically dressed in large floppy hats and long scarves but—apart from the passable accent and the oblique reference to Tom Baker's Doctor Who—not really readable as a stereotypical Brit. Merrick dies in the movie, and his replacement in the series takes an important next step. Rupert Giles (played by Anthony Stewart Head) is a stuffy, tweed-clad, technophobic school librarian whom, among Buffy's new friends, only the computer-nerd Willow thinks is cool because he comes from "some British museum—or possibly *the* British Museum—I'm not sure" ("Welcome to the Hellmouth"). Snyder explains that the significance of this stereotyping of the Watcher in the series lies in his contrast with the Buffy character—he provides a diametric opposite for the fun-loving, shallow, California high school girl.[15]

The implications of this national and generational opposition are important. In the second episode of season 1 ("The Harvest") Giles's position as British and therefore old-fashioned is marked by his technophobia: "It may be that you can wrest some information from that dread machine," he tells Buffy and "the Slayerettes," indicating the computer as they explore the origins of their first opponent, the Master. When they all stare blankly at him he adds sheepishly, "That was a bit British, wasn't it?" "Welcome to the New World," Buffy says wryly. Rhonda V. Wilcox rightly reads this scene as evidence of a "generational division" suggested by "language patterns,"[16] but there are also important national and political implications that she tends to overlook. Within the mythology of *Buffy,* the Watcher is also "called" to his or her destiny, though unlike the Slayer, who is elected by a Higher Order (here readable as the Christian God, if in a feminist version), the Watcher achieves it through heredity. In a comic and crucial exploration of the collision of the worlds of hereditary power and republicanism, Giles explains to Buffy how he came to accept his "destiny" (for which we might, I think, read "role as a responsible citizen"), having initially rejected it when it was explained to him at the age of ten. Though his father and grandmother were Watchers, he had ambitions to become "a fighter pilot—or maybe a grocer" ("Never Kill a Boy on the First Date"). He later dropped out of Oxford in order to dabble in the occult ("The Dark Age") before finally bowing to "destiny."

Giles's past is revealed very slowly through the first three seasons, both to the characters and to the audience. It emerges that not only was he something of a hell-raiser and possibly also a thief (in "The Dark Age" he tries to find a solution to his problems in the bottom of a bottle, and in "Dead Man's Party" he hot-wires his car, a skill that he describes as "like riding a bike"), but he had—and in some cases still has—murderous tendencies ("The Dark Age," "Passion"). In the season 3 episode "Band Candy," while under the influence of the regressive qualities of magic chocolate that has turned the town's adults back into teenagers, he revisits that wild youth, takes up smoking, adopts a Cockney accent, throws a brick through a shop window, steals a coat, and has sex with Buffy's mother on the hood of a police car. These developments point to a complex interplay between national stereotypes and the process of growing up, here inscribed through the slow evolution and maturation of the Buffy character across some thirty-plus hours of television. In effect, as Giles becomes a "naturalized" citizen of Sunnydale, California, the stereotype that he initially represents is gradually broken down. The arrival of a replacement and even stuffier British Watcher after Giles's firing for unorthodox practices in season 3 highlights the extent not just of his change, but of the change in the American teenagers' attitudes toward him as their knowledge and maturity have increased. Within a couple of episodes, indeed, Buffy is able to penetrate the mind of the very "proper" new Watcher, Wesley, and discover his inner teenager—his secret lust for head cheerleader and archbitch Cordelia. This is a revelation that by this stage is a surprise to no one, though it is doomed to failure: Wesley might be referred to as Pierce Brosnan and then James Bond, but he—and they as British action heroes—are also coded effeminate (in "The Prom" he refers to English public school cross-dressing practices, and in "Graduation Day, Part 1" the attraction between Cordelia and himself is ruined by an incredibly awkward first kiss). Within the show's vast metaphoric universe, as I will demonstrate, knowledge and tolerance of (or the decision to reject) difference in the embodiment of a single character frequently relies on his or her nationalized characteristics. Giles's Britishness, like Wesley's, first stands in for the Otherness of adulthood and then for the unacceptable face of history (decadence/adolescence), but in both cases it finally merges into an acceptable version of Americanness. Giles's integration into the New World is complete when he supports Buffy's decision to leave the Council (sever all ties with the Old World) and sums up Wesley's character with the perfect hybrid phrase: "You have the emotional maturity of a blueberry scone" ("The Prom"). Wesley becomes Americanized when he transfers to the spin-off series *Angel* and learns to fight vampires, stand up for what is right, and date a cute rich girl.

It is worth noting here how crucial the Giles character is to Whedon's initial concept. Though Whedon wrote the movie script, Holder and Snyder agree that, unable to direct or develop the vision himself, he was somewhat disappointed in the result.[17] Whedon had a far freer hand in the TV series, directing and writing many episodes himself and playing a central role in all production decisions. The first character to be cast was that of Giles. Marcia Shulman, the casting director, recalls that on first reading the script she called Whedon with a problem: "Everyone I thought of while I read your script is dead [she told him]. And I started naming these really obscure characters from movies of the 30s and 40s."[18] Picking up on the connection with Whedon's initial early-horror concept was shrewd, but casting Anthony Stewart Head on her first day cemented her understanding of the vision and ensured her continuation on the show—Whedon loved the choice. Head's profile with TV fans is crucial to his persona as Giles—and to the metaphors that drive the narrative.

While Susan A. Owen has seen the Giles character as "decidedly feminized,"[19] there are a number of reasons why this reading is reductive. First, his character develops in strength, sex appeal, and action potential as the season progresses. He holds out under torture, he supports Buffy's unorthodox, antiauthoritarian methods, he has relationships with two attractive women, and on more than one occasion he proves himself courageous and skilled in a fight. Second, since he was most recently famous as the gentle, romantic mystery man in the Taster's Choice coffee commercials (Nescafe Gold Blend in Britain), Head's appearance as a stuffy, unattractive English school librarian resonates for TV audiences with that former persona, particularly as he often appears with a cup in his hand. As a consequence of this, Buffy and her friends' dismissal of their Watcher as asexual becomes symptomatic of *their* youth and naïveté, rather than *his* intrinsic nature. "Uh, you do know, right?" Willow asks Giles, regarding Buffy's first sexual encounter. "Oh, good. Because I just realized, you being a librarian and all, maybe you didn't know" ("Passion"). "Now, is it time for us to talk about the facts of life?" Xander asks him as the Slayerettes offer advice about dating Miss Calendar ("Some Assembly Required"). For the audience, armed with the foreknowledge of Head's previous roles, this undermining of the main protagonists' character assessments is richly ironic and invites the witnessing of their awakening as part of the viewing pleasure.

Whedon seized the opportunity presented by the series of revising the film's version of the Watcher. In one of many retrospective scenes, Buffy remembers her first calling to her sacred duty ("Becoming, Part 1"). Remaining true to the film's script and setting, Whedon replaced Swanson with Gellar and Donald Sutherland as Merrick with a stout, be-suited American actor who resembles nothing so much as a tax inspector—a far cry from the eccentric if unstereotypical British Merrick of the film and an even further cry from the tweed-clad Giles. The vision—and the distinction—are sharpened by the switch, as *Buffy* moves away from the camp Californian teen angst of the movie into the complex internationalism of the TV serial.

Giles's slow emergence as more than stuffy, boring, clever, responsible, and good simply because he is British and an adult is just one strand of the show's dense metaphorical matrix, however. At the end of the episode that reveals Giles's past ("The Dark Age"), Buffy makes clear the connection between her initial perception of Giles's good, stodgy Britishness as standing in for adulthood and her growing understanding of the naïveté of this assumption:

GILES: I never wanted you to see that side of me.
BUFFY: I'm not gonna lie to you. It was scary. I'm so used to you being a grown-up, and then I find out that you're a person.
GILES: Most grown-ups are.
BUFFY: Who would've thought.
GILES: Some are even short-sighted, foolish people.
BUFFY: So after all this time, we finally find out that we do have something in common which, apart from being a little weird, is kind of okay.

This moment of recognition is obviously an important turning point in their relationship and the development of their characters: it is the talk Buffy should be having with one of her parents. But if Giles can be seen as a stand-in father whose status as human the teenagers must learn to acknowledge, he can also be seen as representative of American ambivalence about the cultural invasion (past and present) that he embodies. "Maybe that's how they do things in Brit-tain," Principal Flutie warns Buffy, locking the school gates through which she was about to leave illegally on an ostensible errand for Giles, "where they got that Royal Family and all kinds of problems, but here in Sunnydale we don't leave campus while school is in session" ("The Harvest"). Here is a pre-echo, of course, of Giles's own days as a dropout, but it is also a reference to the American perception of European—and particularly British—decadence. In replacing a dangerous British lack of rules with a proud American consciousness of boundaries, Principal Flutie feels he is doing his job as an educator. This scene serves also, however, to ally Buffy-the-teenager with the Brit-without-morals: she is actually lying to the principal about the reason for her attempt to leave campus. On this level she is both an untrustworthy teenager and an intriniscally "good" American: her real errand, after all, is the fighting of evil. In the universe of *Buffy*, this is a simple moral choice—to tell the truth or to lie in order to slay—and she makes the right one. And to unpack the metaphor, her assertion of her right as an individual to defy authority and answer only to her own conscience is an assertion of her rights as a post-Enlightenment human being—or an American citizen.

The complexity of Giles's position as teen/adult, immigrant/Brit, lawless/lawgiver is thrown into sharp relief by his many counterparts on the "purely evil" side of the equation. Monsters frequently appear in *Buffy*, as in many horror movies (*The Blob*, both *Jaws* films, and so on and so on),[20] whenever a couple transgresses moral boundaries. References to the dangerous side of dating are many and frequently comic during the first two seasons of *Buffy*; Xander's love interests (aside from the unattainable Buffy herself) turn out to be a praying mantis ("Teacher's Pet"), a life-draining mummy ("Inca Mummy Girl"), the archbitch Cordelia ("What's My Line? Part 2"), and then his oldest friend Willow ("Homecoming"). While not embodied in monster form, strictly speaking, this last dalliance sets off a whole train of horrific events including the impaling of Cordelia near the region of her heart when she catches the two of them kissing ("Lover's Walk"). By this time, we get the message. In season 4 he sets up home in his parents' basement with an ex-demon, Anya, as he matures into the realization that everyone has a history and maybe also a dark side. Willow's first romance (apart from the oblivious and then forbidden Xander) is with an e-mail demon called Moloch, and her second-season boyfriend

Oz turns into a werewolf three days out of the month. The verdict is still out, but it seems certain that her fourth-season foray into lesbian coupledom is also doomed to be traumatic. Buffy's experiences include a danger-lover with a death wish ("Never Kill a Boy on the First Date"); a wealthy cult-worshipping college boy who plans to sacrifice her to a giant snake demon, which it is hard not to read as an embodiment of patriarchal capitalism ("Reptile Boy"); a jock who turns into a fish ("Go Fish"); and an ongoing love affair with the show's most important liminal figure, Angel, the vampire with a soul. Angel has been her mystery friend and helper since episode 1. True to the monster-as-hidden-desire tradition, he first shows his vampire face when his passion is aroused during their first kiss ("Angel"). Buffy spends several episodes trying to come to terms with the dark side of Angel while fighting other demons, but finally gives in and loses her virginity to him on her seventeenth birthday ("Becoming, Part 2"), not knowing that this will break the curse that makes him half-human, destroy his soul, and turn him into the classic Insensitive Male After Sex, complete with the line "Love ya too. I'll call ya" ("Innocence").

The adults in the series fare no better. Giles's relationship with Jenny Calendar is beset by supernatural difficulties, and its physical side is constantly interrupted by demons. They get together over the shared problem of how to cast Willow's demon boyfriend out of the Internet ("I Robot, You Jane") and bond over an apocalypse threat ("Prophecy Girl"), but their budding romance is interrupted by a demon from Giles's past arriving in Sunnydale and possessing Jenny ("The Dark Age") just as she indicates her readiness to sleep with him. They put things on hold, but their gradual reconciliation is brought to an abrupt halt when Angel, now soulless, breaks her neck and plants her corpse in Giles's rose-strewn bed ("Passion"). Buffy's mother's new boyfriend turns out to be a murderous robot ("Ted"), and her next dalliance is the eternally embarrassing one with Giles under the influence of magic chocolate ("Band Candy"). No one in this universe—as in the classic horror film—gets laid for free.

Crucially, though, more often than not these demons come from Europe. The Moloch episode opens in fifteenth-century Italy. The Master, Buffy's season 1 opponent, is a six-hundred-year-old vampire who has been in the New World for only sixty of them. Eyghon, Giles's nemesis, is Etruscan. Luke, an early season 1 vampire and the Master's right-hand man, had a run-in with a previous slayer in nineteenth-century Madrid. Der Kindestod—a facet of Death itself—is German. Most of the series' most dangerous and enduring vampires (Spike, Drusilla, Angel,

Darla) have European histories and speak of Europe as a veritable play-ground for their kind. This history plays a vital role in the functioning of the metaphors that these monsters embody.

Foremost among the vampires is Buffy's boyfriend, Angel. Unlike most of the other demons, Angel came to the United States not because the "mystical convergence" of dark forces at the Hellmouth promise him apocalypse parties and easy pickings, but in order to find a home for his tortured soul, the restoration of which has made him neither good nor evil, neither human nor wholly demon (a casualty, we might say, of nineteenth-century European social and political upheaval). Hail-ing originally from Ireland—like many of America's immigrants—he was turned into a vampire by Darla in 1753, and for a century and a half he wreaked havoc in Europe until a gypsy curse restored his soul (his conscience), condemned him to eternal torment, and drove him to the New World. There, unable at first to find an identity and living in the gutter, he loses his Irish accent (thankfully for all concerned) and finally becomes "naturalized" with the help of a demon called Whistler who gives him the chance to "become a person" ("Becoming, Part 1"). He then takes up arms against his own kind to help Buffy, abandoning his liminal status for a clear moral stance—until having sex with Buffy turns him back into a bad European. A dangerous immigrant, Angel embodies a whole series of cultural anxieties: not just "sex is bad," but the repressed evil of European decadence returning to tempt young America; the fluidity of immigrant identity and the mutability of bor-ders (like most vampires since Stoker's Dracula, he needs no passport, visa, or green card in order to enter a country); the demon of sexual de-sire transmissible from a monster male to a pure female; the torment of moral choice and the temptation of surrendering to the wrong choice.

Snyder sums up Whedon's concept of the show's monsters in terms that are crucial to an understanding of its political subtext: "People who are evil don't know they are evil [Whedon insists]. They have no choice."[21] Imbued with the myth of European moral decadence and political constraint, the monsters in *Buffy* immigrate to the New World to prey on the inhabitants of a less politically constrained but perpetually morally challenged republic. In Sunnydale, the demon "his-tory" converges on the dark side of the American dream. Giles's job as Watcher then—both narratively and metaphorically—is not only to educate the teenagers in adulthood, providing paternal support in a world of dysfunctional families (Buffy's parents are divorced, Willow's are unrealistic, Xander's are oblivious, and Cordelia's never figure at all except to provide clothes and cars and then to let her down by losing all their money). He must also both embody and help to combat through knowledge the Old (bad) World that here—through the explicit use of national/generational parallels—represents adolescence itself. The value of Giles in the fight against evil is that he has both been there and done that.

There are, of course, many monsters in the series that embody "purely human" concerns, and if these are frequently Western and capitalist, they are at least released by the Hellmouth (life in contemporary America writ large) and owe little or nothing to history and the Old World. In "Nightmares" the repressed that returns and is defeated is the monstrous embodiment of childhood fears. In "Witch" it is pressure from an aspirational parent. In "Out of Sight, Out of Mind" it is the literal invisibility of the unpopular students in the fiercely hierarchical world of high school. In "Ted" it is the powerlessness of a child in the face of the world of parental relationships, and in "Dead Man's Party" it is human relationships in general. But the centrality and endurance of two major monstrous figures in the series tend to overshadow these more general demons. The first is Angel, whose liminality has already been noted as vital to the show's multilevel constructions of meaning. The second is the punk vampire Spike, whose unintegrated Britishness, apparently unredeemable badness, and undeniable presence as the adolescent-as-Other bring me to the second of my main themes here: the complex pleasure of this text for a TV viewer who, judging by the fan mail, might come from almost any country in the world, and whose average age is statistically likely to be closer to thirty than to sixteen.[22]

Spike arrives in Sunnydale with a bleached-blond punk hairstyle, a '57 Chevy, a live-in girlfriend, and an attitude ("School Hard"). He is almost always given the funniest lines and the coolest clothes, and he lives an attractive devil-may-care, after-dark existence. In Robin Wood's terms, he represents the centrality "to the effect and fascination of horror films [of] their fulfillment of our nightmare wish to smash the norms that oppress us and which our moral conditioning teaches us to revere."[23] In episode after episode, Spike returns to enable a thrilling temporary vicarious existence with the "cool," "bad," "rebellious" side of teen age—here resoundingly coded British and Other—while his constant reappearance carries the complementary pleasure of the knowledge that in this universe he will always be defeated. Spike and his fey British girlfriend Drusilla are the show's Sid and Nancy; in one third-season episode ("Lover's Walk") he even departs singing along to Vicious's version of "My Way."[24] The connection is made so explicit, in fact, that an academic article erroneously refers to him *only* as "Sid."[25] It is an interesting mistake. Spike's "badness" is in fact frequently signaled *only* by his British teenage rebelliousness; most of the vampires in Buffy can "pass" (to use Nancy Holder's important racially inflected term)[26] as human, displaying their "vamp" faces only when they feed, feel desire, and/or want to reveal themselves. This aspect reinforces the vamp-as-hidden-desire metaphor in obvious ways. Spike, however, does not need his "vamp" face in order to be coded "bad"; his hair, clothes, and accent do the work. He is, to put it simply, the scary face of adolescence, an adolescence that (unlike that of Giles and—we hope—unlike that of our developing teen heroes) refuses to end. It is an adolescence that is dangerously attractive; Spike's lifestyle leaks disturbingly over into the lives of Buffy and the Slayerettes. Their favorite nightclub, the Bronze—situated in "the bad part of town" ("Welcome to the Hellmouth")—constantly draws vampires to feed, and the diegetic music and MTV video-style segments that frequently signal moments of emotional trauma in the show are indistinguishable from the music played in the trendy gothic setting of Spike and Drusilla's lair ("Becoming, Part 1"). Effortlessly crossing other boundaries, too, Spike is frequently the voice of wisdom, articulating truths about human relationships and comically exploding the other characters' self-deceptions ("Lover's Walk," "Innocence"). Part of his appeal, indeed, is the constant revelation of ambiguity and the constant affirmation of its rejection that he embodies.

Asked what the cultural significance of a vampire narrative like *Buffy* might be, both Holder and Snyder suggest that the 1990s vampire represents the Western—and particularly American (even more particularly Californian)—cult of youth and longevity.[27] This aspect of the vampire myth is referred to several times in the show, though it is also given an interesting twist. In "Lie to Me," Billy Fordham, an old friend of Buffy's, arrives in Sunnydale pretending continued friendship but secretly bent on striking a deal with Spike that will dispel the hopelessness of his inoperable brain tumor—he will deliver Buffy in return for immortality as a vampire. "A couple more days and we'll get to do the thing that every American teenager has the right to do," Fordham tells his vampire-worshipping companions, "die young and stay pretty." This is the attractive side of vampirism—the chance to freeze-frame at one's physical peak, to live the energy, beauty, and irresponsibility of the teen age in perpetuity. In the season 1 finale, "Prophecy Girl," however, Buffy's main opponent is the Master, a six-hundred-year-old vampire who is beginning to decay, whose visage is horrific, and whose only remnants of his teenage years are his cult status and his immorality. The Master kills Buffy and is released on the world, but she is revived by Xander administering CPR. "You're dead!" the Master exclaims as she confronts him once more. "But I'm still pretty," she quips before administering the death blow. This aspect of the series' mythology (even vampires age eventually) creates an important related mythology around an idealized American teen age. Buffy's journey is to adulthood, during which she gains sufficient knowledge not only to defeat evil more effectively, but also to defeat the institutional skeptics who expelled her from her first high school; she achieves a high enough SAT score to progress to college. This knowledge is crucially informed by Old World history—not only the history of demons, but also the history of adults who were once teenagers (frequently Brits who have become naturalized Americans). What her riposte to the Master suggests is that the ideal teen age is characterized by an Americanness in which prettiness and power can go hand in hand and that, with right behind it, it can progress to an adulthood in which power and goodness are beauty that will never fade.

Spike's unredeemable adolescence serves as a contrast to Buffy's character and position as idealized American—and on this level he is too useful to be killed. By season 4 he has been altered by life in the New World through the implantation of a chip that, though it leaves his fundamental badness intact, prevents him from harming anyone. Like Angel, he has benefited from immigration. In Spike's case it is initially the enforced triumph of science over superstition rather than a moral evolution that enables his integration, though by season 5 the implant has begun to reawaken the bad poet in him, drawing latent romance from his self-constructed Gothicism and persuading him that he is in love with Buffy and has a duty to protect her "sister" Dawn. This love might be unrequited—Buffy constantly expresses her profound disgust at the thought—but the alternate possibilities that the show's supernatural premise enables means that the liaison frequently happens anyway. In two separate episodes in season 5, Buffy appears to return his feelings—once in his dreams as she kisses him and declares her desire, and again when she is placed under a spell that has her in love with and engaged to him. In yet another episode, Spike creates a Buffy robot (played, of course, by Gellar) to have sex with, and by the end of that episode the *real* Buffy is pretending to be robot Buffy in order to seduce information out of him. When he shows himself to be honorable after all, she drops the act and kisses him for real, having learned that despite his appearance and four seasons of easy assumptions about his status as enemy, he too has a good side. Like his comic articulation of the truth, this interplay between disgust and desire, bad and good, violence and love perpetuates and reinforces the tensions that underpin the show. Spike, in a similar way to Giles, represents both the threat and its solution, evil (decadence) and the knowledge to defeat it. If from the Old World comes the demon "history," from the Old World also comes the solution "experience." It usually can only be mobilized through New World reinterpretation—both technological (computers, better weapons, microchips) and ideological (morality, hope, religious faith, integration, even consumerism—in "Welcome to the Hellmouth" Buffy spots vampires not by using her inbuilt mythologized Slayer-sense, but by their outdated clothes). But the closure of an episode frequently depends on an uneasy alliance between "history" and "experience," Old and New, bad and good, which have referents in many texts and multiple international media. In *Buffy*, the Sex Pistols and Scooby Doo end up on the same side.

Working knowingly within a paradigm that depends on intertextuality has enabled the producers of *Buffy* to create a world in which multiple and frequently liberal-inflected meanings are not only possible but actively encouraged. The show is packed with pop-culture references both past and present, from the reference to the British punk scene to the naming of dozens of American pop-culture icons. These not only encompass literary and filmic representations of vampires from Anne Rice to *Near Dark*, the *Lost Boys*, and *Nick Knight*, but range gleefully from the Marvel and DC comics, *The Little Rascals, The Wizard of Oz,* and *The Invisible Man*, through *Charlie's Angels, Gidget*, Snoopy, *The Shining, The Exorcist*, Michael Jackson, and *The A-Team*, to *The X-Files, Sabrina the Teenage Witch*, and *Xena: Warrior Princess*. While not recognizing them does not interfere with narrative comprehension and pleasure, spotting them enables both a different kind of pleasure (often the getting of a joke) and a whole new set of meanings. In both situating itself explicitly as existing within a tradition and positioning its characters as fans of that tradition (makers of meaning themselves), *Buffy* invites the carrying of its metaphors across texts and lives. It often uses knowledge of this tradition to signal its own progressive project: in the opening scenes of the first episode, for example, we are given the classic horror movie scenario of a darkened building, a teenage couple breaking in for an illicit rendezvous, and the boy eager to indulge while the girl expresses shyness and doubt. In a startling reversal of the conventions, however, it is the girl who is suddenly revealed as the killer in vamp face, and the boy who is punished.

The positive side of this pop-culture tradition is, of course, as the above list demonstrates, generally firmly American—the *Wizard of Oz* is a stark contrast to the Sex Pistols, and if Buffy's workout music is coded teens only, Giles's alternative—the Bay City Rollers—is coded British bad taste. But the increasing exposure of Giles's own musical skills (he can play guitar and sing), which impress the Slayerettes, is one more facet of the acceptable face of Britishness (its music) emerging in unexpected places. To give another example, in "I Robot, You Jane" Buffy says, "I can just tell something is wrong. My spider sense is tingling," and when Giles looks quizzically at her, she adds, "Pop-culture reference. Sorry." She is implying that this kind of knowledge is nation- as well as generation-specific: she assumes that, being British and a grown-up, Giles won't understand. But the show's interplay between national and generational stereotypes and their exposure as ill-founded implicitly acknowledge its audience's capacity to recognize the fact that Buffy's statement represents naïveté, not truth. Here we—if "we" are the twenty-nine-ish audience—laugh at her as much as with her.

The show also deliberately draws attention to its own techniques with references to textual and psychoanalysis, inviting the exploration of what is really being repressed, returned, and defeated. To give just a few examples, in "Ted" Giles remarks, "Buffy, I believe the subtext here is rapidly becoming text"; also in "Ted" Xander taunts, "You're having parental issues, you're having parental issues—Freud would have said the exact same thing. Except he might not have done that little dance"; in "Welcome to the Hellmouth" Cordelia demands, "God, what is your childhood trauma?"; in "Killed by Death" she asks, "So this isn't about you being afraid of hospitals because your friend died and you wanna conjure up a monster that you can fight so you can save everybody and not feel so helpless?"; and in "When She Was Bad" she tells Buffy, "Deal with it. Embrace the pain. Spank your inner moppet, whatever." By self-parodying some of the pleasures of its text, the show simultaneously concedes the limits to its producers' control of meaning. In showing us some of the wires, it acknowledges our capacity to choose not to see them, to hold the narrative—and the interest—together for ourselves. Nancy Holder's answer to the problem of gaps in her own monster lore indicate the extent to which the whole Buffy project thinks of itself as interactive: "I go on the Web," she explains. "If I don't know something, the fans will."[28]

The universe of Buffy is still in some ways rooted in conservatism. This is a deeply moral and ideologically constructed universe in which violence is "bloodless,"[29] only baddies smoke, the family with all its problems is posited as an ideal, and white American adulthood is the governing norm. But its constant exploration of the difficulties—and the cost—of attaining these ideals undermines any simplistic notion of their "rightness" and "naturalness." The episode in which Buffy reveals her secret identity to her mother is a sensitive handling of a form of coming out, and it was written as such:[30] this gendering of America's ideal future as female owes more to *Ellen* than it does to *Sabrina the Teenage Witch*. The show's producers might balk at portraying lesbian sex with the same freedom as they portray heterosexual sex, but Willow's fourth-season relationship with Tara has become perhaps the show's most stable on-screen pairing. If Christianity is the only workable faith in this universe (feminist though it might be in its adoption of a girl crusader) in that even Willow Rosenberg nails crucifixes to her wall, then it can also be argued that it is merely drawing attention to the hollowness of Christian iconography: it is pagan spells, not crucifixes, which keep the redemonized Angel out of Buffy's house in that same episode. In *Buffy* the cross, like garlic, is of only limited use: the "good" that helps to combat the "evil" of the monster is nondenominational. And the richness of its metaphors enables the mobilization of myriad readings—sufficient to create new fans wherever it is shown in the world. If the Old World is coded "the bad side of adolescence," it is also coded "teacher" and, at the level of viewing pleasure, as pure "fun."

Notes

1. Ken Gelder, *Reading the Vampire* (London: Routledge, 1994), 143.

2. Ibid.

3. I am able to concentrate here only on the first and second seasons, but I will refer where appropriate to later episodes.

4. Quoted from my own interview with Nancy Holder, San Diego, California, 9 August 2000.

5. Taken from my own interview with George Snyder, head of development at Mutant Enemy, Inc., Santa Monica, California, 14 August 2000.

6. Christopher Golden and Nancy Holder, *Buffy the Vampire Slayer: The Watcher's Guide*, vol. 1 (New York: Pocket Books, 1998), 242.

7. Interview with Snyder, 14 August 2000.

8. Carol J. Clover, *Men, Women, and Chainsaws: Gender in the Modern Horror Film* (Princeton, N.J.: Princeton University Press, 1992).

9. Robin Wood, "An Introduction to the American Horror Film," in *Movies and Methods*, vol. 2, ed. Bill Nichols (Berkeley: University of California Press, 1985), 197.

10. Ibid., 201; emphasis in original.

11. Ibid., 207.

12. Ibid., 215.

13. Golden and Holder, *Buffy: The Watcher's Guide,* vol. 1, 224.

14. Interview with Snyder.

15. Interview with Snyder.

16. Rhonda V. Wilcox, "There Will Never Be a 'Very Special' Buffy": Buffy and the Monsters of Teen Life," *Journal of Popular Film and Television* 27, no. 2 (summer 1999): 16.

17. Interview with Holder; interview with Snyder.

18. Golden and Holder, *Buffy: The Watcher's Guide,* vol. 1, 270.

19. Susan A. Owen, "*Buffy the Vampire Slayer*: Vampires, Postmodernity, and Postfeminism," *Journal of Popular Film and Television* 27, no. 2 (summer 1999): 24.

20. Wood, "An Introduction to the American Horror Film," 2: 216.

21. Interview with Snyder.

22. Snyder confirms that the pilot episodes of *Buffy* were shown first in urban college centers in the United States and achieved young-adult cult status before they became popular with younger teens. Intriguingly, the age of the average *Buffy* viewer is now put at twenty-nine.

23. Wood, "An Introduction to the American Horror Film," 2: 205.

24. Although, as Brian Wankum explains in Nancy Holder, Jeff Mariotte, and Mary Elizabeth Hart, *Buffy: The Watcher's Guide,* vol. 2 (New York: Pocket Books, 2000), 441, the sound track which is used is not actually Vicious at all but Gary Oldman playing Vicious in the 1986 film *Sid and Nancy.* There were copyright reasons for this switch, but it is tempting to note yet another strand of the show's intertextuality in that Oldman also played Coppola's Dracula.

25. Owen, "*Buffy:* Vampires, Postmodernity, and Postfeminism," 27–28.

26. Interview with Holder.

27. Interviews with Holder and Snyder.

28. Interview with Holder.

29. Interview with Snyder.

30. Interview with Snyder.

Part III
Fans

9

How to Tell the Difference between Production and Consumption: A Case Study in Doctor Who Fandom

Alan McKee

> Marx considered "productive work" in a very par-
> ticular and specialized sense. . . . There is a very dif-
> ficult passage in the *Grundrisse* in which he argues
> that while the man who makes a piano is a produc-
> tive worker, there is a real question whether the
> man who distributes the piano is also a productive
> worker; but he probably is, since he contributes to
> the realization of surplus value. Yet when it comes
> to the man who plays the piano, whether to himself
> or others, there is no question: he is not a produc-
> tive worker at all. So the piano maker is base, but
> pianist superstructure.
>
> —*Raymond Williams*, Problems in Materialism
> and Culture: Selected Essays

■ Deciding what work counts as "production" and what as "consumption" is a difficult task for cultural theory. This essay emerges from
a sense that this binary category is proving remarkably intractable in
cultural analysis. Particularly—and surprisingly—it seems to me that
research on the "active audiences" of science fiction programs continues to employ this conceptual binary—even as it apparently challenges
it. I attempt to demonstrate that this is the case—and to suggest other
ways in which distinctions might be made between different kinds of

cultural production. Janice Radway, well known for her work arguing that audiences are not made up of passive consumers, suggests,

> Because it has been assumed for so long that consumption is indeed the conceptual opposite of production, scholars have also assumed quite unconsciously that the actual material and social processes of using mass-produced goods must be absolutely distinct from the material and social process of collective production and exchange.[1]

I suggest that, more than this, the very fact of dividing the circulation of texts into binary moments defines the whole way in which we think about culture. Such a binary demands a whole list of other binaries that are associated with production and consumption: active/passive, powerful/powerless, central/marginal, and so on. The consumption/production binary continues to structure our thinking about culture—even though it remains difficult to tell what a moment of production, or a moment of consumption, might be.

Active Consumption

In cultural theory, science fiction fandom has proven to be a particularly attractive object for writers wishing to discuss the "active" nature of audiences.[2] In the work of Henry Jenkins and Constance Penley on the science fiction television series *Star Trek,* in particular, it is obvious that the writers are determined to challenge any belief that audiences are passive consumers. In their descriptions of the practices of these "fans," these writers make them—explicitly—producers. Jenkins, for example, cites and challenges de Certeau who states, "The television viewer cannot write anything on the screen of his set. He has been dislodged from the product. He plays no role in its apparition."[3] Jenkins explicitly disagrees: "de Certeau is wrong to deny the possibility of readers 'writing in the margins' of the television text."[4] Similarly, Constance Penley states of members of these particular fan communities,

> They are not just reading, viewing or consuming in tactical ways that offer fleeting moments of resistance or pleasure while watching TV. . . .
> They are producing not just . . . acts, but real products.[5]

The acknowledgment of audiences as productive is not, in itself, particularly worthy of note. Indeed, in doing so, the writers are promoting what is by now almost an axiom in cultural studies—that there is no contradistinction between production and consumption. As formulated elegantly and clearly by John Hartley, this axiom may be stated thus: "To read texts is also to write them."[6]

What does particularly interest me about these writers, however, is what appears to be a form of *disavowal* about this question: one that I perceive acting more generally in cultural theory. For, having insisted that these fans are—like the makers of the television programs they discuss—"producers," the writers then want (quite correctly, I think) to find some way to *distinguish* between the different types of production under discussion: between the production of interpretations, the production of speech acts, the production of fanzines, the production of television programs. Obviously, if all of these instances were taken to be equivalent—simply because they are all moments of cultural "production"—the term would become meaningless. But in attempting to retain distinctions between "industry" and "fan" production, the writers return to precisely the binaries of "production" and "consumption" from which they explicitly want to escape.

Binary Distinctions

For Jenkins, "semiotic resistance" meets the limits placed on a text by the "producer":

> Semiotic resistance was not always enough to offset the producer's refusal to represent certain groups and concepts within the primary text.[7]

Power

Since Jenkins explicitly names his audience as being involved, in some way, in cultural production, what can he mean by "the producer's refusal to represent certain groups"? If the fans are involved in production, aren't they in some way producers? Similar binaries operate throughout Jenkins's and Penley's accounts of fan culture:

> A model of resistant reading quickly becomes profoundly patronizing if it amounts to telling already socially marginalized audiences that they should be satisfied with their ability to produce their own interpretations and should not worry too much about their lack of representation within the media itself.

Here, the binary distinguishes between the work done by the fans and "the media itself." Fans produce—but within limits set by "institutional power that may satisfy or defer audience desires."[8] And the institutional power under consideration is, presumably, that of mainstream media producers (it should not be understood as that of *fan* institutions, for example). A set of binaries is put in place: the powerful and the powerless. As Penley notes, as she distinguishes between "the SF mainstream" and "amateur writers," "the relatively powerless [are] attempting to resist, negotiate or transform the system and products of the relatively powerful."[9]

The question of power is one that continually recurs in writing about fan audiences. It is instructive that Jenkins gives readers the ability to produce interpretations, but it is to the institutions that produce broadcast texts that he grants power. Jenkins cites the work of coauthor John Tulloch when he goes on to characterize fans as a

> powerless elite . . . who claim a privileged relationship to the series by virtue of their mastery over its materials and yet who have little or no influence on "the conditions of production or reception of their show."[10]

He notes

> the fans' powerlessness over the narrative's development, of the degree to which the fans' own pleasures are often at the mercy of producers who operate from a very different agenda.[11]

In this, Jenkins is retaining some of the terms of a consumption/production binary. The fans may produce interpretations—but finally, there is the text, which is produced by the institutions of the media.

This idea is addressed more fully by John Tulloch. In his work on Doctor Who fans in the coauthored book (with Jenkins) *Science Fiction Audiences,* Tulloch suggests that the "powerless elite" of fans has "little control over the conditions of production . . . of 'their' show."

> We . . . asked the [Doctor Who Appreciation Society] executives . . . whether they had any influence on the production of the show. . . . "No, they don't take a great deal of notice."

For Tulloch, this demonstrates fans' "absence of power over . . . production of the series."[12] The fans do not produce the series. They produce only interpretations. Tulloch notes:

> the primary text [of *Doctor Who*] retained an authority, an aura which could not be successfully met by the home-made secondary texts which circulated around it. Local forms of grassroots cultural production at the site of the consumption were not substitutes for getting access to the mainstream media.[13]

Industries

Another binary used to structure the interpretation of fan culture by these writers is that of industry versus various forms of nonindustry.

They repeatedly make the distinction between the work of fans and that of the industry, insisting that these are quite different—again, binary opposite—forms of cultural production.[14] Fans do not have an industry—or if they do, it is a "mini-industry" or a "cottage industry."[15] Fan production is thus characterized in terms understood to be opposite to mainstream industrial production. For example, in this account, fans do not produce in order to make a profit; indeed, fan production is characterized by "a distaste toward making a profit."[16] Similarly, fan production is more open and democratic in organization.[17] In short, the attempts made by these writers to retain distinctions between different moments of cultural production rely on a series of familiar boundaries:

Producers	Fans
The media	Their own interpretations
Powerful	Powerless
Owners	Readers
Industry	Non/cottage/mini-industry
[production]	[consumption]

My point is that in these writings, a distinction is retained that is not that between different *kinds* of texts being produced by various groups or individuals—as might be suggested by the assumption of audiences as "productive." The distinction rather takes the form of a binary: one that retains the idea that fans are, finally, the consumers—*not* the producers—of the text (although they may be producers of zines and interpretations).

Disputations

My unease with this approach to distinction between forms of cultural production is basically an empirical one, although it can also be sustained by appeals to theoretical writing. From my analysis of *Doctor Who,* it seems that the distinction between the cultural production of fans and that of television producers is not nearly so distinct as these accounts might suggest. In attempting to trace the "power" of various groups, the status of the texts that are produced, and the relationship of all of these to modes of production, there is no clear dividing line. It is not simple to decide what counts as the primary text, the media itself. And ultimately, there can be no firm boundary set, I suspect, between the fan and the producer. John Tulloch quotes Gary Russell, the secretary of the Doctor Who Appreciation Society, who feels powerless in the production of *Doctor Who*: "they [the producers of the program] don't take a great deal of notice [of fans' wishes]"[18] However, by dint of the fact that Tulloch's research was completed several years before its publication in 1995, we are presented with a startling fact: by the time that Russell is presented publicly proclaiming his powerlessness, he has already been the editor of the official BBC-licensed *Doctor Who Magazine,* a commercial publication; the BBC has published several of his original Doctor Who novels; and he is only a year away from writing the official novelization of the only new episode of *Doctor Who* produced by the BBC in 1996. In 1997, he would go on to script the BBC's *Doctor Who* CD-ROM—the only new official Doctor Who audiovisual product produced by the BBC that year. In 1999, his production company, Big Finish, would be licensed by the BBC to produce a new series of Doctor Who (in an audio format). The question is a simple one—at what point did Russell stop being powerless? When did he stop being a fan and start being a producer? Can he be a producer, in the media itself—indeed, in the mainstream—and still be a fan?

Similarly, the accounts cited above of the differences between the fans and the industry do not seem entirely accurate. I think the authors are interested in the forms of production more than the texts themselves.[19] And if it were indeed the case that the mode of production determined the relation of the text to the mainstream, industry, the media itself, then it would only be necessary for a fanzine to be produced in a nondemocratic manner, for profit, and it would have equal status with the industry's texts. Obviously, this is not the case. More than this, empirical evidence makes clear that this account does not adequately explain the difference of fan production from industry production. There are tendencies within fandom to professionalism that stretch all the way up to the production of the broadcast television programs themselves. Many fan producers sell zines and audio or video productions for profit, and there are hierarchies of cultural status and earning power within fandom, just as there is in the media.[20] And fandom itself is by no means a democratic ideal:

> There is a recognised hierarchy, led by Trufans and BNFs (Big Name Fans) for whom Fandom is a Way of Life (FIAWOL). . . . British BNFs . . . may well be invited to join the masonic elite of the Knights of St Fandom.[21]

So while the ideal of the participatory-democratic, non-profit-making fan publishing collective is an understandably attractive one for any model of culture that relies on the production/consumption binary and thus the Marxist ideals with which it is associated, this is simply *not* the same thing as discussing fan production. Such models of production are indeed a part of fan work, but not all of it. In short, these writers claim to be writing about the difference between fans and producers—whereas, in fact, what they map out in their account of the differences of modes of production is a distinction between collective, non-profit-making modes of cultural production and capitalist modes of cultural production—a binary that maps quite poorly onto the fan/producer binary.

More than this, focusing on the lack of charge for many of the fan products does not necessarily mean that they are of a kind different from those texts produced by the mainstream. John Frow has pointed out that the distinction between the commodity and the gift is a slippery and difficult one that requires more sophisticated definitions and thinking than is usually the case. On close examination, he suggests that "the concepts of gift and commodity seem to partake of each other."[22] Working from Appadurai, he goes on to note that there is no simple distinction between forms of exchange, from commodity exchange to barter to the gift: "there is a calculative dimension in all these forms of exchange."[23] He suggests that "[t]he . . . stress laid by Appadurai and Kopytoff on the possibilities of movement between different contexts makes it difficult to continue using the notion of the commodity form as a sign of essential identity."[24] We cannot use modes of production as an accurate way of describing the different status of various kinds of texts.

Doctor Who—Binaries and Boundaries

A close study of the ways in which various kinds of Doctor Who texts have been circulated illustrates the difficulties with these binaries that these writers have used in order to understand fan culture. For example, the *Doctor Who Magazine* is the official, licensed BBC monthly magazine, professionally produced, for profit, by a major international publisher. It is edited and written by self-proclaimed Doctor Who fans—Gary Gillatt, Alan Barnes, Scott Gray—all of whom regularly write in the magazine as fans, for fans. Is this fan publishing? But in that case, how can we reconcile that with its capitalist status? On the other hand, is it mainstream? If so, how do we explain that a group of fans are creating the primary text that should, logically, belong only to the faceless and powerful producers?

Similarly, the most recent "serious" television production of *Doctor Who* was a one-off telemovie in 1996. It was produced by Philip Segal:

> Segal had watched *Doctor Who* as a child, at the side of his much-loved grandfather. The ideas and images of the programme had been jangling about in the back of his mind throughout his television career.[25]

Segal himself states:

> I feel exactly the same way about *Doctor Who* as I did before—I believe
> in it passionately. . . . It's a great programme. . . . It deserves to be loved
> the world over. . . . I think it should always be in the hands of people
> who are enthusiastic about it.[26]

The producer of the television program *Doctor Who* is a fan.

Doctor Who, as a television series, stopped *regular* production in
1989. One of the writers in the last, twenty-sixth season of the program
was Marc Platt:

> Platt had been a fan of *Doctor Who* since it first began, and had been
> submitting ideas to the production office since the mid-seventies.[27]

After the television series stopped production, the BBC licensed Virgin
Publishing to produce a series of original novels. Platt also wrote two of
these: *Cat's Cradle* and *Lungbarrow* (the latter based on an unproduced
television script on which he was working when the series was canceled).
The entire series of novels is written by self-named "Doctor Who fans."
One of the most prolific authors of this series of BBC-licensed Doctor
Who novels is Paul Cornell, who states in an interview, "A lot of fans
have a lot of trouble admitting it and parading it, but I'm quite proud
of it."[28] Cornell is also a professional television scriptwriter, part of the
industry, writing for *Coronation Street,* a British soap opera that regularly reaches sixteen million viewers.

As noted above, the "powerless" fan Gary Russell is one of the most
prolific writers in the range. Mark Morris—a professional horror writer and self-confessed fan—has also contributed to the range:

> The BBC took over production of the novels in 1997. The BBC em-
> ployee who works as the editor of the range is Steve Cole. Not only is
> he a fan, but a fan who has previously produced fanzines: "I had really
> atrocious artwork and letters published in *Skonnos* when I was about
> 13. In 1990 I wrote stuff for *TV Zone.*"[29]

In short, fans produce the television program, edit and write the official
novels, edit and write the official magazine. But what of the other unofficial fan productions that are not simply fanzines, not produced as
part of a democratic, anticapitalistic enterprise? What of, for example, unofficial videos and audio productions? What about the "Professor" audio
dramas produced with the stars of *Doctor Who* by BBV Productions?

> It's been nearly ten years since . . . former *Doctor Who* stars Sylvester
> McCoy and Sophie Aldred . . . played opposite each other; now, together

again in the science fiction dramas *Republica* and *Island of Lost Souls,* they are experiencing déjà vu playing a time-travelling Professor and his associate, Ace. Not only do they feature two of the show's most popular actors, the plays intend to emulate the style and appeal of *Doctor Who* in their storytelling.[30]

What of *The Stranger* videos, also produced by BBV, featuring the stars of *Doctor Who* playing roles similar to those played in the television program? And then there are the fanzines. And bulletin board comments about *Doctor Who,* often involving the producers, editors, and writers of the program.[31] And casual conversations over drinks. And private interpretations made of programs. At what point do we draw the line, claim here is production, the industry, and here are fans, the powerless, those who may produce, but do not really produce? Of course, we do not. We must find other ways than such simple binaries by which to distinguish between the cultural objects produced by different people. One way might involve employing the concept of canonicity.

The Canon

To make a short detour (simply to reject what I see as an obviously unhelpful possibility): we cannot simply use the number of people in the audience for a particular text in order to work out whether it is part of "the text." The *Doctor Who* television series reached, in its final season, around three million viewers. The magazine reaches only ten thousand, the official novels about the same number. Surely the texts have a different status culturally? Well, yes. But these numbers cannot be used to argue for a qualitatively different status for these texts. In America, a successful television program reaches tens of millions of viewers. In Australia, a program can be counted a success if it has one million viewers nationally, a spectacular success if it has two. There is no number above which the producers suddenly become powerful. The reach of a text is an element that must be borne in mind—but that does not, I think, provide a useful way of distinguishing between those texts that are products of the industry and those that are products of fans.

I find that the concept of canonicity—the decision as to what constitutes "real" *Doctor Who*—provides a more helpful way to approach these questions. Constance Penley suggests the point I am getting at here when she notes the importance of a moment in the Star Trek film *The Final Frontier,* which seems to play out the concerns of "slash" fanzine writers—the homoerotic relationship of James Tiberius Kirk and Mr. Spock:

Near the end of *Star Trek V: The Final Frontier,* Captain Kirk, thought
to be dead but rescued finally by Spock and some exceptionally helpful
Klingons, stands facing his first officer on the bridge of the Klingon ship.
Glad to be alive, he moves toward Spock and reaches for him with both
hands. Spock interrupts the embrace with "Please, Captain—not in
front of the Klingons."

Analyzing this moment, Penley suggests that

It is not yet clear what it will mean for the fans to have their desires
recognized, their fantasies ratified, not only by William Shatner, but,
indirectly, the Great Bird of the Galaxy, the fan's pet name for Gene
Roddenberry, who created *Star Trek.*[32]

It is a "fleeting public recognition of their illicit desires."[33] The difference between the slash fanzines discussed by Penley and the feature
film produced by the industry is not, in fact, one of mode of production. Rather, it is one of the filmic text's "ratified" status. It seems to
me, though, that previous writers have too easily mapped this canonicity back onto the binaries already noted. For example, Tulloch and
Jenkins state,

Semiotic resistance was not always enough to offset the producer's
refusal to represent certain groups and concepts within the primary
text: the primary text retained an authority, an aura which could not
be successfully met by the home-made secondary texts which circulated
around it.[34]

They recognize the "aura" that I am discussing, but see it as distributed according to a simple binary: the primary text has an aura; the
secondary text does not. Once again, producers have the power; the
fans do not. An analysis of *Doctor Who* suggests that, again, this is not
the case: that canonicity—aura, reality—is not distributed in a binary
manner according to modes of production. The question of what constitutes the program's canon is one that is hotly debated within Doctor
Who culture. In an article titled "Spiking the Canon," published in
the *Doctor Who Magazine,* the Doctor Who novelist Steve Lyons ex-
amines the concept of the canon. His discussion is a suggestive one
for any attempt to distinguish between those texts that are seen to be
authoritative—the products of those who are powerful, the industry—
and those that are not—the products of the powerless:

Ah, how well we all remember the Doctor's thrilling third encounter
with the Zarbi . . . Published in 1965 in the very first *Doctor Who* an-

nual. . . . Strangely though, I've yet to view a subsequent episode—or read a book or a comic strip—which refers back to "The Lair of Zarbi Supremo." . . . And why? You're probably screaming the answer at this page right now: it's not canonical!

So, er . . . What does that mean, exactly?

. . . *Doctor Who* has many grey areas. Its writers change regularly, as do its producers and stars. We disregard "The Lair of the Zarbi Supremo" even though it was written . . . by the series' first script editor, David Whitaker. Likewise, if a future episode of the series referred back to the events of [BBC radio Doctor Who production] "The Paradise of Death," [the *Doctor Who Magazine* letters page] would doubtless be filled with complaints from people who don't consider that radio drama to be canonical. But why should we exclude it, when it was written by seventies producer Barry Letts and starred [the *Doctor Who* cast]?[35]

Steve Lyons refers to "grey areas." And these should be borne in mind. Binaries—production/consumption, fan/producer, powerful/powerless— do not allow for gray areas. In attempting to map the canon—the primary text—it might at first seem commonsensical that its boundaries will be clear and well-defined. As the analysis of fan writing proceeds, however, it becomes obvious that such an assumption is mistaken. This can be seen, for example, in the comments of Doctor Who fan/BBC author Mark Morris:

> The first thing I ever wrote were three or four 250-page *Doctor Who* novels when I was about 11. I can't believe I've got a real *Doctor Who* book out now and become part of the mythos.[36]

The official BBC novels are "real" for this producer/fan. So if we accept that Penley's and Tulloch and Jenkins's accounts of the powerlessness of fan producers is in fact about powerlessness to affect the canon, then we see a significant shift: for the canon is *not* simply what is produced by the industry. It is a status granted to texts—of being real, of carrying authority—that is, finally, validated by *the fans themselves*—and not by the producers. For there is no simple production context that guarantees canonicity. Jenkins, writing about canonicity, sees it as a relatively weak tool of the "powerless elite" of fans:

> Constructing the program canon: the selection of a particular television series is simply the first stage in a larger evaluative process. Not every series episode equally satisfies the interests that initially drew fans to the program. . . . A primary function of fan publishing, then, is to

provide a public forum for evaluating and commenting on individual episodes.[37]

Here, the fans choose the canon from the real—i.e., transmitted television—text. In this view, canonicity is simply about choosing from an already existing text those elements that are to be validated. In short, fans make their own canon—but not under conditions of their own choosing. However, in studying Doctor Who fandom, it becomes apparent that the text—the program itself with which the fans have to work—is not as simple, pregiven, and industry-determined as this reading might suggest. Hartley proposes, "Television is recalcitrant when it comes to deciding where the text should stop,"[38] and in the case of Doctor Who, this occurs not only within television, but also outside of it. Take, for example, the problems Steve Lyon experiences as he attempts to decide what the canonical version of Doctor Who might include:

> The only possible justification [for rejecting the BBC radio Doctor Who] is that those stories didn't appear on the television screen. But where does that leave Children in Need's two-part EastEnders/Doctor Who crossover "Dimensions in Time"? Unfinished Fourth Doctor story "Shada"? Sixth Doctor, Tegan and Jimmy Savile-starring skit "A Fix with the Sontarans"? If you accept that "Shada" is canonical, then why not "The Nightmare Fair," that unproduced but in active preproduction Sixth Doctor versus the Toymaker saga intended to kick off Season Twenty-Three? . . . If you accept "The Nightmare Fair" on the basis of its subsequent Target Books novelisation, then why not the BBC books? They are official BBC productions, after all. And if you accept the BBC books, then why not Virgin's New Adventures . . . the official continuation of Doctor Who? Why not 1986's "secret origins" Companions novel Turlough and the Earthlink dilemma? Why not the PROBE videos which feature Carolyn John as Liz Shaw? Why not Richard Franklin's Recall UNIT fringe stage production? I could go on, but arguments about what comprises the Doctor Who canon have raged for years, and there are no easy answers.[39]

"[T]here are no easy answers," and this is indeed apparent when one reads the texts produced (sometimes officially, sometimes informally) by members of Doctor Who fandom. A review of an unlicensed audio adventure starring the seventh Doctor and his television companion states:

> In another medium, straight-to-video drama, Bill Baggs has previously presented the pairing of "the Stranger and Miss Brown" as portrayed by the Doctor/Companion team Colin Baker and Nicola Bryant—and

there was an ambiguous possibility that these people could be the Sixth
Doctor and Perpugillium Brown. . . . Here, the actors who played the
Seventh Doctor and Ace are playing characters with identical personalities to their television alter egos. . . . Is this really *Doctor Who* on
these CDs? I think so. . . . If they're not "real" *Doctor Who,* then I'm a
banana.[40]

Debates about what texts should be accorded this sense of ratification,
of being real or authentic texts—canonical texts—were particularly
visible on the newsgroup rec.arts.drwho during 1998:

Some of you old-timers may remember a survey I did last year on the
subject of canon. . . . I thought it might be interesting to try it again.
Obviously, I'd prefer simple "yes" or "no" answers, but I learned from
last year's responses to expect almost anything from you people. . . .

  1. *Everything* is canon
  2. Nothing is canon except the bits I like
  3. The original BBC television series
  4. The Paul McGann telemovie
  5. Virgin's New Adventures
  6. Virgin's Missing Adventures . . .[41]

This post goes on to suggest thirty-nine different categories of possibly canonical Doctor Who text. And it is instructive to note, in the responses to this post, not only a lack of agreement on what constitutes a
canonical—real, authentic—part of *Doctor Who,* but also a sense of uncertainty in individual responses. One post suggesting that "Everything
with *Doctor Who* on it is canon" was met with the response, "Even the
underpants?"; these underpants became an important symbol in this
debate about policing the boundaries of Doctor Who canonicity. All
posters agree that there must be limits. But how were these to be established? Consider a representative response:

  4. The Paul McGann telemovie
      Yes, unless a new series says it isn't . . .
  17. the DWM comic strip
      Some of it.
  18. other comics
      Probably not
  19. The Pescatons
      Not to me but that's not saying it isn't . . .
  22. Dimensions in Time

Er I'll get back to you . . .
24. The PROBE series
Not sure, don't see why not . . .
25. the Professor & Ace series
To me yes . . .
29. The Target novelizations
Not if they contradict canon elsewhere . . .
31. The Radio Times comics & specials
 · Not sure.[42]

For these fans, then, some of what the BBC publishes is canon—that is, some of the books have a status that is as real, authentic, and central as the original television series. The BBC coproduced telemovie (1996) appears to be slightly less canonical than the original television series. The books featuring the eighth Doctor produced by the BBC seem to be slightly more canonical than the books featuring previous Doctors produced by the BBC. The books of short stories produced by the BBC—same editors, same writers, same designer, same publisher—are uniformly regarded as less canonical. But throughout this thread, the most noticeable tendency is that toward uncertainty: "not sure," "don't know," "suppose so"—and a concomitant relativism—"to me, they are." In response to this survey, Daniel Gooley writes:

2. Nothing is canon except the bits I like.
Yes.

So far, this seems to be the only element that everyone emphatically agrees is a "No!" And yet, it's the only one that makes any sense to me. That's because (I think) everyone is accepting "canon" as an actual, discrete thing, rather than a personal belief, whereas option 2 above only works on the personal level. I've been jumping frustratedly up and down for the last few days, unintentionally sounding like Paul Cornell on a bad day, shouting : "There is no such thing as canon!"
Except on your own terms.[43]

It is apparent throughout the debates in rec.art.drwho that the fan community does not see all televised television programs as the "text" of the show (the Children in Need "Dimensions in Time" story, despite being a televised BBC production, starring the actors who have played the Doctor, and being made by the producer of the television series, proves particularly problematic for fans trying to decide on the canon), and not *only* televised programs as canon. And if the difference between fan production and industry production is not the mode of production, but the "realness" that is accorded those texts as part of the program's canon, then those decisions on the part of the fans become intensely important.

Gay Books

This is not simply an exercise in nitpicking. For Tulloch, Jenkins, and Penley, fans are relatively powerless because they cannot influence the "real" text. But what if the texts that fans are producing are indeed regarded as part of the real text? Not only the television program itself, but affiliated—official, BBC, and industrially and capitalistically produced—novels, for example? Both Jenkins and Penley explore in some detail the ways in which alternative forms of sexuality—both mention homosexuality—are included in fan writing while being excluded from the canonical texts of science fiction television. In the production of Doctor Who texts, gay sexuality has now become canonical. Indeed, there are gay, lesbian, or bisexual characters in a large number of the official, BBC-licensed Doctor Who novels—including *Love and War, Sleepy, Human Nature, Damaged Goods, Tragedy Day, Deceit, Death and Diplomacy, Bad Therapy, Return of the Living Dad,* and *The Also People*—to name only a few. Indeed, two of these—*Bad Therapy* and *Damaged Goods*—place homosexual characters at the center of the narrative—as in this description of cruising in the latter:

> Harry had been so engrossed in thoughts of his late wife that he had not noticed the man circling round then stand[ing] opposite the bench. Generally Harry found himself with men of his own age or older, and encountered clean, young, silent men only in his fantasies. But this man was staring at Harry, and he smiled, and Harry felt his stomach twist. As if responding to Harry's desire, the man lit a cigarette. The yellow flare revealed thick black eyebrows as straight as a slash of felt-pen, a sharp nose and jaw, and eyes that were definitely looking at Harry. The light died, but Harry could still see the man gesture with a flick of his head—come with me—and then disappear into the solid shadow of the copse.[44]

Once again, it is obvious that the distinction between the fan and the industry does not work as a simple binary, but must be managed in other ways—such as through the concept of canonicity. These fans are not powerless, producing only secondary texts. Many of the fan community accept these gay stories as canonical—as real Doctor Who. Of course, not all fans do. But that is precisely the point—the status of being canonical, having the aura described by Penley, is not industrially determined—it is produced discursively, within the fan community, and it is always provisional.

Advantages of the Canon

Marx attempted to categorize moments in the circulation of culture as either production or consumption. As Raymond Williams points out, the decisions on taxonomy Marx makes are open to question. I would go beyond this and suggest that the binary classification with which Marx works—where every moment must be either one of production or consumption—is simply not a useful one as we attempt to make sense of the complexity and variety of situations involved in the circulation of culture. In part, this may be due to the proliferating communications technologies of the early twenty-first century, which demand new ways of theorizing culture. If access to means of production (computer, Internet) is possible for a large percentage of the population of a Western country, then binaries that rely on the difficulty of gaining that access can no longer be easily accepted. More than this, a theoretical turn that allows us to acknowledge that all moments of consumption can also be understood as moments of production demands new ways to account for the specificity of different cultural moments. In the case of Doctor Who fandom, I think that the concept of canonicity does this work well. We must, however, note the specificity of this case. *Doctor Who* is not *Star Trek,* and neither is it *Coronation Street. Doctor Who* has an active subculture organized around the program; many of the fans become producers of physical cultural texts (which seem particularly to invite commentary about the "active audience"—see Penley's distinction between "readings" and "real products").[45] The fact that *Doctor Who* ceased regular television production in 1989 has profoundly altered the forms taken by fan culture: it has removed an easy center and made more commonplace debates about canonicity of the various products that have replaced it. So, in the case of *Doctor Who,* self-proclaimed fans—consumers—have become particularly involved in the production of more or less canonical texts.

This insight may not help us finally to decide whether the man who plays the piano is in fact a productive worker—but it does help to focus on the ways in which we might consider specific cultural situations with a full acknowledgment of their specificity, as well as the reality of inequality between different kinds of cultural production. It may seem that this essay has taken a long time to make a relatively simple point. However, I feel that the tenacity of the production/consumption

binary is an important issue for current cultural criticism. It is necessary to show that if there is a serious desire to account for the difference
in status between the texts produced at various moments of cultural
production, the retention of a simple binary between the powerful and
the powerless, between the fans and the producers, is a misleading one,
which draws attention away from the complexity of the differences between, for example, unspoken interpretations, fanzines, official magazines, unofficial audio productions, official books, and episodes of a
television program. Entry to the canon is discursively managed, and it
is this, finally, which enables it more accurately to account for the difference in status of various texts. Modes of production cannot be relied
on to determine the importance of or to understand the circulation of
texts. The canon is never absolute. Its definition is achieved by consensus within various groups, but it is never stable. It is always open to
challenge, is different for different groups—and can, of course, change
over time. And it is the fans, finally, who make those decisions. It is
they who are ultimately the powerful ones.

Notes

Many thanks to Mark Gibson and Lelia Green for their helpful comments and
suggestions on an earlier draft of this paper. All responsibility for errors and
stupidity remains my own.

1. Janice Radway, "Reading Is Not Eating: Mass-Produced Literature and
the Theoretical, Methodological, and Political Consequences of a Metaphor,"
Book Research Quarterly 2 (fall 1986): 10.

2. See, for example, Adrian Mellor, "Science Fiction and the Crisis of the
Educated Middle Class," in *Popular Fiction and Social Change,* ed. Colin
Pawling (London: Macmillan, 1984), 20–49; Joanna Russ, "Pornography by
Women, for Women, with Love," in *Magic Mommas, Trembling Sisters, Puri-
tans, and Perverts: Feminist Essays* (Trumansburg, N.Y.: Crossing, 1985); Pa-
tricia Frazer Lamb and Diana L Veith, "Romantic Myth, Transcendence, and
Star Trek Zines," in *Erotic Universe: Sexuality and Fantastic Literature,* ed.
Donald Palumbo (New York: Greenwood Press, 1986); Camille Bacon-Smith,
"Acquisition and Transformation of Popular Culture: The International Video
Circuit and the Fanzine Community," paper presented at the International
Communication Association conference, New Orleans, 1988; Constance Pen-
ley, "Brownian Motion: Women, Tactics, and Technology," in *Technoculture,*
ed. Constance Penley and Andrew Ross (Minneapolis: University of Minne-
sota Press, 1991), 135–61; Constance Penley, "Feminism, Psychoanalysis, and
the Study of Popular Culture," in *Cultural Studies,* ed. Lawrence Grossberg,
Cary Nelson, and Paula Treichler (New York and London: Routledge, 1992),

479–500; Constance Penley, *NASA/Trek: Popular Science and Sex in America* (London: Verso, 1997); Henry Jenkins, *Textual Poachers: Television Fans and Participatory Culture* (London and New York: Routledge, 1992); Henry Jenkins, "'Strangers No More, We Sing': Filking and the Social Construction of the Science Fiction Fan Community," in *The Adoring Audience: Fan Culture and Popular Media,* ed. Lisa A. Lewis (London and New York: Routledge, 1992), 208–36.

3. Michel de Certeau, quoted in Jenkins, *Textual Poachers,* 152.

4. Jenkins, *Textual Poachers,* 155.

5. Penley, "Brownian Motion," 139.

6. John Hartley, *Tele-ology: Studies in Television* (London and New York: Routledge, 1992), 9.

7. John Tulloch and Henry Jenkins, *Science Fiction Audiences: Watching Dr. Who and Star Trek* (London: Routledge, 1995), 21.

8. Ibid., 264, 265.

9. Penley, "Brownian Motion," 138, 132.

10. Jenkins, *Textual Poachers,* 87.

11. Ibid., 118.

12. Tulloch and Jenkins, *Science Fiction Audiences,* 145, 150.

13. Ibid., 21.

14. See, for example, ibid., 144; and Penley, "Brownian Motion," 135.

15. Penley, "Brownian Motion," 139; Jenkins, *Textual Poachers,* 158.

16. Jenkins, *Textual Poachers,* 160; see also Penley, "Brownian Motion," 139.

17. Penley, "Brownian Motion," 143; Jenkins, *Textual Poachers,* 159.

18. Tulloch and Jenkins, *Science Fiction Audiences,* 150.

19. Perhaps it is the very category of "zines" that attracts this form of analysis. To treat fanzines as the privileged cultural product of fan culture leads to a certain image of that culture, for the category of "zines" brings with it a history of a form that is antiestablishment, anarchistic, anticapitalistic. See, for example, Stephen Dunne, "Inter/erupt! Queer Zine Scene?," in "Queer Media," ed. Jodi Brooks, Michael Hurley, and Leigh Raymond, special issue, *Media International Australia,* no. 78 (November 1995): 53–68. However, not all fanzines neatly fit this "ur"-zine category, and—importantly—there are many more forms of fan production than simply zines.

20. Lamb and Veith, "Romantic Myth," 237.

21. Mellor, "Science Fiction," 24.

22. John Frow, *Time and Commodity Culture: Essays in Cultural Theory and Postmodernity* (Oxford: Clarendon Press, 1997), 102, 132.

23. Appadurai, cited in ibid., 143.

24. Ibid., 147.

25. Gary Gillatt, "The Mourning After . . .," *Doctor Who Magazine,* no. 246 (December 1996): 6.

26. Philip Segal, "Philip Segal," *Doctor Who Magazine,* no. 247 (January 1996): 6, 7.

27. David J. Howe, Mark Stammers, and Stephen James Walker, *Doctor Who: The Eighties* (London: Virgin, 1996), 126.

28. Dave Owen, "We are Time's Champions," *Doctor Who Magazine,* no. 267 (July 1998): 51.

29. Steve Cole, "Q&A Steve Cole," *Doctor Who Magazine,* no. 259 (December 1998): 31.

30. John Ainsworth, "Is This the Doctor and Ace?" *Doctor Who Magazine,* no. 268 (August 1998): 44.

31. The newsgroup rec.arts.drwho can be accessed from the Web site http://west.pair.com/dw/.

32. Penley, "Brownian Motion," 135.

33. Ibid., 137.

34. Tulloch and Jenkins, *Science Fiction Audiences,* 21.

35. Steve Lyons, "Spiking the Canon," *Doctor Who Magazine,* no. 267 (July 1998): 6, 12.

36. Mark Morris, "Talking Books," *Doctor Who Magazine,* no. 255 (August 1997): 24.

37. Jenkins, *Textual Poachers,* 95.

38. Hartley, *Tele-ology,* 22.

39. Lyons, "Spiking the Canon," 6.

40. Dave Owen, "Shelf Life," *Doctor Who Magazine,* no. 268 (August 1998): 42.

41. Allen Robinson, "The 1998 Canon Survey," posting to rec.arts.drwho, 22 September 1998.

42. Si Jerram, "Re: The 1998 Canon Survey," posting to rec.arts.drwho, 23 September 1998.

43. Daniel Gooley, "Re: The 1998 Canon Survey," posting to rec.arts.drwho, 23 September 1998.

44. Russell T. Davies, *Damaged Goods (The New Doctor Who Adventures)* (London: Virgin, 1996), 16.

45. Penley, "Brownian Motion," 139.

10

Trainspotting *The Avengers*

Toby Miller

I made this beer in honor of Mrs. Peel. Like the character played by
Diana Rigg on *The Avengers,* this beer kicks you in the butt, but you
don't mind.

—*Jennifer Gutzbehal*

■ Gutzbehal's "Emma Pale" comes complete with brewing instructions,
down to ingredients, mash and sparge specifics, boiling details, and
fermentation.[1] The beer testifies to the enduring significance of a forty-
year-old TV series that dates from the days when film was rarely used
to record British television because the medium was not deemed worthy
of archiving, let alone commemoration. But it lives on.

The Avengers ran on British TV from 1961 to 1969 and was exported
to scores of other nations—in fact it was the first UK show during
prime-time sweeps on the U.S. networks. A hybrid of espionage and
thriller, the program was notable for its lead characters. John Steed
(Patrick Macnee) was a dandyish gentleman who embodied both a fop-
pish style harking back to the Regency and a modish 1960s chic. The
successive women leads, Catherine Gale (Honor Blackman) and Emma
Peel (Diana Rigg) personified modernity *tout court:* hip, leggy, sexy,
brilliant, physically competent women who took nonsense from no
man and were Steed's superiors intellectually and his equal in combat.
Gale and Peel were single women, flirting with Steed, and they were not
reduced "to a metaphor for national affluence." Allowed to serve as
self-actualizing subjects, they drew appreciative female audiences as a
consequence.[2] Perhaps women viewers witnessing uninhibited female
stars who dressed for success through power saw the flip side to the

uncompromising but sexy figures that leaped out to male fans.[3] Both in the UK and elsewhere, the program garnered ratings and acclaim as a harbinger of feminism and a sign that television drama could be stylish and knowing as well as popular. In the 1990s, Diana Rigg continued to receive letters from women for whom she had been a feminist icon *avant la lettre*,[4] while in the year 2000, the program could be seen and heard regularly on the U.S. Mystery cable channel, Radio Canada, Foxtel cable in Australia, and TF1 in France, and as *Agenti Speciali* on Italy's satellite Channel Jimmy and *Los Vengadores* in Argentina on Uniseries.[5]

When I first planned to write this essay, I intended to address issues of gender and empire in *The Avengers,* arguing that what looks like escapist spy television is also a significant allegory that resonates with progressive political practice and viewing protocols. My reading was—and is—that the series materializes a transcendent new world, one after patriarchy (or at least on the way to "after patriarchy" via a utopian alternative universe) and after empire (an unfurling narrative: TV series, 1961–1969; independence of Britain's "possessions," 1957–). Mrs. Gale and Mrs. Peel are figures of high modernity, reacting against and with the constraints of femininity even as they play with them. They are also representatives of a ruling-class white background from the former empire, with "winds of change" blowing through their political and domestic lives. Steed is on the cross-benches of tradition and modernity, a playboy who destabilizes conventional masculinity and signifies both a disappearing genteel world and a new, brash one. But I came to believe that my account of the series, and that of many non-cultish fans (for example, casual viewers enchanted by Rigg's challenge to standard femininity, or cultural historians interested in TV gender innovations) bore minimal relation to the reactions of the true cultists, whose sensemaking practices owed much more to practical criticism than cultural politics. In any event, the renewed attention given to *The Avengers* in the late 1990s derived from two helpful happenings in any cultural studies researcher's life: the emergence of the World Wide Web (ethnography direct to your home) and the release of a new film inspired by the series as well as videos and DVDs of the show.

As word spread about the upcoming 1998 movie, spectacular rumors emerged that boded ill for the revival: Sean Connery was a sexual harasser; the set caught on fire; Connery was injured in his limousine; Uma Thurman and Macnee were hauled back from the United States to redub some sound; the date of release was postponed from June to August; a lost soul in Arizona told Internet readers that he had been accosted en route to *The Devil's Advocate,* offered a free ticket to a preview of *The Avengers,* and been horrified; magazine cover stories on Thurman queried whether she could fill Rigg's boots; and critics asked whether Ralph Fiennes was a credible marquee name for a "popcorn movie." Much of this anxiety derived from the affection in which the old series was held. People just didn't want to see something that they had owned, at least as an item of popular memory, distorted and lost to future generations. Meanwhile, Web sites were awash with speculation about how the new text would match up to the old.

Where does this affectionate connoisseurship of cult fans sit along-side how media audiences are conventionally classified? There have been two main forms of audience analysis: audience research and spectator-ship theory. The former is primarily concerned with the number and conduct of people seated before screen texts: where they came from, how many there were, and what they did as a consequence of being present. The audience is understood as an empirical concept that can be known via research instruments derived from sociology, demography, social psychology, and marketing. Spectatorship theory is also concerned with speculation about the effects of films on people, but instead of questioning, testing, and measuring them, it uses psychoanalysis to explore how supposedly universal internal struggles over the formation of subjectivity are enacted on-screen and in the psyches of watchers. The spectator is understood as a narratively inscribed concept that can be known via a combination of textual analysis and Freudianism.

There are three primary sites for defining the audience: the culture industries, the state, and criticism. In this sense, the audience is artificial, the creature of various agencies that then act on their creation. As John Hartley says, "The energy with which audiences are pursued in academic and industry research . . . [is] larger and more powerful than the quest for mere data. . . . it is the search for . . . knowledge of the *species*."[6] There is something quite eerie about audience research and researchers; they are their own cults—of numbers, neurones, neuroses, and negativity.

Many discussions of the audience are signs of anxiety: laments for civic culture in the United States correlate an increase in violence and a decline in membership of parent-teacher associations with heavy film viewing—as true today as it was when the Payne Fund Studies of the 1930s inaugurated mass social science panic about young people, driven by academic and familial iconophobia and the sense that large groups of people were engaged with popular culture beyond the control of the state and ruling classes, such that they might be led astray.

"The audience" is never available in a pristine form, because our knowledge of it is always in some relationship to these particular perspectives[7]—hence the link to panics about education, violence, and apathy, supposedly engendered by the screen and routinely investigated by the state, psychology, Marxism, neoconservatism, the church, liberal feminism, and others. The audience as consumer, student, felon, voter, and idiot engages such groups. This is Harold Garfinkel's notion of the "cultural dope," a mythic figure "who produces the stable features of the society by acting in compliance with pre-established and legitimate alternatives of action that the common culture provides." The "common sense rationalities . . . of here and now situations" used by people are obscured by this condescending categorization.[8] The emergence of public education in the West, allied to the disciplines of literary criticism (to distinguish the cultivated from others) and the psy-complexes (to distinguish the competent from others), has seen the rhetoric of audiences shift since the nineteenth century. At that time, audiences were read as active, given their unruly and overtly engaged conduct in public space at cultural events.[9] But when the audience is invoked today by the industry or its critics and regulators, it immediately becomes a "dope."

Of course, there is another tradition of audience studies, which picks up on Garfinkel's cultural dope insight and takes the reverse position from rat-catching psy-doomsayers and armchair (not couch) humanities "psychoanalysts." Instead of issuing jeremiads, this line claims that audiences, like neoclassical economics' consumers, are so clever and able that they outwit the institutions of the state, academia, and capitalism that seek to control and measure them. In one sense, this has a venerable tradition, via literary theorists like old SS man Hans Robert Jauss's aesthetics of reception, and old Marxism man Jean-Paul Sartre's philosophy of the mutual intrication of writer and reader in making meaning. In communications and culture, especially television, the ideas really spread with Umberto Eco's notion of open texts and encoding-decoding, as later picked up by Frank Parkin and then Stuart Hall, on the left, and on the right, in a psychological frame, by uses-and-gratifications functionalists such as Elihu Katz.[10] Today, this position has been elevated to a virtual nostrum in cultural studies TV history, at least when applied to fans.

While fans are sometimes regarded as, literally, fanatics (in keeping with the concept's origins in nineteenth-century U.S. professional baseball and its madcap followers), they are invested by this position with the role of exemplary reader and critic. Today, the term "fan" covers the establishment of imagined links to stars and popular culture characters.[11]

Eco suggests that fans make a text into a cult when they thoroughly "own" it (psychologically if not legally), disarticulating the program from its origins and making it anew as part of their everyday worlds.[12] This is what ethnomethodologists refer to as manufacturing the "personalized stranger," a figure the public assumes to know at a quite intimate level—not in terms of secrets, but as someone with whom diurnal interaction is taken for granted.[13]

After publishing a book about *The Avengers* television series,[14] I encountered some of this fervor and sense of ownership or entitlement, right down to the creation of a Web site that lists my mistakes of fact and interpretation and invites fans to contribute additional instances.[15] Members of an Internet discussion group about another television series sought to prevent me from joining them because they believed that the placement of shudder or bastard quotes around the term "Miller's 'informants'" by the *New York Times'* book reviewer implied that I had not obtained consent from viewers before printing their words.[16] I also encountered stern reactions from British newspapers, which assumed that, as I taught in New York, I must be "an American." This licensed some amusing (albeit condemnatory) reviews in newspapers such as the *Guardian,* which explained my failings as a by-product of the U.S. education system, as well as the pleasurable mockery of conservative bastions like the *Daily Telegraph,* which gave a column over to quoting my prose each day for a week.[17] The story was always the same—there ought to be a mimetic relation between popular culture and its chroniclers, if the culture is worth chronicling at all. When this historic mission fails, or politics is brought to bear on the texts in question, mockery or a tongue-lashing are the only correct responses. When I noticed similar critiques across the Web and various other U.S. media, such as *Entertainment Weekly, Television Quarterly, Elle Singapore,* the *Washington Post* and *International Herald Tribune, Marie Claire, HQ,* and *Playboy* (along with several endorsements and encouragements), I began to wonder whether, authorial ego aside, something was going on here that I should pay attention to in terms of the active-audience/critic relation.[18]

Consider the egregious reactionary politics of Ayn Rand, an early advocate of the active-audience school of readers' liberation. Responding to *TV Guide*'s suggestion that British viewers of *The Avengers* were so unsophisticated that they overlooked the kinky undertones of women in leather adorning the program, she defended the audience as uniquely able to see through the series' (to her mind, undesirable) irony and modernity to its transcendent themes of heroism and morality.[19] Rand's

latter-day ideological confrere, Virginia Postrel, editor of the ultraliber-
tarian *Reason* magazine, wrote a 1999 op-ed piece for the *Wall Street
Journal* in which she welcomed the TV side of cultural studies, describing it as "deeply threatening to traditional leftist views of commerce"
because notions of active media consumption by fans were so close
to the sovereign consumer beloved of the right: "The cultural-studies
mavens are betraying the leftist cause, lending support to the corporate
enemy and even training graduate students who wind up doing market
research."[20] Ouch.

There was something to investigate here, and it found me wondering
about Todd Gitlin's accusation that some sectors of cultural studies were
in synch with the discourse of neoclassical economics and the right:
"What the group wants, buys, demands is *ipso facto* the voice of the
people. Supply has meshed with demand."[21] As Herbert I. Schiller puts
it, the direct opposition drawn between political economy and active-
audience theory assumes that the fragmentation of audience niches and
responses obviates the necessity for concern about the concentration
and reach of economic power in mass cultural production—pluralism
ensures diversity. This amounts to an endorsement of market values
under a situation of monopoly capital.[22] That made me wonder whether
the literary-critical corollary of such capitalism might thrive in Avengers
cultism.

Many critics who wrote about the TV series in the 1960s and since
are themselves unabashed fans. Monica Furlong of Britain's *Daily Mail*
described herself as "addicted" to the program.[23] The *Chicago Sun-
Times'* Mary Houlihan-Skilton confided her love for Steed.[24] The *New
Musical Express* said "anyone with a memory of 60s television has *The
Avengers* bound up in it,"[25] while the *Village Voice* looked back on the
frisson between Steed and Mrs. Peel as a guide to good sexual relations.[26] At the same time, several critics of the day felt that the series
looked trivial alongside the "kitchen-sink" school of British social-
realist television, film drama, and documentary because of its links to
the fantastic and a depthless form of characterization that privileged
style over substance.[27]

Behind and alongside these popular intellectuals lies a more inchoate,
anti-intellectual, profoundly apolitical, but perfectly pleasurable take on
the series. "The Avengers TV Show Mailing List" is, rather ominously,
available to join via avengers@suburbia.com.au. This address testifies to
the ongoing Australian fixation on suburbia as the country's domestic
utopia and fate (versus its touristic image) and, more important for our
purposes here, to a search for friendship in the face of isolation and a

TRAINSPOTTING *THE AVENGERS* ■ 193

sense of, well, fun associated with the program that eschews the stress on questions of postmodernity and empire that preoccupied me in my book. Consider the first move required of a subscriber to the list:

> Tell us who you are, what you are and why you think you are. Let us know where you're from, what your favourite episode is and why, etc etc etc. It will help stimulate discussion and debate as well as provide a sense [of] community.

It would be easy to dismiss these folks as trainspotters—losers and nerds lacking a fulfilling life who compensate through a search for like-minded geeks. But what they engage in is sweet and joyous—it's just not an instance of resistive reading that challenges prevailing conservative cultural politics. The annual "Avengers Dead Man's Treasure Hunt," for example, sees fans gather in Hertfordshire, where many exterior scenes were shot during the Rigg period. Aficionados re-create a car rally from one episode, visit numerous shooting locations, then put themselves through an evening of quizzes and champagne.[28] This kind of event has drawn not-altogether gentle parodies from other followers of the series, who spoof the idea of fan conventions via the mythic "BowlerCon," a reference to Steed's habitual bowler hat. The faux convention features lost footage found in an Aberdeen toilet, a star appearance by Fang the dog from an old episode, and auction bids of up to two hundred pounds for a cobweb used in another program, plus a "Dead Man's Trolley Dash," in which participants boldly race one another in supermarket carts.[29] Meanwhile, a (real) "Young Avengers" fan site specializes in rating shows, listing the make of car driven by *all* characters, and penning fan fiction. The site is dedicated to reproducing the series' following.[30] There are sophisticated sites aplenty, notably in Argentina.[31]

Throughout, the problem remains of the "typically inward-looking" orientation of these sites and the formations of fans/cultists around them. A "shared interest in the show is an end in itself and seldom leads to some action beyond that interest, some larger political purpose."[32] Fans of Mrs. Peel and Mrs. Gale who are clearly not cultists have an obvious and important gender politics ("I liked the show, they were great, what fabulous role models"). But I am unable to unearth any politics other than a conventional literary-critical style appreciationism among Avengers cults ("Why hasn't my 2001 *Avengers* calendar arrived in the mail yet and why is this site taking so long to load?"). Such cults are entirely self-directed forms of life—self-formation is their alpha and omega. Collective consciousness about the show does not lead to collective investigations of gender politics on TV, or postcolonialism, or the fashion industry and tie-ins, or product placements, or the politics of fun.

Meanwhile, the inevitably complex interdependency between these fans and *The Avengers* rights-holders adopts its customary form—*that might spark a critique of capitalism.* The fans sense that they "own" the text—they understand it, they honor it, and they sustain it as consumers and historians. But corporations own the text in a legal sense. This has become especially sensitive since the advent of the Web. Sounds and images borrowed from programs and stories created from characters in original texts often lead to legal problems. At the same time, corporations sell merchandise (often directly) thanks to fan Web sites, and the free advertising and public relations that keep "their" commodity in public view amounts to a classic free ride in economic terms.

So Studiocanal/Canal+ Image UK Ltd, which owns the worldwide rights to *The Avengers,* sends ambivalent missives to contributors to Web sites. On the one hand, it must assert an ongoing right to the series, lest the latter fall into the public domain ("These sites use mainly material that belongs exclusively to our company, be it in the form of photos, sound or video, and whose use should have imperatively required our prior consent"). On the other hand, "the comments on your sites are of great interest and contribute to enriching common knowledge of the series." Some Web authors are even invited to offer their handiwork to "the official site." But they must recognize that the decision to hold off on issuing a "cease-and-desist order" or embarking on prosecution is not "a waiver of our rights," but rather "a gesture of CANAL+ IMAGE UK Ltd opening up to the community of net surfers who are fans of the series."[33] Warming to this latter point, A&E, the cable channel that markets *The Avengers* videos and DVDs in the United States, has sought from the beginning to make alliances with Internet fans. Its own site has several segments dedicated to trainspotter norms: introduce yourself, list your favorite season/episode/scene/technology, compare and contrast series to film, and outline whether or not Steed and Mrs. Peel "did the bad thing." Of course, the main purpose of this activity is to encourage sales.[34]

As Justin Lewis rightly says, "TV viewing is a cultural practice, and like all cultural practices, it involves not only 'doing it' but 'ways of doing it.'"[35] For those of us schooled in pub talk or Leavisite talk, whether it be about sport, politics, literature, or friends, there is of course nothing startling or new about this kind of evaluation by fans/litterateurs. To invest it with some political significance or theoretical importance is basically to reinstate the very canonical norms that the left should be seeking to do away with. These forms of fandom are straightforwardly dedicated to replicating a college of aficionados, who by their knowledge of the great elevating texts are somehow superior. This sounds familiar and, if anything, somewhat regressive to me. It replicates the very forms of quality discourse that were supposedly toppled by anti-canonical cultural studies. Instead, the best readers of the best texts are back, armed with their best interpretations. No, thank you. I'll try the Emma Peel beer, and occasionally peer at the Web site listing my foibles as a scholar, but other than that, count me out of cultism as a supposedly progressive tendency. Leave spotting trainspotters to trainspotters.

Notes
Thanks to Marie Leger for comments.

1. Jennifer Gutzbehal, *Jen & Rehmi's Emma Pale,* at http://i.fix.org/~jennyg/beers/emmapale.html, accessed September 2002.

2. Moya Luckett, "Sensuous Women and Single Girls: Reclaiming the Female Body on 1960s Television," in *Swinging Single: Representing Sexuality in the 1960s,* ed. Hilary Radner and Moya Luckett (Minneapolis: University of Minnesota Press, 2000), 293.

3. Brigid Keenan, *The Women We Wanted to Look Like* (New York: St. Martin's Press, 1977), 73.

4. Adam Sweeting, "Back with a Vengeance," *Guardian,* 16 October 1993, 26.

5. "On the Air," at http://davidsmith.com/avengers/air.htm, accessed September 2002.

6. John Hartley, *The Politics of Pictures: The Creation of the Public in the Age of Popular Media* (London: Routledge, 1992), 84.

7. John Hartley, *Tele-ology: Studies in Television* (London: Routledge, 1992), 105.

8. Harold Garfinkel, *Studies in Ethnomethodology* (Cambridge, England: Polity Press, 1992), 68.

9. Richard Butsch, *The Making of American Audiences: From Stage to Television, 1750–1990* (Cambridge: Cambridge University Press, 2000), 3.

10. Armand Mattelart and Michèle Mattelart, *Theories of Communication: A Short Introduction,* trans. Susan Gruenheck Taponier and James A. Cohen (London: Sage, 1998), 119–20, 123.

11. Laura Leets, Gavin de Becker, and Howard Giles, "Fans: Exploring Expressed Motivations for Contacting Celebrities," *Journal of Language and Social Psychology* 14, no. 1–2 (1995): 102–23.

12. Umberto Eco, *Travels in Hyperreality: Essays,* trans. William Weaver (London: Picador, 1987).

13. Rod Watson, "The Public Announcement of Fatality," *Working Papers in Cultural Studies* 4 (1973): 16, 19 n.19.

14. Toby Miller, *The Avengers* (London: British Film Institute, 1997).

15. David Smith, "Book Bloopers," at http://davidsmith.com/avengers/bloop-1.htm, accessed September 2002.

16. Liesl Schillinger, "English Leather," *New York Times Book Review*, 22 February 1998, 34.

17. Vera Rule, "Take a Footnote, Mrs Peel," *Guardian*, 31 October 1997, Screen section, 11; Peterborough, "Any Old Irony," *Daily Telegraph*, 21 October 1997, editorial page.

18. David Browne, "The Avengers," *Entertainment Weekly*, no. 425 (3 April 1998): 88; Fritz Jacobi, "Review and Comment: Books in Brief," *Television Quarterly* 29, no. 4 (1998): 71–73; John Sosnovski, "Mrs Peel, We're Needed," *Elle Singapore*, August 1998; Carolyn Banks, "Catsuits and Champagne," book review, *Washington Post*, 22 March 1998, X03; Alison Boleyn, "The World Is," *Marie Claire*, November 1997; Franz Lidz, "My Dear Mrs. Peel," *HQ*, no. 61 (November–December 1998): 42–46; "Avenging Angels," *Playboy*, July 1998.

19. Ayn Rand, *The Romantic Manifesto: A Philosophy of Literature*, rev. ed. (New York: Signet, 1975), 137–38.

20. Virgia Postrel, "The Pleasures of Persuasion," *Wall Street Journal*, 2 August 1999, 18.

21. Todd Gitlin, "The Anti-Political Populism of Cultural Studies," in *Cultural Studies in Question*, ed. Marjorie Ferguson and Peter Golding (London: Sage, 1997), 32.

22. Herbert Schiller, *Culture Inc.: The Corporate Takeover of Public Expression* (Oxford: Oxford University Press, 1989), 153.

23. Monica Furlong, untitled, *Daily Mail*, 15 October 1965.

24. Mary Houlihan-Skilton, "Slick 'Avengers' Series is Making Cable Comeback," *Chicago Sun-Times*, 9 November 1990, Weekend Plus, 3.

25. Richard Cook, "A Thoroughly British Affair," *New Musical Express*, 20 November 1982, 6.

26. Bruce Eder, "A License to Thrill," *Village Voice*, 5 February 1991.

27. James Chapman, "*The Avengers*: Television and Popular Culture during the 'High Sixties,'" in *Windows on the Sixties: Exploring Key Texts of Media and Culture*, ed. Anthony Aldgate, James Chapman, and Arthur Marwick (London: IB Tauris, 2000), 46–47.

28. "Avengerland," at http://www.kikgraphics.demon.co.uk/avengerland.html, accessed September 2002.

29. "BowlerCon," at http://members.aol.com/hehehedc/bowlercon.html, accessed September 2002; "Dead Man's Trolley Dash," at http://members.aol.com/hehehedc/avengertroll.html, accessed September 2002.

30. "Young Avengers," at http://davidsmith.com/avengers/yav/yav-welcome.htm, accessed September 2002.

31. "Los Vengadores," at http://www.isurf.com.ar/98-07-julio/veng_des.htm, accessed September 2002.

32. Butsch, *The Making of American Audiences*, 291.

33. Michael Schmidt, letter to Net surfers, 5 July 2000.

34. A&E, at http://www.aande.com/perl/www.heads.pl?action=boards& topic=The+Avengers, accessed September 2002.

35. Justin Lewis, *The Ideological Octopus: An Exploration of Television and Its Audience* (New York: Routledge, 1991), 49.

Star Trek, Heaven's Gate, and Textual Transcendence

Jeffrey Sconce

> To help you understand who we are, we have taken
> the liberty to express a brief synopsis in the vernacu-
> lar of a popular "science fiction" entertainment
> series. Most readers in the late 20th century will
> certainly recognize the intended parallels. It is really
> quite interesting to see how the context of fiction
> can often open the mind to advanced possibilities,
> which are, in reality, quite close to fact.
> — *Jwnody, "Overview of Present Mission,"*
> *Heaven's Gate Web site*

■ On 27 March 1997, police in San Diego discovered thirty-nine people
dead in an upscale home on the city's north side. The bodies were identical in every detail: a purple shroud covering each corpse—heads shaved,
black pants, black Nike shoes, and black shirts. Detectives originally
believed all of the victims to be male, but subsequent investigation revealed the majority of the bodies were those of women. In preparation
for this "final exit," many of the bodies had overnight bags filled with
toiletries and clothing at their side, money and passports in their pock-
ets. Confirming police suspicions, autopsies revealed that most of the
victims had perished in a mass suicide—overdosed on phenobarbital
mixed in applesauce with a vodka chaser.

Who were these unfortunate souls? Though each victim had worked
hard to erase his or her gendered identity, each also wore a patch on the
makeshift black uniforms that proclaimed a common bond: "Heaven's
Gate Away Team." These ID patches merged two disparate strains of

science fiction. Heaven's Gate: the rather infamous "UFO cult" that had for many years wandered across the United States telling of the imminent return of the "Representatives," citizens of an ethereal plane known as T.E.L.A.H. (The Evolutionary Level above Human). In college auditoriums and in the pages of *USA Today,* the Heaven's Gate collective recruited new members with the dream of a coming repatriation to T.E.L.A.H., a vision of transcendence trading in images drawn from Christian theology and dystopic science fiction.

> Planet About to be Recycled—
> Your Only Chance to Survive—
> Leave with Us
>
> The Shedding of our Borrowed Human Bodies May Be Required in
> Order to Take Up Our New Bodies Belonging to the Next World[1]

For reporters investigating the history of Heaven's Gate, all that was needed was a quick trip to the news morgue for a fact check. There was plenty to work with—arrest reports, previous coverage in *Time* and the *New York Times Magazine,* and even a made-for-TV movie based on the lives of the UFO cult's founders.[2] Understanding the other half of the patch, however, required a more subtle knowledge of American television and the "vernacular of a popular 'science fiction' entertainment series." Away Team: Captain Picard, Commander Riker, the U.S.S. *Enterprise—Star Trek.* In the mythos of Gene Roddenberry's extraordinary pop-cult franchise, the "away team" designated a group of crew members dispatched from the ship on hazardous missions to strange planets, often to walk among primitive, barbaric, and otherwise threatening civilizations. Reviewing the extensive literature of Heaven's Gate, it quickly became apparent that members strongly identified with this conceit. They, too, considered themselves superior alien beings, "E.T.'s presently Incarnate" sent to Earth in messy mortal form to prepare the willing few for eventual evacuation by spaceship. Tabloid reports of a UFO spotted in the wake of a comet passing by earth in the spring of 1997 provided the final trigger for the group's transcendence. When police found the corpse of the group's sixty-five-year-old leader, Martin Applewhite, he was alone in bed; on the mantel next to him was a framed picture of a silver-skinned space alien. "Beam me up, Scotty," went the running joke of day, "there is no intelligent life on this planet."

When police searched the Heaven's Gate compound in the wake of the suicides, they discovered two lists of videotapes inside a living room cabinet. One list contained titles approved for viewing by the group;

the other, titles that were forbidden. Sanctioned series included *Star Trek: Voyager, Deep Space Nine, The X-Files,* and *Millennium,* while *The Island of Dr. Moreau* and the recent Bond film *Golden Eye* "were considered inappropriate and hastily forbidden, as was everything that promoted a mammalian or human point of view."[3] Unlike the many cults that seek to remove themselves from the distractions of the everyday world, Heaven's Gate had an active (if discriminating) interest in television and popular culture. As Rodney Perkins and Forrest Jackson opine in their account of the group, "They surfed the Media, looking for signs of any sympathetic ideas"[4] (true of all television viewers, no doubt). As an away team, members of Heaven's Gate clearly found particularly sympathetic ideas in the world of *Star Trek.* Over the following weeks, as the press pieced together the group's activities and beliefs in the months leading up to their departure from this mortal plane, the Star Trek angle became a popular lead in the reporting. Along with the concept of the away team, Heaven's Gate members had apparently integrated all manner of Star Trek lore into their daily lives. Viewings and discussions of the series were a centerpiece of the group's activities. Lieutenant Commander Data, the childishly innocent yet incredibly brilliant android of the series, served as a favorite role model of the group. An advanced being housed within the alien trappings of human form and struggling to make sense of human illogic, Data provided the group with a prime figure of identification. One doomed member of the group, Norma Jeanne Nelson, occasionally claimed to baffled neighbors in Dallas that she was actually *from Star Trek.* "We just looked at her in surprise. It just didn't dawn on us that she was in a type of cult," observed one acquaintance. "We thought that maybe she was crazy."[5] Finally, in the most perverse coincidence of all, one of the victims of the mass suicide turned out to be the brother of Nichelle Nichols, the actress who played Uhura in the original *Star Trek* series.

These connections to *Star Trek* helped the American public better understand these "cult" members, especially when the press reported that the group's primary means of financial support had been through working as computer consultants. The Heaven's Gate members were, in short, "Trekkies," a label that positioned them in a larger culture profile as mindless geeks overly invested in what was, after all, only a TV show. They were not, of course, the first group to gravitate toward Gene Roddenberry's influential vision of a liberal-humanist utopia in space—a classless society that had transcended sexism and racism to dedicate itself to knowledge, exploration, and infinite diversity in infinite combinations. But they soon became the most notorious Trekkies on the planet (or off), having seemingly made the ultimate sacrifice to travel through the stars. Despite the fact that the group's beliefs, bizarre as they were, had no actual foundation in the *Star Trek* series, and that members clearly understood *Star Trek* to be fiction (even as they believed their own mythology of T.E.L.A.H. to be real), their interest in the series aligned them with generations of Trekkies ridiculed for their "unhealthy," "wasteful," and even "psychotic" investment in the TV series. Fans of *Star Trek,* notes Henry Jenkins, have been consistently maligned as "brainless consumers" and infantile, desexualized "social misfits" dedicated to the "cultivation of worthless knowledge" over "devalued cultural material."[6] Jenkins adds that Star Trek fans are also often accused of being unable to distinguish fantasy from the real world, becoming so obsessed with the Star Trek universe as to "lose themselves" in a permanent haze of syndicated televisual reality. So strong is this image of the deluded Trekkie that many fans are reluctant to profess their affinity for the series, fearing that others will take such an interest to be the defining characteristic of their social identity. Indeed, in a perverse twist on contemporary "identity politics," many fans of the series have fought in vain to replace the infantilizing, derisive term "Trekkie" with the more dynamic label of "Trekker."

A recurring question in the now copious critical literature surrounding *Star Trek* concerns the basis of the show's extraordinary appeal. Why has *Star Trek* spawned such an active and invested group of viewers, many of whom are eager to attend annual conventions, dress in Star Trek costumes, compose fan fiction, sing "filk" songs, master the wholly imaginary language of the Klingon empire, and even don "Away Team" patches before embarking on a final exit to the final frontier? Several critics, including Jenkins, Constance Penley, and Camille Bacon-Smith, have already explored in great depth and sophistication the often-complex politics of identity at work in the Star Trek fan community.[7] In the following pages, I would like to use the example of Heaven's Gate as a means of examining the Star Trek phenomenon, using it as a limit case in discussing the now extensive literature surrounding the series and its fans. In addressing these questions, I hope to contribute to an ongoing debate over the series' continuing appeal, as well as mediate the at times acrimonious exchanges between those who idealize Star Trek fandom as a wholly "progressive" phenomenon and those who legitimize larger cultural stereotypes about the "emotional retardation" of the Trekkie. What *are* we to make of the Heaven's Gate cult's veneration of Data, their identification with the mission of an away team, their belief in delivery and transcendence through the stars? Why did this series "speak" to them in such compelling terms, and is there a difference in degree or in kind between the followers of Heaven's Gate and the attendees of a typical Star Trek convention?

While it would be ridiculous to blame *Star Trek* for the mass suicide at Rancho Sante Fe, the fact remains that these dysfunctional followers of Applewhite were indeed energetic Star Trek fans. What are we to make of such dedicated viewing? Ever vigilant for answers that are both easy and sensational, the press is always eager to link misfortune and tragedy to causal factors in popular culture. This article will consider the merits of the exact opposite argument. I maintain that the problem with the Heaven's Gate cult was not that they were *too obsessed* with *Star Trek*; rather, *they were not obsessed enough*. If their devotion to *Star Trek* had been stronger, they would still be alive today—healthier, happier, and reasonably better adjusted than most Americans.

To Boldly Repeat . . .

For over a decade now, those who have chosen the path of Star Trek in life have found themselves the center of popular and academic speculation. What is the seemingly limitless appeal of the series and its various sequels? When *Newsweek* magazine pondered "the enduring power of *Star Trek*" in 1986, it came to the conclusion: "Like music, it appeals to man's love of repetition. The same characters do basically the same thing in each show." Later in the same piece, *Newsweek* offered that "the fans, after seeing the crew on film and at conventions for 20 years, feel relaxed around the characters, who they know will do nothing surprising," a condition that "offers the possibility of near-total mastery of the facts" of the series.[8] Here we have a rather typical abstraction of Star Trek fans—fixated on meaningless facts and afraid of any form of change that might impinge on their infantile pleasures.

Embedded in a larger cultural mythology of television and passivity, such stereotypes of the Trekkie have been so strong that one of the major tasks of Star Trek scholarship has been to interrogate and thus disarticulate the popular fusion of Trekkie equals geek. On the very first page of *Textual Poachers,* for example, Jenkins relates an infamous moment in Star Trek fandom—William Shatner's turn as guest host on *Saturday Night Live.* In the obligatory sketch of Kirk appearing at a Star Trek convention, Shatner "is bombarded with questions from fans who want to know about minor characters in individual episodes, . . . who seem to know more about his private life than he does, and who demand such trivial information as the combination to Kirk's safe."[9] In the sketch's most famous line, Shatner finally explodes,

"Get a life, will you people? I mean, I mean, for crying out loud, it's just a TV show!" Addressing a particularly geeky thirty-year-old fan (played to perfection by Jon Lovitz in Spock ears), Shatner delivers the most cutting insult of all: "You, there, have you ever kissed a girl?" Jenkins opens with this familiar broadside in order to refute it, mounting a counterargument of fans appropriating the raw materials of the original series and elaborating them into a more extensive narrative universe. Their mastery of narrative details is not born of some encyclopedic anal retention, but instead allows them to produce new fan fiction that supplements and expands the original diegetic boundaries of the series. For Jenkins, Star Trek fandom does not mean slavish devotion. "The fans' response typically involves not simply fascination or adoration but also frustration and antagonism, and it is the combination of the two responses which motivates their active engagement with the media. Because popular narratives often fail to satisfy, fans must struggle with them, to try to articulate to themselves and to others unrealized possibilities within the original works."[10] Borrowing from Michel de Certeau, Jenkins refers to this process as "textual poaching," fans raiding and reworking the property of Paramount Studios into a textual vehicle more accommodating of their meanings and pleasures. Most dramatic in this regard is the practice of "slash fiction," where a small group of fans has rewritten the adventure narrative of Star Trek into a homoerotic romance between Kirk and Spock. Other scholars of Star Trek fandom have also argued against the image of Trekkers as "social misfits" and "cultural dupes," and in so doing have emphasized the "active" interest of these fans in generating creative play from what seems to outsiders an endless cycle of repetitive consumption.

Despite such efforts to empower Star Trek fans through appeals to the dynamic process of "rerunning, rereading, and rewriting," the image of the fan as deluded misfit continues to echo throughout popular and academic culture. Paramount's very own documentary on the Star Trek phenomenon, Trekkies (1997), attempts to balance emic and etic views of the fan culture, hooking mainstream viewers by opening with rather merciless portraits of various "dysfunctional" fans before conceding, in the second half, that Star Trek viewers are actually often rather intelligent. Predictably, ridicule precedes respect as the studio endeavors to exploit its fan base before flattering it, an afterthought no doubt designed to keep them from jumping ship to Xena or Babylon 5.

In the realm of academic criticism, meanwhile, Saturday Night Live's attack on the perceived asexuality of Trekkies (long a staple of schoolyard taunts) finds institutional validation in the work of psychiatrist Ilsa Bick. To begin her "diagnosis" of Star Trek pathology, Bick opens with a jab at Jenkins. "Although the breadth of Jenkins's work is impressive and resists homogenization of the diverse facets of fan culture," she notes, "he may be exaggerating the fans' independence." After this opening nod to the "poacher" position, Bick then proceeds with her real project: confirming with professional authority the already reigning cultural suspicion that Star Trek fans are indeed a pack of emotionally and sexually retarded dweebs. Bick argues that the central appeal of *Star Trek* (its "master narrative," as she calls it) resides in Freud's concept of latency, that period of homosocial relations separating the often traumatic childhood discovery of sexual difference from puberty and more adult forms of sexuality. During this period, children express suspicion and discomfort with the opposite sex. "For latency-aged boys in particular," argues Bick, an "emphasis upon commonality and narcissistic mirroring involves an almost ritualized shunning of girls, regarded by these boys as disease-riddled vessels of contaminants (such as 'cooties') and malevolent, seductive interlopers intent upon the destruction of the solidarity of male chums."[11] For Bick, Star Trek fandom is a regressive pleasure, taking developmentally immature adults back to a time when, much like the lost boys of *Peter Pan,* they did not have to face the uncertainties of change and the impending challenges of adulthood.

While some aspects of Bick's reading seem rather contrived (such as interpreting the translucent transporter beams of the Enterprise as evocative of male ejaculate at the ultimate primal scene), her latency interpretation of the program has a certain merit in describing the foundations of the original series.[12] The first *Enterprise was* essentially a boy's club where each week Kirk, Spock, and McCoy beamed down to a new planet only to encounter women who quite frequently turned out to be disguised, monstrous, conniving, or otherwise evil. These episodes, finally, concluded with the punishment of the "cootie-creature" followed by the "discovery of home" and the primal reunion with "Mom" (a k a the *Enterprise).* Moreover, her diagnosis of the Star Trek fan seems to eerily prefigure the social profile of the Heaven's Gate cult (as the most notoriously dysfunctional of Star Trek fans). As has been well documented, members of Heaven's Gate also had significant issues related to their adult sexuality. Leader Applewhite had himself institutionalized after a series of homosexual affairs with students in the late 1960s and early 1970s, culminating in his new "mission" and a wholly platonic marriage with Bonnie Lu Nettles. Throughout its twenty-five-year history, sex was the cult's greatest taboo. All members were to remain celibate, a cause aided by the erasure of all markers of sexual difference—unisex haircuts and baggy clothing kept minds on the more metaphysical tasks at hand. For those male members still tempted by another's loins, there was of course the option of castration—a most drastic latency strategy adopted by several members of the group. Though not a boy's club in the manner of the *Enterprise,* the Heaven's Gate community did view themselves as a genderless homosocial group often forced into contact with the sexual confusion of Earth. As one member griped,

> [The] "lower forces" have succeeded in totally addicting humans to
> mammalian behavior. Everything from ads for toothpaste to clothing
> elevates human sexuality. Being from a genderless world, this behavior
> is extremely hideous to us. Even if we go on an outing as harmless as
> visiting the zoo, the tour guides lace their commentary with sexual
> innuendoes, even when the group they are addressing is full of small
> children.[13]

As mentioned before, the group's favorite character in *Star Trek: The Next Generation* was Lieutenant Commander Data, the rather asexual android continually baffled by the illogical ways of humans, particularly in relation to issues of emotions and sexuality.[14] Finally, like Kirk, Spock, and McCoy, this away team's ultimate goal was a primal reunion with the all-protective "mother ship," which they eventually discovered surfing in the wake of the Hale-Bopp comet.

Despite its seeming utility as a diagnostic tool, however, Bick's article remains troubling on a number of levels. First, as the opening jab at Jenkins and the overall tone of the piece indicate, Bick does seem to relish confirming the cultural stereotype of the Star Trek fan rather than problematizing it. Toward this end, she treats fans not as social subjects but as dysfunctional effects read off a text. Second, and related to this first problem, is the familiar psychoanalytic gambit of diagnosing media viewers based on textual evidence alone without reference to the social and historical specificity of the viewer's position in relation to those texts. Diagnosed via plot points and series architecture, the problem with Star Trek fans, ultimately, is that they *haven't* ever kissed a girl. Freud himself, of course, adamantly reminded budding psychoanalysts to avoid the temptation of reading dreams (and, one might presume, television shows) in terms of universal symbols divorced from the analysand's individual psychic history. Jenkins and the other scholars who defend Star Trek fandom have at least engaged Trekkers in conversation about their specific interests in the series. While those who argue for an active/progressive rather than passive/regressive portrait of Star

Trek fandom would probably agree that many of the fantasies and pleasures of the series are (or can be) expressive of sexualities (especially
in the case of slash fiction), few would engage in a totalizing argument
that "explains" all varieties of fan interest in the series in terms of a
master narrative drawn from Freud.

For those hoping to understand the extraordinary appeal of *Star Trek*
by examining its fans, the Jenkins-Bick dichotomy presents somewhat
of a conundrum. Who are we to believe—Jenkins's portrait of the empowered bricoleur or Bick's diagnosis of the regressive neurotic? Did
the members of Heaven's Gate pursue the latency narrative implicit in
Star Trek to its nightmarish conclusion, or were they active authors
of their own psychotically idiosyncratic universe? One might regard
their entire cosmology as a form of "poaching" reality, Christianity,
and the speculative "science" of ufology. Staying at a campground in
the mid-1970s, Applewhite and cofounder Bonnie Lu Nettles provided
the group with a highly structured experience that depended on science
fiction as a means of organizing their world. "The campground was
arranged in 'star clusters,' which were intended to simulate life within
a spacecraft," observed one reporter. "Each cluster was named after a
galaxy and arranged in a similar manner with identical equipment. To
leave one's cluster required a 'flight plan' that explained one's reasons
for exiting." Those on their way to Safeway or the post office left from
a parking lot dubbed a "docking zone."[15] At the time of their suicide at
Rancho Sante Fe, their rented home had been for sale on the real estate
market. After the deaths, a real estate agent who had frequently been in
the home noted "the stark metal bunks, computers and TV screen made
the place seem like an 'earthbound spaceship.'"[16] Recruiting materials
released to the public over the years did little to dispel such science-
fictional associations, as in this description of the group's history posted
on the Heaven's Gate Web site: "An 'away team' from an Evolutionary
Level Above Human, an 'Admiral,' His "Captain," and crew, during
the 1920s to 1950s, picked and prepped the human bodies which they
would wear for the task we are about to describe."[17] That task, of
course, was to convince as many hapless humans as possible that the
UFOs of T.E.L.A.H. would soon be here to evacuate the planet of its
more enlightened citizenry. Not unlike the slash writers so frequently
venerated in Star Trek critical literature, members of Heaven's Gate
also found raw materials with which to work in *Star Trek,* and the series undoubtedly helped them better understand (if not negotiate) their
unique position in social/cultural space. It is doubtful, however, that anyone would applaud this particularly idiosyncratic mode of "poaching."

Self-castration in the service of alien transcendence may be the ultimate form of slash, but few would consider it "resistant" or "progressive."

It may well be that attempts to understand fans by appeals to total-izing theories is a futile endeavor, much like efforts to understand audi-ences by placing them in the crosshairs of social-scientific media effects research. Perhaps, too, this dichotomy posited as a divide separating Jenkins and Bick is somewhat fallacious. Although Bick's critique of the "exaggerated independence" of Star Trek fans remains rather ab-solutist, Jenkins does allow that not all "poaching" is necessarily to be celebrated. Discussing de Certeau in relation to Stuart Hall's influential encoding/decoding model, Jenkins writes, "Readers are not always re-sistant; all resistant readings are not necessarily progressive readings; the 'people' do not always recognize their conditions of alienation and subordination."[18] Despite their differences, Jenkins and Bick may share common ground in engaging issues of "alienation and subordination." At the crux of their debate, I would argue, is the status one assigns repetition and fantasy in understanding popular narrative and its role in social life. In this respect, Jenkins and Bick are simply rehearsing a long-standing methodological impasse between cultural studies and psychoanalysis in engaging the narrative product of commercial capi-talism. Exactly what is the status of repetition, fantasy, and popular narrative in social life? Should we regard the fantasy life offered by the culture industries (one often based on repetition of narratives, genres, and formats) as yet another mode of mystification and misrecognition that prevents us from considering our own personal alienation and social subordination? Or are these fantasies, especially when actively reworked by fans, the only thing that makes our day-to-day alienation and subor-dination bearable? If Jenkins and Bick embody a methodological impasse between cultural studies and psychoanalysis, they also serve as advocates in the competing calls for a progressive versus radical politics.

And therein lies the true schism structuring debates over Star Trek fans, as well as the grounds for a potential compromise. Are Star Trek fans empowered bricoleurs or regressive neurotics? Is *Star Trek* a semi-otic resource or a lingering symptom? A more sober consideration of the average Star Trek fan would probably demonstrate that the franchise has now nurtured generations of "empowered neurotics." While some fans have chosen to integrate *Star Trek* on a path toward empowerment (if only in limited terms of expanded community and personal pleasure), others have turned to the series as fuel for neurosis and even (in the case of Heaven's Gate) raving delusion. In either case, for better or worse, television becomes a vehicle of transcendence, evacuating troubled, marginalized, maladapted, disaffected, or just plain bored audiences from the terrain of everyday life. Or, as one fan wrote in describing the "discovery effect" of *Star Trek,* "There you are, in the midst of whatever personal demons or small annoyances haunt your own life, and the rather large problems that haunt the planet, and then—suddenly there is *Star Trek.*"[19]

A Federation of Narratives

As this discussion demonstrates, most examinations of *Star Trek*'s appeal have focused almost exclusively on either story elements (Bick) or fan activities (Jenkins). While both are important, of course, there has been relatively little attention given to *Star Trek* as a *television* show; that is, while Star Trek mythology has been interpreted and its fans analyzed, few have addressed in any detail *Star Trek*'s historical importance in contributing to a new mode of televisual narrativity. In part, this reticence to confront the televisuality of *Star Trek* is a function of the general lack of literature (and interest) in the formal and narrative analysis of television itself. Long regarded by both social scientists and critical theorists as a problem, few have been willing to engage television in the rigorous aesthetic analysis found in film and literature. And yet questions of television form are pivotal in understanding the larger cultural phenomenon of *Star Trek.* One might begin by asking, for example, why it is that television, more so than film, seems to inspire such fanatical investment in its narrative worlds. Beyond the Star Wars franchise and the *The Rocky Horror Picture Show,* it is difficult to think of films that have fostered such intense fan involvement as *Star Trek* (or *The X-Files, Babylon 5, Friends,* or even a daily soap opera for that matter). There are no doubt people who have read certain novels by Tom Clancy or Jacqueline Susann thirty or forty times—and yet conventions devoted to *The Hunt for Red October* or *Valley of the Dolls* remain rare. Any consideration of *Star Trek* and its audience must contain a more general discussion of television textuality itself. Without invoking some essentialist notion of televisual specificity, I do believe there are certain historically and culturally unique formal characteristics in commercial U.S. television that encourage and reinforce audience involvement with its diegetic worlds. In many ways, the fan community around *Star Trek* has both anticipated and perhaps even contributed to the development of a now wholly dominant textual strategy in U.S. television.

As a starting point, one might consider the often staggering number of episodes generated by a successful open-ended series such as *Star*

Trek. There are just 79 episodes of the original series, making it only a modest success in terms of its initial network run, but even this limited metatext makes over three full days of continuous programming available to viewers and fans. *Star Trek: The Next Generation* and *Deep Space Nine* contributed another 353 episodes, and *Voyager* added another 172 episodes by the end of its seventh season. All told, that's approximately 604 hours of time spent with various crews in the Federation— exploring space, battling, and/or bonding with alien civilizations, and perhaps most important, just hanging around the ship. If one were to watch every episode of the Star Trek franchise (which many have) back-to-back (which few would probably survive), it would take twenty-five days of twenty-four-hour viewing to complete the run (and that's not even counting the hours of Star Trek motion pictures, or the nearly endless number of hours one could spend reading Paramount-approved novelizations, not to mention endless volumes of fan fiction). Paramount's newest installment in the Star Trek franchise is *Enterprise,* which will no doubt contribute another seven-year run to the story vault.

Sheer textual volume, while important, does not completely explain such intense involvement from fans. *Star Trek,* after all, had to engender devoted fan interest before making such duration and depth possible through endless syndication and spin-offs. *Gunsmoke* ran for over twenty seasons on American television without creating opportunities for fans to gather dressed as Festus or Miss Kitty. Genre is clearly a consideration here. A list of the television series that have developed the strongest fan communities include *Star Trek, Dr. Who, Twin Peaks, Xena, The X-Files, Beauty and the Beast, Blake 7,* and *The Prisoner,* to name just a few. As many have noted, elements of science fiction and the fantastic allow for more active fan identification and engagement with a TV series; indeed, the fantastic as a genre (or a series of subgenres) actively encourages audience speculation and the elaboration of alternate narrative worlds. While one could wonder what lay beyond the textual confines of Dodge City on *Gunsmoke,* such musings about the plains of nineteenth-century Kansas are not nearly as rewarding as learning the history of the Klingon Empire or extrapolating the customs of Romulan diplomacy. Science fiction's ability to displace the terrain of fantasy, allegory, social commentary, and other modes of critically engaging the real world also makes for more active forms of speculative investment. The mysteries of Vulcan physiology, for example, allow for a freedom of sexual scenarios not so apparent in potential Dillon/Doc stories.

And yet, not all science fiction programming begets a fan community (most, but not all), and few create communities as intense as that of Star Trek. While the strength of Star Trek fandom is in large part a function of genre and an increasingly elaborate narrative universe, its original success may well be a function of the program's unique place in the historical development of television narrative. In his original pitch of the series to NBC, for example, Gene Roddenberry referred to *Star Trek* as a "one-hour science-fiction series *with continuing characters.*"[20] The fact that Roddenberry chose to emphasize continuing characters demonstrates that such a development was somewhat of a novelty in mid-sixties science fiction television. Science fiction to that point had primarily meant anthologies in the vein of *One Step Beyond, The Twilight Zone,* and *The Outer Limits.* Roddenberry's series, on the other hand, was to offer "all the advantages of an anthology with none of the limitations."[21] Such comments suggest the pure anthology format had fallen into industrial disfavor by the mid-sixties. As Mark Alvey argues of this period, "some continuity was considered essential to encourage repeat viewership—the extreme form of 'self-closed' narrative, the anthology, was shunned. Repeated elements designed to make the series familiar and 'habitual' were institutional givens: an established premise, a genre foundation, and above all, continuing characters."[22] Episodic television offered a number of economic and scheduling advantages to the networks. Familiar genre formulas could be raided and adapted to the overall series architecture, a structure of recurring characters and sets that provided continuity in scheduling/viewing while also maximizing narrative and material economy in production. Wooing cost-conscious NBC executives who were no doubt reluctant to confuse their viewers or stockholders with weekly excursions in outer space, Roddenberry referred to *Star Trek* as "*Wagon Train* to the stars" and described the U.S.S. *Enterprise,* perhaps the most beloved spaceship in science fiction history, as little more than "a basic and amortized standing set."[23]

When *Star Trek* arrived on network airwaves in 1966, then, it did so as an *episodic* series, following weekly, self-contained adventures of a continuing cast of characters as they guided the U.S.S. *Enterprise* on a mission of intergalactic exploration in the twenty-fourth century. Christopher Anderson argues that by the late 1950s two narrative models dominated episodic television. In what Anderson terms the "disguised anthology" format, a recurring protagonist "entered a new community" and "either witnessed or provoked a new story in which he would participate to varying degrees" (examples might include *Route 66* and *The Fugitive*). The other option was a format based on a recurring community impacted by outside forces, a structure that "generally involved the potential disintegration and ultimate reintegration of the community structure" (such as *Bonanza* or *Gunsmoke*).[24] *Star Trek*'s primary narrative innovation, then, was to combine these two narrative options, following the community of the *Enterprise* as it traveled from planet to planet provoking a series of episodic adventures. As the many studies of Star Trek fandom have demonstrated, fans were far more interested in the *continuing community* of the story world than in the isolated (and often quite ridiculous) plots of individual episodes. In fact, an early survey of Star Trek fans found that the show's status as an "action/adventure" series was its least engaging element.[25] While many isolated characters and alien worlds remain central to Star Trek fan culture, fan interest has long focused primarily on the various incarnations of the *Enterprise* (and related vessels), their crews, and the historical genesis of the Federation. With the original series, the already speculative genre of science fiction now had a vehicle for centrifugal elaboration of a larger universe and centripetal elaboration of character and character relations. Almost immediately after cancellation of the original series, Star Trek fans began the now decades-long project of such textual elaboration, speculating about gaps in the narrative, providing more detailed accounts of minor characters, and generating wholly new tales within the "rules" of the overall metadiegesis.[26] As Jenkins notes, "For the fans and perhaps many regular viewers . . . *Star Trek* is experienced as something closer to a serial. No episode can be easily disentangled from the series' historical trajectory; plot developments are seen not as complete within themselves but as one series of events among many in the lives of the primary characters."[27]

This promotion of the Star Trek universe as "real" began with the producers themselves from the earliest days of the series. Exploiting growing fan interest in the reality of Roddenberry's vision of the future, Stephen Whitfield and Roddenberry's *The Making of Star Trek* (published in 1968) is replete with anecdotes reinforcing fan conceptions of the Federation as the earth's "real" future.

> After reading through a few lines of dialogue with Bill Shatner and Leonard Nimoy, the director turned to George [Takei] and said, "Okay, and at this point, Sulu fires the phasers. So you hit this button and fire the phasers." . . . George promptly replied, "No, that's not the right button. The phaser button is the one over here." . . . The director gave him kind of a funny look and said, "What are you talking about? What difference does it make? This is a sound stage, remember? Push

the button and let's get on with the scene." George steadfastly refused
to push that button, saying, "If I push that button, it will blow up the
Enterprise!"[28]

Cultivating viewer interest, participation, and belief in the Star Trek
metaverse has remained a central project for producers ever since Paramount realized the franchise still had life in movies and spin-offs.

In essence, these first fans of the original installment in the franchise
anticipated and perhaps even contributed to a gradual shift in commercial television's predominant narrative format. Throughout the 1970s
and 1980s, television moved toward what Horace Newcomb has termed
"cumulative narrative."[29] In series such as *M.A.S.H., The Mary Tyler
Moore Show, All in the Family, Hill Street Blues, Magnum, P.I.,* and *St.
Elsewhere,* television began to balance self-contained episodic stories
with long-term progression of various serial story arcs.[30] Such a format
has provided producers and programmers with the advantages of both
episodic *and* serial narrative formats, accommodating the habits and
pleasures of two distinct audience groups. Episodic elements allow new
and infrequent viewers to enjoy an isolated story while the more serial,
cumulative aspects of the series allow for the pleasures of investing
more profoundly in that particular series' metadiegesis. This format has
proven so effective for commercial television that by the 1990s, cumulative narratives came to dominate almost all of prime-time television in
the United States.[31] Appropriately, then, when the Star Trek franchise
generated its first spin-off in 1987, *Star Trek: The Next Generation,* the
series dropped the wholly episodic structure of its predecessor so as to
acknowledge, accommodate, and court the cumulative interests of Star
Trek fandom developed over the previous two decades. The new *Star
Trek* was a model of cumulative design, integrating episodic adventures
with longer, more character-based arcs of melodrama. Guest aliens and
love interests returned for encore appearances or enjoyed multi-episode
runs. Overall, great care was taken to suture the original series and
the new series together as equally legitimate and related installments
in a coherent metaverse, an impulse that has guided development of all
subsequent Star Trek properties.[32] The Star Trek franchise, in short,
generally works *with* fans in order to police textual consistency and expand textual boundaries. As Jenkins notes, "While *Star Trek: The Next
Generation* makes occasional explicit references to program history,
fans are capable of reading that history into a look, a raised eyebrow,
the inflection of a line, or any other subtle performance cue that may be
seen as symptomatic of what the character 'had to be thinking' at that

moment."[33] The same might now be said of *ER, NYPD Blue,* or even *Friends,* all of which feature characters and narrative worlds informed by their own textual history.

One might argue that any narrative, regardless of medium, allows for extension at the margins and elaboration of a narrative world. That may be true, but I would still argue television provokes a specific and highly intensified form of such elaboration. For example, the serial elements of TV narrative, whether implicit as in the original *Star Trek* or made explicit in the cumulative mode, encourage two forms of fantasy engagement in viewers. On the one hand, serial narrative by its very nature creates gaps, hesitations, and delays that foster fantasy elaboration. This is true whether viewers consume a series in the real time of its original sequencing across months and years or as a block of programs made available in syndication years after its cancellation. In either case, one encounters windows on a narrative world that omit as much as they include. On the other hand, the episodic qualities of cumulative design allow for weekly rehearsals of a particular fantasy structure related to genre or character. Fans of a series, be it *Star Trek* or *Seinfeld,* tune in each week to see favorite characters enact a specific set of character functions. In many cases, plot is secondary to premise in television, giving rise to the standard industry maxim that TV is a more character-based medium than film.

In addition to television's powers of seriality, duration, and depth, the medium also exudes a certain presence of "liveness" that is significant in constructing its narrative worlds. Elsewhere, I have argued that the seemingly live and even living qualities of television make it a far different narrative medium than film.[34] Television's perpetual sense of "nowness," even as it broadcasts shows from the distant past, infuses its programs with a wholly different realism than that of the cinema. Whereas film viewers recognize that movies are by definition stories trapped in the past, television trades on its sense of always instantaneous transmission in the present. Contemporary television series often take great care to orchestrate the illusion that the diegetic world unfolds parallel to that of the viewers, as in *ER*'s practice of sending a second-unit team to Chicago to pick up seasonal shots of their principal characters in the city. One might argue that even episodes of the original *Star Trek,* now some thirty years old, appear within the unending flow of television as living transmissions from another world, direct from the series diegesis of the twenty-third century. This quality, I would argue, is reinforced by a decades-long process of syndicated repetition. Stumbling across the "Tribbles" episode of *Star Trek* ten or twenty times in one's lifetime tends to reaffirm its status as a living window on the Federation in the twenty-third century.

Elsewhere in this volume, Sara Gwenllian-Jones argues that televisual metaverses, be they of *Star Trek, Buffy,* or *The X-Files,* constitute our culture's true form of virtual reality. In contrast to the crudely realized shapes and awkward movements of contemporary virtual reality technology, the nexus of a textual, intertextual, and extratextual metaverse can be, for those willing to make the investment, a truly living reality. Significantly, this is a reality that exists more within mental architecture than electronic, and therein lies its power. Putting aside the various progressive and regressive scenarios offered by Jenkins and Bick, a central and in many ways unparalleled pleasure offered by *Star Trek* is the audience's opportunity for collective elaboration and maintenance of the Star Trek metaverse, a psychic structure one can choose to inhabit at will. And, like the physical universe, the Star Trek metaverse is one that (for the moment anyway) is continuing to expand.

This requires rethinking the significance of repetition and mastery in relation to Star Trek fans. In his famous piece on the cult status of *Casablanca,* Umberto Eco suggests that cult texts must "provide a completely furnished world so that its fans can quote characters and episodes as if they were aspects of the fan's private sectarian world." Such activity—a function of mastery through repetition—is certainly true of *Star Trek.* Eco then adds, "I think that in order to transform a work into a cult object one must be able to break, dislocate, unhinge it so that one can remember only parts of it, irrespective of their original relationship with the whole."[35] This seems less applicable to Star Trek fans who, despite often individualistic, idiosyncratic, and even aberrant interests in the series, are brought together in a mutually sustaining fantasy of a textual totality. *Star Trek* is one of the few series to make available the series "story bible" to the public, providing readers with the time lines and character biographies that govern its textual universe. Paramount has also cashed in on fan interest in designing and diagramming the various ships in the Federation fleet, publishing blueprints in the days of print, and more recently issuing a CD-ROM that allows prospective shipbuilders to design their own crafts. Role-playing games and Klingon language camps can help round out days and months spent in the Star Trek metaverse. Finally, whether staged for public relations or a sincere effort to engage fans (or perhaps both), producers also boast that *Star Trek* is the one place in Hollywood that has an open-door script policy, supposedly considering for possible production all unsolicited scripts submitted by fans. Taken together, the United

Federation of Planets is thus also a federation of narratives where, as in all true federations, characters and subplots are autonomous—divided by discrete episodes, series, or quadrants of the galaxy—and yet all contribute to the strength of a whole that is greater than the sum of its parts.[36] Considered in this respect, the desire to repeat and master the textual worlds of Star Trek is not necessarily about regression into psychosexual stasis, but constitutes instead the enabling foundation for more multifaceted forms of textual play. In this respect, Bick's critique of Star Trek fans sides with the wrong character in that other famous latency narrative, *Peter Pan*. The most appropriate metaphor for *Star Trek* and its fans is not the lost boys, forever stuck in the psychosexual limbo of latency, but Tinkerbell, that fantastic creation held together only by the collective investment of belief, an entity made real through sheer force of imagination and will.

Some Desire to Advance Even BEYOND All HUMAN Behavior

All narrative, it might be said, asks its readers to become temporarily delusional. Most popular novels, movies, and television shows require a suspension of disbelief for maximum enjoyment—the reader must allow him- or herself to be temporarily transported to a fictive elsewhere. In rare cases (as with Heaven's Gate),[37] popular narratives so colonize the mind as to suspend belief in reality, leading to any number of potentially hazardous "conversion" experiences. Is there a common profile to those who make such deep investments in narrative worlds? What is the line dividing faith and delusion?

Hours before one member of Heaven's Gate ingested his fatal applesauce, he confessed to a video camera, "I think everyone in the class wanted something more than this human world has to offer." Another member added, "If humans were told the truth about what was going on on this planet, they'd be shocked and wouldn't continue in their eight-to-five slavery and ignorance."[38] How many of us, I wonder, would agree wholeheartedly with such statements, even if we do not harbor fantasies of hitching a ride to another plane of existence on a passing comet? Many fans of *Star Trek* would certainly second these statements. If Star Trek fans and the Heaven's Gate cult share anything, then, it is the desire to transcend the more brutal and limiting features of our planet. Why this bond? Those preparing to make an offensive statement often preface it by arguing that stereotypes have some basis in fact. That said, it would probably not be a misstep to say that many (if not most) Star Trek fans (and science fiction fans for that matter) are "misfits" of one kind or another. Jenkins, of course, works strenuously against such conceptions, arguing that the "stereotypical conception of the fan" as nerdy, asexual, and infantilized may have "a limited factual basis" but is actually "a projection of anxieties about the violation of dominant cultural hierarchies."[39] Trekkies have been ostracized, in other words, because their veneration of "Amok Time" scandalizes bourgeois taste, which would prefer such energy be invested into Shakespeare or Faulkner. And yet, I would imagine an adolescent boy pummeled daily in the schoolyard for his fascination with Vulcan culture or a girl ostracized for reading Star Trek novels on the bus would have a different perspective on their social status. Those administering the pummeling or the ridicule could probably care less about bourgeois cultural hierarchies except for how they manifest themselves in terms of current dress codes and "appropriate" behavior in their own peer culture.

Whether *Star Trek* is a cause or a symptom, most Trekkies have probably experienced the phenomenon of not fitting in at some point in their life. Rather than reject this misfit label, perhaps it would be better to embrace it, recognizing that "nerdism" is in fact a form of nonconformity that can present a certain friction in the normative operation of social power. Though it may lead to disenfranchisement in certain arenas of the social order, it can also foretell of rewards in other venues. For example, while I have no empirical data to support this claim, I would hazard to guess that very few Trekkies have been captain of the football team or homecoming queen, and yet many high school and college valedictorians have been Trekkies—this in a culture where America's long-running populist traditions can often translate into a profound anti-intellectualism. As "empowered neurotics" (or perhaps nerds), a great number of Star Trek fans are no doubt individuals who possess an intelligence in excess of that required by their station in life and the economy. In short, the metaverse of Star Trek becomes a fictional enclave for smart people in a dumb world.

And what smart person wouldn't want to live on the U.S.S. *Enterprise,* especially in the *Next Generation* incarnation so favored by Heaven's Gate? Instead of spending your workday typing memos for a cranky boss or crunching numbers for some soulless retail project, you get to map new star systems, study the ecosystems of new planets, and learn the ways of exotic civilizations. Indeed, the Federation is one of the few places left in the universe where anthropologists, historians, and other intellectuals are actually valued rather than reviled and ridiculed. No need to worry about money or other material resources. Everyone, regardless of gender, race, or species seems to get along (at least within the Federation). The only trauma one seems to face is in the eternally baffling arena of romantic relationships, but even if you get dumped, it will no doubt be a humane and respectful process since no one in the twenty-fourth century seems overly neurotic. People seem a lot less superficial in the future. Who knows? You might even get a date with Seven-of-Nine once she appreciates your true inner beauty. At night you retire to your stylishly appointed suite complete with a view of the galaxy and decorated with interplanetary bric-a-brac collected on your recent missions. Can't sleep? Perhaps a completely nonfat yet wholly convincing hot fudge sundae or a shot of synthohol sake will help make you drowsy. If not, there's always a stroll along the ever-active corridors of the *Enterprise,* where something or someone interesting waits just beyond every curve in the hallway. Friends always await in Ten-Forward to discuss the politics of the ship and its crew—not in vicious, backstabbing gossip, but rather out of a sweet concern and interest in the personal well-being and happiness of every crew member. The holodeck is always a tempting distraction. Hang out for a couple of hours in a French salon with Jean-Paul Sartre. Program a life-or-death adventure in the land of ancient Vulcan. And through it all, be secure in your knowledge that Captains Kirk, Picard, Sisko, and Janeway are in their own quarters enjoying a cup of Earl Grey, reading *Moby Dick,* thinking through the next day's mission. Tomorrow will be another day of untold excitement and adventure, where a rational application of science and democracy will actually work.

In this respect, the Star Trek metaverse is a compensatory future, a coping mechanism for enduring the daily grind of contemporary life. As a coping mechanism for empowered nerds, Star Trek functions very much like a secular religion. What are the implications of making this conversion, of becoming washed in the green blood of the Vulcan? Like other religions, one faces continuing marginalization and even persecution (of a kind), but one also enjoys the community of faith, a mutual dedication to a more rational and meaningful existence in the distant future. Of course, one could easily critique such faith by continuing the parallel and pointing out that Star Trek presents another "opiate for the masses." It may well be that Star Trek (like academe) is a perfect cultural mechanism for disempowering smart people by distracting them with a fantasy world so as to prevent them from intervening meaningfully in the real operations of social power. And yet, Star Trek fandom does retain a fundamental difference from traditional organized religions. Despite the stereotypes, Trekkies in the end do recognize that their metaverse is a *fantasy,* not a deferred reward that will be encountered one day in the clouds.

This, of course, returns us at last to the members of Heaven's Gate, seemingly the most dysfunctional Trekkies to have ever walked the planet. And yet, like so many other famous kooks of this century, the roots of the Heaven's Gate cult can be found not in the adventures of Kirk and Spock, but in Applewhite and partner Bonnie Lu Nettles's perverse reading of the Book of Revelations. Down on their luck in the early 1970s, spiritually bankrupt, sexually confused, and in search of a more "divine truth," Applewhite and Nettles began piecing together a new religion from scraps of theosophy, New Age spirituality, Christianity, and ufology. They believed that two thousand years ago, a representative of T.E.L.A.H. occupied the body of Christ to teach humans how to transcend their mortal shells. In a slightly displaced version of the common Christ delusion, Bo and Peep (as they came to call themselves) believed that two more representatives of T.E.L.A.H. arrived in the early 1970s to occupy their own bodies. When in their transcendent form, members of T.E.L.A.H. greatly resembled the now ubiquitous schwa image of the extraterrestrial—hairless bodies, almond-shaped eyes, giant foreheads.[40] Though their eventual interest in Star Trek was an echo rather than a source of this belief system, few newspapers or critics were willing to blame Christianity for the couple's misguided mission. As always, pop culture fixations make for better press and better villains.

Far from being a symptom of insanity, Heaven's Gate's interest in Star Trek was perhaps their last hope. If only they had spent less time reading the Bible and more time watching *Star Trek,* they might still be alive today, free of the metaphysical mumbo jumbo that made them take the ultimate leap of faith in the wake of the Hale-Bopp comet. As Trekkies, they would have had a community, a language, and a metaverse that might have made their daily lives and failed ambitions (for themselves and the planet) more bearable. As one member said in his taped good-bye the day before the mass suicide:

> We watch a lot of *Star Trek* . . . it's just like going on a holodeck. . . . We've been on a holodeck, we've been in an astronaut training program. . . . We figured out a day equals one thousand years . . . played it out mathematically . . . it's roughly thirty minutes. . . . We've been training on a holodeck for thirty minutes, now it's time to stop and put into practice what we've learned . . . so we take off the virtual reality helmet, we take off the vehicle that we've used for this task. We just

set it aside, go back out of the holodeck to reality to be with the other members in the craft, in the heavens.[41]

This member of Heaven's Gate clearly saw *Star Trek* and the holodeck as a metaphor, "the vernacular of a popular 'science fiction' entertainment series" that one might use to converse about other social possibilities. Rather than "live long and prosper" by investing in the power of fiction and textual transcendence, however, Heaven's Gate chose to believe in the more dangerous illusions of a religious transcendence. Therein lies the true tragedy. Rather than put their faith in a forlorn comet and confused charismatic, television could have been their true means of deliverance.

Notes

1. Heaven's Gate Web site, at http://www.trancenet.org/heavensgate/misc/ovrview.htm, accessed August 2000.

2. See "Flying Saucery in the Wilderness," *Time,* 27 August 1974, 58; James Phelan, "Looking for the Next World," *New York Times Magazine,* 29 February 1976.

3. Rodney Perkins and Forrest Jackson, *Cosmic Suicide: The Tragedy and Transcendence of Heaven's Gate* (Dallas: Pentaradial Press, 1997), 55.

4. Ibid.

5. Staff of the *New York Post, Heaven's Gate: Cult Suicide in San Diego* (New York: Harper Paperbacks, 1997), 272.

6. Henry Jenkins, *Textual Poachers: Television Fans and Participatory Culture* (New York: Routledge, 1992), 10–12.

7. For a cross section of such work, see (in addition to Jenkins's *Textual Poachers*) Camille Bacon-Smith, *Enterprising Women: Television Fandom and the Creation of Popular Myth* (Philadelphia: University of Pennsylvania Press, 1992); Constance Penley, *NASA/TREK* (London: Verso, 1997); Constance Penley, "Brownian Motion: Women, Tactics, and Technology," in *Technoculture,* ed. Penley and Andrew Ross (Minneapolis: University of Minnesota Press, 1991); Joanna Russ, "Pornography for Women, by Women, with Love," in *Magic Mommas, Trembling Sisters, Puritans, and Perverts: Feminist Essays* (Trumansberg, N.Y.: Crossing Press, 1985).

8. "Star Trek's Nine Lives," *Newsweek,* 22 December 1986, 66, 71.

9. Jenkins, *Textual Poachers,* 9–10.

10. Ibid., 23.

11. Ilsa Bick, "Boys in Space: Star Trek, Latency, and the Neverending Story," *Cinema Journal* 35, no. 2 (winter 1996).

12. Bick wisely—or perhaps disingenuously—ignores the Star Trek spin-offs and their more complicated architecture since they would almost certainly compromise her argument.

13. Glnody, "Earth Exit Statement," at http://www.heavensgatetoo.com/exitgln.htm, accessed August 2003.

14. Such "asexuality" was based on a wholly selective reading of the series by the members of Heaven's Gate. Data lost his virginity early in the very first season.

15. Perkins and Jackson, *Cosmic Suicide*, 43.

16. Staff of *New York Post, Heaven's Gate: Cult Suicide in San Diego*, 26.

17. Perkins and Jackson, *Cosmic Suicide*, 72.

18. Jenkins, *Textual Poachers*, 34.

19. Quoted in Jacqueline Lichenberg, Sondra Marshak, and Joan Winston, *Star Trek Lives! Personal Notes and Anecdotes* (New York: Bantam Books, 1975), 9.

20. Stephen E. Whitfield and Gene Roddenberry, *The Making of Star Trek* (New York: Ballantine Books, 1968), 22.

21. Whitfield and Roddenberry, *The Making of Star Trek*, 23. It should be noted that Roddenberry was joined in this new narrative form by Irwin Allen, whose series *Voyage to the Bottom of the Sea* and *Lost in Space* also melded science fiction with episodic structure during this period.

22. Mark Alvey, *Series Drama and the "Semi-Anthology": Sixties Television in Transition* (Ann Arbor: UMI Dissertation Services, 1995), 39–40. For an excellent summary of these issues, see the entire chapter "Series Imperative/Series Narrative."

23. Whitfield and Roddenberry, *The Making of Star Trek*, 28.

24. Christopher Anderson, *Hollywood TV: The Studio System in the Fifties* (Austin: University of Texas Press, 1994), 208.

25. Lichenberg, Marshak, and Winston, *Star Trek Lives!*, 48

26. Jenkins provides a useful summary of these activities in *Textual Poachers*, 162–77.

27. Ibid., 99.

28. Whitfield and Roddenberry, *The Making of Star Trek*, 380–81.

29. Horace Newcomb, "Magnum, PI: The Champagne of Television," *Channels*, April/May 1985.

30. See Christopher Anderson, "Reflections on Magnum P.I.," and Thomas Schatz, "St. Elsewhere and the Evolution of the Ensemble Series," in *Television: The Critical View*, 4th ed., ed. Horace Newcomb (New York: Oxford University Press, 1985).

31. For a more detailed discussion of the issues addressed below, see Jeffrey Sconce, "What If? Diegetic Space in Contemporary Television," in *The Persistence of Television*, ed. Lynn Spigel and Jan Olsson (Durham, N.C.: Duke University Press, 2001).

32. This strategy has been most manifest in various crossover episodes, where characters in one series appear on another. Notable episodes include "Relics" from *Star Trek: The Next Generation* (featuring Scotty from the original series) and "Trials and Tribble-ations" from *Deep Space Nine* (wherein

members of the *Deep Space 9* crew find themselves inserted into the episode "The Trouble with Tribbles" from the original series). *Deep Space Nine* also imported *Next Generation*'s Worf in an attempt to bolster sagging interest in the franchise.

33. Jenkins, *Textual Poachers*, 99.

34. See Jeffrey Sconce, *Haunted Media: Electronic Presence from Telegraphy to Television* (Durham, N.C.: Duke University Press, 2000).

35. Umberto Eco, *Travels in Hyperreality* (London: Picador, 1986), 196, 197.

36. As anecdotal proof of this theory, I would point to the spectacular misunderstanding of the Star Trek metaverse made by the architects of *Star Trek: Voyager,* the third and certainly least successful spin-off from the original. In its initial design, *Voyager* was conceived as somewhat of a "Swiss Family Robinson" narrative. After an inexplicable interstellar mishap, the crew of the Federation vessel *Voyager* are flung seventy thousand light years away from home. Now stranded in an uncharted part of the universe (and metaverse), their cumulative series goal was to return home to Federation space. While one can certainly see how Paramount executives were enamored of this return to an action-adventure premise of exploration for the series (especially after the more stagebound *Deep Space Nine*), such a series foundation cut *Voyager* off from the franchise's chief narrative strength—namely, the hours, days, months, and years fans had invested in elaborating the familiar, communal metaverse of the Federation. Gone were the complexities of character arcs and relations, the intrigue of interspecies rivalries, the history of Federation politics and protocol. Recognizing this, the producers of the series soon concocted ways to inject elements of the previous Star Trek metaverse into *Voyager,* but since the very premise made such injections unrealistic, obvious, and contrived, they only amplified the overall defects in the series design. *Voyager*'s "failure" serves as a reminder that while book and film narratives reward temporary suspension of disbelief, a television series demands a more free-floating form of suspended disbelief, asking us to invoke the existence of an alternate, parallel reality that we will occupy in weekly televisual installments and through ongoing psychic investment.

37. "Some desire to advance even BEYOND all HUMAN behavior," at http://www.trancenet.org/heavensgate/book/610.htm, accessed August 2003.

38. Good-bye videotape, as quoted in *Heaven's Gate: Cult Suicide in San Diego,* 212, 7.

39. Jenkins, *Textual Poachers,* 17.

40. Perkins and Jackson, *Cosmic Suicide,* 31–33.

41. "Farewell Tape," as quoted in Perkins and Jackson, *Cosmic Suicide,* 72.

A Kind of German *Star Trek:*
Raumpatrouille Orion and the
Life of a Cult TV Series

Eva Vieth

■ Imagine that *Star Trek* consists of just seven episodes. Imagine it had all stopped back in 1967: a first glimpse of the crew and the Klingons, a hazy outline of a different world and time, and nothing more. No films, no second-generation spin-off series, no merchandise. How many fans would there be? How many people would turn up for conventions? How many people would even remember that there had been a science fiction series called *Star Trek* on television back in the sixties? How many people would have incorporated Trek lore into their daily lives? How many scholarly studies would have been published?

Star Trek appeared on American television on 8 September 1966. Nine days later, on 17 September 1966, on German television, a different starship left its (submarine) base to cruise the universe: the *Orion,* on space patrol to protect Earth from attacks from outside our solar system. Yet while the original *Star Trek* made it through three seasons and gradually established its own universe, *Raumpatrouille Orion* went out of production after seven episodes. Apart from its continuation in a series of pulp novels, a handful of merchandise products, and the occasional rerun on television, there was little to feed into fandom. Despite this lack of narrative development, *Orion* today has a small but dedicated fan following on the Internet. Recent video and DVD releases sold tens of thousands of copies, and the quirky music used in the series is still recognizable enough to be used as a jingle in a current radio advertisement for a popular brand of beer.

This essay has three aims. First, it introduces the German sister ship of the *Enterprise* to an anglophone public. Second, it (roughly) traces the codevelopment of *Orion* and its fandom between 1966 and the present day, asking how such a limited text has fascinated ardent fans for thirty-five years. Third, the chapter explores Orion fandom as it exists today, examining contemporary Orion fan cultures and their activities in order to shed light on the nature and development of science fiction television fandom in general.

The Beginning—*Orion* Appears on TV

Until 1962, West Germany had only one national television channel— the public broadcasting station ARD controlled by the television stations of the various German Länder.[1] In 1962, however, a second channel was launched. This was ZDF, directly under the influence of the national government. The so-called third channels, produced by the Länder stations, were added from 1964 onward. All channels subscribed to a notion of television as a medium for both public education and entertainment and were closely regulated by public agencies. Nevertheless, they also saw themselves as competitors and so were reaching for innovative program formats that would attract bigger slices of the audience pie. This was one reason why the unusual experiment of a science fiction television series found interested producers.

During the 1960s, the West German television audience grew rapidly. In 1960, there were 3.4 million television sets in West Germany; by 1965 there were 10 million, and by 1970 there were 15.1 million. In 1969, 84 percent of the West German population could be reached by television. It quickly became the major medium of social integration and the center of private rituals. Television programs were topics of conversation and the television schedule shaped peoples' daily routines.

Approximately 30 percent of the channels' content consisted of information programs, 15 percent of entertainment shows, just under 20 percent of films and TV plays, just over 10 percent of youth programs, and around 10 percent of sports. Many films were imported and dubbed, most from America and Britain, some from France and Italy. It was the same with serials, a form that was seen as vulgar and trivial and was therefore only gradually adopted by German production houses.[2] The most popular serial genres were the crime series (such as *77 Sunset Strip, Perry Mason,* and *FBI*) and family westerns (such as *Bonanza*). Though some 1950s science fiction films were dubbed and broadcast, German television was relatively science fiction–free—the *Twilight Zone* was not broadcast in Germany until 1968, *Doctor Who* had to wait until 1989. While it cannot be claimed that fiction in general was scorned, "folksy," realistic, and/or comedy forms of reality representation were preferred.

Into this setting came the idea for a series about a space ship and its crew—first conceived by Rolf Honold in the early 1960s, inspired by the American science fiction wave, and planned as an alternative to "the ever-present crime serials."³ A first draft, titled *Terra Calls Andromeda,* was bought by Bavaria Studios, but the production costs were deemed too high and the series was never made. A coproduction with American producers was suggested but, according to one of the later coauthors, failed because the German team could not answer the question "Who are the heroes and who are the Indians?"⁴ In response, Honold and a team of experienced writers wrote a second, less expensive version of the series. Financed by the four major German Länder stations and the French station ORTF, the entire seven-episode series was shot in black-and-white by Bavaria Studios for a total cost of just over DM 3 million. In contrast, *Star Trek* (which was filmed in color) had a budget of $300,000 or DM 900,000 per episode.

Although the production costs for *Orion* were about half those of *Star Trek,* the producers did not skimp. Well-known German actors such as Dietmar Schönherr, Eva Pflug, and Wolfgang Völz were hired, set design was handled by the respected Rolf Zehetbauer (who was later awarded an Oscar for his work on *Cabaret*), and the starship *Orion* was furnished with chairs, glassware, and tables from established designers such as Mies van der Rohe, Harry Bertoia, and Charles Eames. The series' special effects are one reason for *Orion*'s present-day cult status; they include the use of aspirin to create the fizz as the *Orion* makes its underwater launch and a "planet explosion" in which flying coffee beans substituted as debris. What today seems charmingly inadequate was the best to be had at the time—special effects technician Theo Nischwitz was one of the best in German cinema. Similarly, the unique astro sound of the *Orion* was created by famous film composer Peter Thomas. Style and quality were what was aimed for, and to this day, "style" and "quality" are cited by *Orion* fans as a key part of the series' attraction.

When the series finally hit TV screens, its time slot demonstrated that *Orion* was not perceived as a cheap production. It was shown first on the ARD channel on Saturday evenings at 8:15—a prime slot usually reserved for the film of the week or serious German productions, the programs described as *Straßenfeger* or "street-sweepers" because the German streets emptied as people went home to watch them. *Orion* initially was perceived as general family entertainment; only in later reruns was it moved to the afternoon or late-night slots that are today reserved for science fiction. During its first run, each episode was tuned in by 36 to 56 percent of the West German audience.

Set in the year 3000, *Orion* reaches farther into the future than *Star Trek* but makes little use of the technology gap this would imply. Even though color technology was available, the series was still made in black-and-white. The audience encounters the Orion crew for the first time at the moment when they are relegated to patrol duty for the insubordinate behavior of their captain; against orders, Commander McLane had landed on a planet considered impossible to reach. An officer of the Galactic Security Service (GSS), Tamara Jagellovsk, is assigned to "keep an eye on them." Much of the tension (and the humor) of the series draws on the conflicts between the maverick McLane, the militaristic bureaucrats of the GSS, and Jagellovsk's attempts to mediate.

The rest of the crew consists of three men and a woman, identified as international through Asian, Italian, French, and Scandinavian surnames, though undeniably German in appearance and behavior. The relationship between captain and crew is informal; the once-used phrase "McLane and his gang" is appropriate in its suggestion of adolescent companionship. This atmosphere is confirmed in the closing scenes of the episodes, which are usually set in the submarinean Starlight Casino, where the success of the individual missions is celebrated with whiskey and champagne.

The first episode also introduces the main "baddies" of the series, the Frogs, mute, glittering shadows who possess vastly superior weapons technology and are intent on invading Earth, though their motives are never elaborated. Four of the seven episodes take their cue from an act of aggression by the Frogs, who apart from creating an artificial nova and directing it toward Earth are also able to influence human behavior through "telenosis rays." This strand of the narrative culminates in the last episode of the series, when one of the main officials of the GSS turns traitor. With his telenosis-gained help, the Frogs attempt an invasion of Earth, an attempt that at the last minute is wrecked by McLane and his gang.

Other themes include robots suffering from "robot neurosis" and thus turning against humans (a conscious homage to Asimov's Three Laws of Robotics); a conflict between the interests of Earth and the planet Chroma, governed exclusively by women; and a rebellion on a prison planet. Though McLane is obviously the hero of the series, both the crew and Jagellovsk have considerable input in the solutions to these problems. The use of weapons usually forms a significant part of these solutions, but intelligence and negotiation skills are also emphasized.

Though the militaristic bureaucracy of the GSS is often ridiculed, it is not refused outright; on the contrary, long scenes visualize and humanize relatively democratic decision-finding processes at the round tables of the military. While McLane's insubordination is celebrated, it is also questioned—once quite graphically by Jagellovsk forcing him to obey orders at gunpoint and thus leading the mission to a successful conclusion.

Female roles in the series are ambiguous. Female assertiveness in "masculine" roles—such as the female GSS officer, McLane's female teacher Lydia van Dyke, or the ruling matriarchs on the woman planet Chroma—is celebrated, but these constructions are interspersed with scenes that foreground the more emotional, girlish nature of the female characters. In a sense, this romantic side is even granted victory—the tensions between McLane and Jagellovsk are resolved in the last episode by turning them into a couple. Yet the series equally pokes fun at the overly boyish behavior of male characters, so a tongue-in-cheek confirmation of private gender roles with a simultaneous embrace for gender equality in professional functions might be the most adequate description.

First Reactions

Program magazines cited enthusiastic responses from *Orion*'s audience:

> This is how you normally imagine the future.

> The sophisticated, brilliant special effects of the series *Raumschiff Orion* are easily as good as foreign productions of this kind.

> The richness of ideas, the cast, and the original future-music fascinate me anew with every episode.[5]

Despite the series' popularity with its audience, professional critics found little to praise. Though the program announcement in one of the leading TV magazines, the *Hör Zu,* still recognized tongue-in-cheek irony in some of the more militaristic episodes of the series, the press reaction in general was less than kind:

> We are being served the old stories, well-known from pulp novels and cartoons: about spaceships encountering—obviously hostile—gnarled aliens on alien planets; about the aggressions of these aliens against Earth; about robots conquering mankind; about old soldier's jokes that apparently haven't changed since the forties; about Tarzan's battle with the Amazons who finally surrender to male superiority; about quests, order, courage, humor and love, about technology, tricks and light.[6]

> The *Orion* stays in the magnetic field of the twentieth century. Commands are usually bellowed, the ray guns are used with the same old trigger-happiness. Robots provide a homespun kind of crime story tension.[7]

The majority of critics, even those accepting the film technology as interesting, were offended by the militaristic setting of the series. Whether it was denounced as German-made fascism or as imperialism imported from America, the ideological content of the series was considered unacceptable for German public television. Partly, the series was judged to be too simplistic; other commentators thought the techno-jargon was too complicated for the average viewer. Criticism in the presses of neighboring countries was even harsher:

> What a pity that it is de facto a gruff German fabrication that in its unintentional realism reminds us too strongly of a not quite forgotten, disgustingly petty-bourgeois "Orders are orders" past.[8]

> Those who are imprisoned in the mindset of the imperialist system can imagine an encounter with aliens only as terrifying. . . . those who have got used to "Overkill"—thanks to West German TV—can see modern mass destruction weapons only as harmless, like the club of a Neanderthal.[9]

It would take a study in itself to analyze the different cultural preconceptions, stereotypes, and fears that were expressed in these criticisms and that offer vivid insight into the West European cultural and political climate of the late 1960s. Militaristic Germans in black uniforms,[10] no matter how ambiguous or ironic, were not welcome on German television.

There were a variety of reasons why production of *Orion* was canceled after just seven episodes. The series' most reliable chronicler, Josef Hilger, lists the problems of getting the expensive cast back together, the difficulties of continuing the story line after it had come to a conclusion in the seventh episode, and disagreements between the various television stations that were sponsoring the program. However, there are also clear indications that the series originally was intended to last much longer—the raw material for more episodes was there, and the special effects scenes had been shot in color so that they could be reused in a possible continuation at a later date with more advanced television technology. The almost uniformly negative reaction of professional critics played a significant part in the decision to discontinue the series. The progressive aspects of the series—its critical construction of militaristic hierarchies, its commitment to gender equality, its representation of the victory of diplomacy over an arms race—were completely disregarded. As far as television was concerned, the adventures of the *Orion* were over.

Orion Strikes Back

But *Orion* wasn't dead yet. Just fifteen months after its first run, the series was repeated due to popular demand. It was again repeated in 1973, then in 1975 and 1979, a further four times on different regional channels in 1980, and yet again in 1987 and 1988. Since 1991, it has run five times on the private channel SAT 1 and another five times on various regional stations. To date, the number of broadcasts totals twenty—a very respectable number for German television, which adopted the strategy of rescreening popular series much later than American TV. Audience shares for the reruns range from 0.1 percent (late night reruns) to 40 percent (prime-time reruns), though the last time *Orion* broke the one-million-audience barrier was when it was rerun at Saturday lunchtimes in 1996. *Orion* was released on video in 1993 and on DVD in 1999; its availability, coupled with widespread use of home video recording equipment, has made further reruns of the series less appealing. Nevertheless, the relatively high ratings before this decline suggest that there was still considerable interest in the series' vision of the future.

But unlike *Star Trek,* this continuing interest has not led to the production of new series. "New" Orion stories appeared only in the form of paperbacks (35 new stories), then pulp novels (a total of 145 new stories). They lacked the visual and aural appeal of the TV series, and there was little to differentiate them from competing series like Perry Rhodan.[11] Nevertheless they became the basis for the formation of fan clubs. Officially produced Orion merchandise was minimal. In the 1960s, available merchandise consisted of a set of signed photos, several decks of cards with Orion pictures, and a tin toy model of the *Orion.* In 1989, two plastic models of the *Orion,* a toy ray gun, and posters were available, produced to promote and capitalize on the cinema release of the *Orion* series. The year 1990 brought an Orion rubber stamp. In 1991, to celebrate the twenty-fifth anniversary of the series, Goldmann published a book of Orion trivia. This was followed by a set of postcards and a phone card in 1995. In 1996, a laserdisc set was released. The list ends in 1998 with a set of envelopes stamped with a picture of the *Orion.*

Only the card decks and the trivia book were marketed by an established merchandising company; everything else was strictly limited edition fare. The range of available Orion products was slightly extended by fan-produced Orion paraphernalia, and a handful of musical homages. As far as merchandising goes, Orion merchandise is meager. But this was all that fans of the series had to work with.

Orion Fandom—A Short History

Orion fandom evolved in distinct stages. The first fan club was founded in 1966 in the wake of the original television broadcast. But most Orion fan clubs were founded in 1977, their creation triggered by the introduction of a readers' letters page in the pulp novels. Provided for the first time with a platform for communication, fans began to exchange information and merchandise, organize conventions, and discuss the details of the Orion universe.

Over the next five years, around a dozen fan clubs were established; some of the clubs appeared and disappeared rather quickly; others changed their name or merged into larger organizations. From the beginning, the clubs focused on knowledge about the actors and writers, collectors' items, and the technical aspects of the series. Neither the ideological implications nor the greater narrative of the Orion universe found much resonance, though the series' imagined future technologies and its special effects were discussed at great length. Fan fiction took second place to the building of *Orion* models, the designing of blueprints of the ship, and similar activities.

The mission statement of one of the most stable fan clubs, Uraceel, founded in August 1982 and still in existence (up to 160 members), sums up this interest rather neatly:

> Mission statement: To maintain the series *Raumpatrouille Orion* in its essence and to be open to new ideas. This refers to ideas for a cinema film, the collecting of old props and photographs, newspaper articles and models; interviews with the actors, writers and Bavaria Film Studios; DIY-kits built on the basis of photographs of the TV series; contact between its members.
>
> Ultimate aim: To revive the *Orion* for the cinema and in new episodes (in color).

Though new fan clubs were founded—and folded—in the intervening years, no club reached beyond this sphere of activities. The last stage of Orion fandom, to date, was sparked by the advent of the Internet. The availability of new communication technologies has prompted increased fan activity and has slightly changed its nature. Dozens of Orion-influenced home pages can be found. The Starlight Casino, one of the biggest, offers downloads of music, screensavers, and so on. This home page also feeds into the most active virtual fan club, the F.R.O.G.s (founded in 1998), which has a mailing list of sixty-four members, which will be discussed in more detail.

With the Internet, the writers of fan fiction also began to reach a greater audience and receive more attention. Orionspace[12] offers a fan fiction archive. Some stories continue the series' story line; others focus on seasonal jokes (Christmas on the *Orion*); still others introduce new crews, imitating *Star Trek*'s progression from the original series to *Next Generation*. Cross-over stories mix the universes of Orion and Star Trek. "Shadows of the Past"[13] describes a meeting between the Frogs and the *Enterprise;* "Sky Hunter"[14] brings the crew of the *Orion* face to face with Star Trek villain Khan.

Orion fan culture is invigorated by the dedication of a small number of key individuals who have made the *Orion* their personal mission. Josef Hilger, avid collector of Orion history and trivia, maintains contact with the producers, writers, and actors of the series, and is the proud keeper of "the" Braun iron, the prop that served as the main steering unit in the series; Michael Lange published an independent fanzine for ten years before it folded in 1999; Ralf Kramer founded Uraceel and organizes Orion conventions; Michael Höfler maintains the Starlight Casino Web site; Karl-Josef Adler maintains the F.R.O.G. mailing list. These individuals are widely accepted as the experts on the series. They seek and maintain contact with regional and national media in order to keep *Orion* in the public eyes and are invited to participate in events and talk shows. In general, it is these fans who keep the *Orion* "going."

The Fanscape Today

Here I want to turn to the interviews and activities on the mailing list to give a more detailed picture. I will use Abercrombie and Longhurst's model of the five different fan types or stages[15] as a basis to group the reactions of the fans I spoke to. First, the "consumer" expresses a liking for a particular series but would not go much out of his or her way to do something with it. Second, the "fan" sees himself as a dedicated follower of a particular series but has no contact with a productive fan culture. Third, the "cultist" lives inside a fan culture and is engaged in regular exchanges with other fans. Fourth, the "enthusiast" produces fan paraphernalia to gain respect within a fan culture (the latter two are perhaps what most people have in mind when they use the term "fan"). Fifth, the "petty-producers" begin to use their fan knowledge and expertise to produce economically viable items, publish fan stories in a professional context, and so on.

Abercrombie and Longhurst categorize different types of fan mainly in terms of the differential distribution of skills, i.e., what they do and how these activities are placed within the general frame of reference of fan culture. This in turn forms the basis for their analysis of fan identity; the scale reaches from fandom as an extra that is set apart from everyday activities (the consumption of a series) to the gradual incorporation of fan activities into everyday life and the core of the fan's identity, to the "final" stage when the material production for the market forms the basis of the economic existence of the petty-producer. As Abercrombie and Longhurst emphasize, this scale should not be treated as a fixed grid of identifiable fan specimens, but rather as typifying abstractions of a fluid fan continuum.

Abercrombie and Longhurst also stress that their model can be read both as a synchronic analysis of fan culture—i.e., different types of fans existing at the same time—and as a diachronic description of how an individual fan might develop from interested observer to fully engaged semiprofessional. As *Orion* can be seen as a phenomenon specific to a particular time, but also continuing into the present, we will have to flip from one perspective to the other while analyzing the Orion fanscape. We shall see that the first stage of fandom might look slightly different if interest in the series begins during childhood or in adolescence.

When I initially randomly canvassed friends, acquaintances, and people on the street, it became clear quickly that *Orion* is familiar only to a certain age group—from about twenty-five to about sixty—people who were children or teens in 1966 or during the 1980s reruns, or the parents of children hooked on the series. Many of those who saw their children watching *Orion* had only hazy memories of the series: many could not name characters or actors, or confused the series with *Star Trek* although recognizing the title, pictures, or key names. Though readers' letters published in magazines show that there were adults engaging intensely with the series in 1966, I could not locate a single person who had seen the first episode of *Orion* as an adult and was still active in fan culture.[16]

Similarly, I could not find any fans of the series younger than the mid-twenties. Two fans reported that their teenage sons had developed quite a liking for the series by watching *Orion* with their parents or accompanying them to conventions, but they are exceptions in that they grew into the social life of fandom without first developing a fascination with the series. In general, it seems the series has lost its appeal for people who were children from the mid-1980s onward. This might partly be explained by the change German television went through when it opened to the independent channel market and a greater number of American and Japanese productions competed for the attention of the younger audience. However, as the original *Star Trek* series does not seem to suffer from a lack of a "Next Generation" of young fans, it has to be assumed that *Orion* as a text has finally lost its appeal, that it has simply become too dated to attract the interest of today's younger generation.

The first age bracket that shows interest in and knowledge about *Orion* is the twenty-five-to-thirty age group. Some cultists can be found in this group, though the majority are consumers or fans (to use Abercrombie and Longhurst's terms). They are not active in fan groups and, generally, do not use the text as a basis for production. However, this age group identifies *Orion* as "cult television" and uses the series as a basis for social events—as the background to a party or in themed Orion nights and similar private events. When asked to explain why the series is "cult," they focused on the "weird" and "outdated" trick technology, the style aspects, and the 1960s flair of the series. Their affection for these aspects is indicative of an amused, postmodern nostalgia for the Cold War period. It is here, in the antechambers of fandom proper, that *Orion* achieves cult status. That status is awarded for "trashiness," for its use of an iron as a steering unit, for the "flying coffeebean" planet explosions, for the sometimes cheesy dialogue and the outdated gender roles.

When we move into the heart of Orion fandom, into the group of thirty-to-forty-five-year-olds from whom the cultists, enthusiasts, and petty-producers are recruited, the picture changes completely. The more intense the engagement with text and fan culture becomes, the more emphatically the notions of "trash" and "cult" are refused. To understand what it is replaced by, we need to look at the development of an Orion fan. All the fans (or cultists) that I spoke to (about twenty) had encountered *Orion* in their childhood or early teens. *Orion* was the reward they got for finishing their homework, a privilege fought for at home or enjoyed secretly while staying at a friend's house, the Saturday afternoon pleasure that still tasted of weekend and excitement. Most of them had adapted and used *Orion* as a basis for their own games and stories, asked their mothers to make them astronaut costumes, and generally submerged themselves in an Orion world. The borderlines with other science fiction worlds, especially in the 1970s when *Star Trek* had also reached German television, were thin but jealously guarded. As one fan reported:

> As a kid, I liked *Orion* a lot better than *Star Trek*. Might have had something to do with our role-sharing—when we played *Star Trek*, I always had to play Pille [the German nickname for Leonard "Bones" McCoy], but when we played *Orion*, I could be commander McLane.

The next step, for most of the cultists, was a move from willing submersion to the acquisition of power through knowledge. It began to matter to them how things were done in the series, what kind of special effects were used, what the *Orion* should "really" look like. The text, while still held in high respect, was no longer sacrosanct. It could be controlled, judged, criticized—very much as Abercrombie and Longhurst suggest happens as the analytical and interpretive skills of fans grow. Engagement changed from intense identification through childhood reenactments to more distanced practices like building scale models, attempting to write viable sequels, and creative criticism through pastiches and caricatures. These activities require a peer group with similar interests and commitment, and it is at this stage that most cultists join some sort of fan group. The process should not be imagined as linear, however—it might be interrupted by long phases of disinterest in *Orion* and only rekindled through meetings with other fans.

Fans describe how, within fan groups, knowledge and expertise become the currency that buys respect and inspires jealousy. While newcomers who accept their "newbie" status are welcomed, those who challenge the knowledge hierarchies encounter distrust and aggression. This form of competition was—and still is—strongest among *Orion*'s enthusiasts and petty-producers. Fans describe long-lasting feuds over the abuse of information given or received, disappointment when the fan community or other enthusiasts respond unenthusiastically to their ideas, and temporary allegiances with other enthusiasts against outsiders attempting to monopolize the text for ends seen as egotistic. Although these conflicts were more often alluded to than expressed explicitly, and though they were balanced by descriptions of synergetic effects and long-lasting friendships, they make clear that the pecking order at the enthusiast end of the fan continuum is tough. Fandom is not necessarily the cozy haven of community it is often described as being; the more central it becomes to the fan's identity, the more it is threatened by struggles for authority and power within the fan community.

Social competition within fandom is even more apparent in a small universe like Orion fandom than in a big universe like the Star Trek fan continuum. Star Trek fandom—as studies such as Tulloch and Jenkins show[17]—allows for a wide range of fan identities and fan positions: appropriations by the scientific community of the Massachusetts Institute of Technology, queer readings, feminist readings, readings of black emancipation, adaptation of the Klingon and Vulcan culture, and so on. The limited diegetic universe of Orion allows less room for maneuver—while some appropriations are common among Orion fans, others, such as queer readings, find little or nothing in the text to work with. Though the pulp novels attempted to open the universe and introduce new elements, the television series as ultimate authority offers little invitation to imagine other worlds, other futures. Consequently, there are no alternative fan cultures guided by Frog or Chroma philosophy. The field of fan activities engendered by *Orion* is mostly limited to exchanges of technical knowledge, keeping track of actors and producers, creating Web sites and similar derivative texts, and constant speculations about new episodes of the series.

I am not suggesting that *Star Trek* somehow engenders a "better" fandom than *Orion,* or that the Orion fans are just a bickering bunch of egomaniacs. Far from it—surveying the F.R.O.G.s mailing list, it becomes obvious that most contact between fans consists of friendly exchanges of information, helpfulness (such as offering a fellow fan a place to stay during a convention), and attempts to expand the painfully small text base (for example, by producing an Orion radio play). Equally, once I had established that I had no interest in deriding *Orion* as "trash," I received full support from the fans. While friendly banter is common in e-mail exchanges, "flame wars" are a rarity. The only serious outbreak of hostilities that I witnessed was directed against an outsider—a nonfan who had downloaded pictures from fan Web sites and was trying to make a profit by auctioning them off on an "*Orion* CD-ROM" through eBay. Here, the fan community drew together and became active by complaining to eBay and stopping the auction—in other words, protecting their communal intellectual property. When the thief was revealed to be a "sad git" teenager attempting to augment his pocket money, the outrage abated and the community moved on to other topics. Nevertheless, the limited room for maneuver and the small, intimate community heighten the potential for direct, personal conflict.

The smallness of the Orion universe also accounts for two last points: (a) fan interest in speculating about "new" *Orion* episodes, and (b) the increasing signs that the Orion fan proper is a dying breed. Both have their immediate cause in the small text base. In his book on fan culture,

Hilger dedicates a whole subchapter to the cycles of hope and disappointment the fan community went through whenever there were rumors of a continuation of the series. As the actors aged, and one of them even died, these rumors became less and less likely to be true, but they still continue. One of the last topics of the mailing list was a discussion of fully computer-animated films like *Final Fantasy* and *Shrek*; the point of interest was the potential of the technique for a continuation of *Orion* with the familiar faces at the helm.

This, as much as the mission statement of Uraceel, reveals the "direction of desire" for most of the Orion fans—to be able to experience more of the fascination and excitement they experienced on first viewing *Orion*, to continue and extend their relationship with the series' characters. It remains speculation whether an *Orion: The Next Generation* would be accepted as an alternative by fans, as *Star Trek: The Next Generation* was, eventually, by Star Trek fans. From the current perspective of the fans, it would be a supplement—better than nothing, but not what is really longed for. What is desired is more of the old crew, a nostalgic desire that also highlights the real structures of authority. Even though Orion fan culture has survived and thrived for thirty-five years, the original series remains the point of reference, the universe to be expanded. Fan culture did not manage to emancipate itself fully from the text that inspired it.

This leads us to the last point, the gradual extinction of Orion fandom. In my interviews with two of the leading Orion petty-producers/ enthusiasts, both stressed that they had recently retreated from their intense fan activities of earlier years. For health and family reasons— both had small children—they had decided to become observers rather than activists. To this end, they had reduced their collections and/or moved them to more peripheral places within their houses. They both mentioned feeling that they had "reached a limit" where yet another review of the familiar series would add little new to their pleasures of reception. If taken together with the lack of young fans, this suggests that *Orion* might have reached its final reception stage—when fewer and fewer fans are active producers of new material and revert to being only interested consumers. From being a defining point of these fans' identities, *Orion* has become only one of many interests, a status it also has for many participants of the mailing lists. Increasingly, the series is losing its capacity to generate fans—to function as a basis of identity, a reference point for self-definition. Whether anything—a continuation in whatever form, or the rise of an engaging enthusiast/petty-producer

within the fan community—can reverse this process cannot be predict-
ed. At the moment, the signs are discouraging.

Across the Universe—Orion versus Star Trek fandom

Many things make *Orion* unique—its textual limitations, its strong
ties with German culture, the production circumstances that made a
continuation of the series problematic. On the other hand, similar arguments of uniqueness might be listed for *Star Trek,* and yet one cannot
evade the impression that we are dealing with parallel histories here—
if *The Next Generation* and the three other Star Trek spin-off series
hadn't rejuvenated Star Trek fandom,[18] we might be writing a similar
epitaph for the most popular science fiction series ever. Nevertheless,
quite apart from the respective development of the two series, there
is a vital difference that might also account for the different kinds of
fandom they inspired: the central element that organizes narrative and
characters into a coherent, meaningful whole.

In *Star Trek,* this element might be described as Roddenberry's vision, neatly summed up in the series' philosophy of "infinite diversity in
infinite combinations." *Star Trek* engages intensely in cultural, ethical,
and moral debates, employing the science fiction backdrop and its technological possibilities to revisit and rewrite central moments in history,
to tell fables about poignant cross-cultural encounters. The quest of the
different Star Trek starships *(Enterprise, Voyager)* is the classic quest
of mankind, the journey into strangeness and toward a deeper understanding of the self and the other. It is this resonance with "deep" questions that makes *Star Trek* such an attractive text both for a significant
proportion of its fans and for academic studies, a parallel history of the
changing views on multiculturalism of the past three decades.

Orion has no such depths to offer. Though a background ideology
can be discerned that in some respects is similar to the Star Trek one—
distrust of military authority, a celebration of wit and companionship, a
preference for peaceful solutions[19]—it is neither as explicit nor as elaborate. Even given that a bigger text base might have developed a more
detailed credo, there is nothing that suggests *Orion* might have set out
to discuss philosophical questions. If deeper questions are given space,
such as the processes and dangers of military decision making, they are
handled pragmatically, shown rather than discussed. When explicitly
asked what *Orion* was about, one of the fans commented hesitantly:

> It's not really the right question for *Orion*—or maybe, if you want
> to put it like that, it's about orders. Not about following orders or not

following orders, but rather about thinking about the orders you are given and deciding whether to follow them or not.

There is coherence in the ideology resistance of the series—adequate in a culture and time that regarded most explicit ideologies with suspicion—and the loose organization of the Orion fans. A more structured and elaborate system, like one of the Star Trek MUDs[20] that established a "Star Fleet Academy" and expected its members to behave according to their rank and status, does not seem to appeal to the fans attracted by *Orion*.

Nevertheless, *Orion* does have a focus element, even if it cannot be found in its ideology. Style takes its place: the elaborate and distinctive settings and props, the music, the rituals—such as back-to-back dancing in the Starlight Casino—are rated as essential among the fans. Home pages collect Orion designs in the form of photographs of original props or in photographs of items that have similar aesthetic qualities. Several bands have used the Orion theme in their songs or created variations. While the fans might not be into role playing, loving attention is given to the re-creation of costumes or drawing pictures and creating models.[21] Where *Star Trek* is almost cerebral in its contemplation of good and evil, *Orion* is much more visual, aural, sensual in its celebration of strangeness, of futuristic style. The casual, often quirky dialogue and acting combine with this to make not an ideological but a fashion statement. Even after thirty-five years, Orion is "cool." It is little surprise that a number of Orion fans have occupations relating to fashion, advertising, or design.

The Life of a Cult TV Series

Reading *Orion* as a possible "alternative" to *Star Trek* offers several conclusions. First, science fiction fandom seems to follow a general outline in terms of fan types and behavior. The Abercombie and Longhurst model fits the structure of the fan communities of both series if adjustments for the age of the fans and the time of "first contact" are taken into consideration. Second, a cult series has a "life" that is based in the changes in the culture surrounding the text but can be relatively independent of marketing efforts, as long as there is a communication base for a fan culture to build on. Although *Orion* was not supported by an interested industry, a surprisingly enduring fandom was and still is in existence. Means of communication, rather than merchandise, can be isolated as the decisive factor for changes within the fan community.

Third, beyond general fan typifications, different texts engender different kinds of fan activities and identities. The points of interest for fans are not arbitrary readings but in fact coincide with central textual structures. Despite some striking similarities both in the text base and in fan behavior, Star Trek and Orion fans are different, they are fans of different aspects of their favored texts, and these aspects for the main part are those prioritized in the production of these series.

The complexities of the relationships between producers, texts, and audiences cannot be reduced to a single one of its components, nor can purely active or passive roles be assigned to either the industry or the consumer. Fandom, or rather a cult phenomenon, happens at the fragile interface of production and consumption. The analysis of a limited, non-mainstream cult series like *Orion* highlights the similarities between large and small fan communities, but also draws attention to their ultimate differences.

Raumpatrouille Orion offers rich hunting grounds for textual analysis and cultural studies. While many of the themes are common both to *Orion* and *Star Trek*—allusions to the Cold War, to female emancipation, and to man/machine conflicts—the emphatically German interpretation of these themes invites comparisons between different cultural contexts within the Western powers of the 1960s. Uhura might have happily traded places with Jagellovsk regarding the advancement of female emancipation, while questions of race and ethnic origin couldn't even be visualized at that stage of German popular culture.

Notes

All translations by the author.

1. Knut Hickethier, *Geschichte des Deutschen Fernsehens* (Stuttgart, Weimar: Metzler, 1998), 235.

2. This synopsis of German TV history is taken from ibid., 110–280.

3. Rolf Honold, cited in Josef Hilger, *Raumpatrouille: Die Phantastischen Abenteuer des Raumschiffes Orion* (Berlin: Schwarzkopf & Schwarzkopf, 2000), 8. Most of the information on the history of *Orion* comes from Hilger.

4. Hilger, *Raumpatrouille*, 14. Among ardent fans, this interlude is seen as the occasion where Gene Roddenberry might have seen the script, and thus found the inspiration for *Star Trek*. Much to the chagrin of the fans, these rumors could never be substantiated.

5. All audience and magazine quotes taken from Hilger, *Raumpatrouille*, 200–201.

6. Dresp, Filmreport, 1966.

7. Hassencamp, Hör Zu, 1966.

8. De Tijd, Netherlands, 1966.

9. Wochenpost, East-Berlin, 1967.

10. In fact, the uniforms were blue but appeared to be black because the series was shot in black-and-white.

11. The most successful German pulp novel science fiction series.

12. At http://www.Orionspace.de.

13. Christian Heyer, "Schatten der Vergangenheit," 1993, at http://www.Orionspace.de/sc0771.htm.

14. Christian Heyer, "Der Himmelsjäger," 1993, at http://www.Orionspace.de/sc0772.htm.

15. Nicholas Abercrombie and Brian Longhurst, Audiences (London, Thousand Oaks, New Delhi: Sage, 1998), 121–57.

16. As this is a "homemade" study done on very limited resources, this does not mean that there aren't any—I might have simply missed them. Nevertheless, as I contacted the main fan groups about this question, it can be safely assumed that they are pretty rare.

17. John Tulloch and Henry Jenkins, Science Fiction Audiences: Watching Dr. Who and Star Trek (London: Routledge, 1995).

18. The German Star Trek fandom is so similar to the American one that no separate discussion is necessary here—there are literally hundreds of fan clubs, conventions have three thousand participants or more—including Vulcans and Klingons—and the universities have adopted the analysis of Star Trek as a cultural phenomenon in seminars and conferences. For the reception of Star Trek as a specifically American series, see http://ikarus.pclab-phil.uni-kiel.de/daten/deutsch/litwiss/dat_lit/PopST/00journa.htm#Sektion2.2.

19. At least in some episodes like the Chroma incident.

20. Multi-Use Dungeons, Internet role-playing virtual communities.

21. For example, see http://dspace.dial.pipex.com/town/terrace/kag15/page2.htm.

Contributors

Karen Backstein is an independent scholar who has taught at various institutions in the New York City area. She has published several articles on dance and film.

David A. Black is associate professor of communication at Seton Hall University. He is author of *Law in Film: Resonance and Representation,* and his work has appeared in *Yale Journal of Criticism, Media, Culture, and Society,* and *Literature and Psychology.*

Sara Gwenllian-Jones is lecturer in television and digital media at Cardiff University. Her publications include articles in *Screen, Journal of Television and New Media,* and *Continuum.* She is coeditor of *Intensities: The Journal of Cult Media* and is currently writing another book about cult television and working on a documentary project about tribal peoples.

Mary Hammond is lecturer in English literature at the Open University. Her research interests include nineteenth-century popular fiction, horror, and fan cultures.

Nathan Hunt is a Ph.D. student at the University of Nottingham. He researches fan culture, particularly issues of production and consumption of science fiction fan media and the practices of cult film and television viewing.

Mark Jancovich is reader and director of the Institute of Film Studies at the University of Nottingham. He is the author of several books, including *The Place of the Audience: Cultural Geographies of Film Consumption* (with Lucy Faire and Sarah Stubbings) and *Rational Fears: American Horror in the 1950s.*

Petra Kuppers is assistant professor in performance studies at Bryant College. She works mainly in performance and disability studies, and often links these areas of investigation to popular culture, cultural politics, and issues of representation. She is the author of *Disability and*

Contemporary Performance: Bodies on Edge, and also a community artist, a horror and sci-fi fan, and a former foreign correspondent for German genre magazines.

Philippe Le Guern is senior lecturer in media studies at the University of Angers, France. His work looks at television and its audiences from a sociological perspective, with a particular emphasis on fan culture. He edited a collection on media and contemporary cults and is currently studying the Eurovision Song Contest and its audiences.

Alan McKee is a failed Doctor Who novelist but a successful academic writer. His most recent book is *Textual Analysis: A Beginner's Guide.* He is currently the chief investigator of the Australian government-funded Understanding Pornography in Australia research project.

Toby Miller is professor of cultural studies and cultural policy at New York University. He is the author of several books, including *The Avengers, Technologies of Truth: Cultural Citizenship and the Popular Media* (Minnesota, 1998), and *SportSex*; editor of *Television Studies*; and co-editor of *SportCult* (Minnesota, 1999). He is an editor of *Television & New Media.*

Roberta E. Pearson is reader in media and cultural studies at Cardiff University and the author, coauthor, or coeditor of numerous books and articles. She has been a Star Trek fan since the original series premiered in the United States and is currently coauthoring a book titled *Small Screen, Big Universe: Star Trek as Television.*

Jeffrey Sconce is associate professor in the School of Communications at Northwestern University and author of *Haunted Media: Electronic Presence from Telegraphy to Television.* His work on film, television, and popular culture has appeared in numerous anthologies and journals, including *Screen, Science as Culture,* and the *International Journal of Cultural Studies.*

Eva Vieth, Tom Hopkinson Scholar, completed her doctorate in the School of Journalism, Media, and Cultural Studies at Cardiff University. She has lectured at Utrecht University (Netherlands) and given guest lectures at the Richmond American University in London. She coedited *American Cultural Studies: A Reader* with John Hartley and Roberta Pearson and has published several articles on Second World War iconography, illustrated magazines, and popular photojournalism.